John Slocum
and the
Indian Shaker Church

JOHN SLOCUM
AND THE
INDIAN SHAKER CHURCH

by Robert H. Ruby
and John A. Brown

Foreword by Richard A. Gould

University of Oklahoma Press : Norman

By Robert H. Ruby and John A. Brown

Half-Sun on the Columbia: A Biography of Chief Moses (Norman, 1965)
The Spokane Indians: Children of the Sun (Norman, 1970)
The Cayuse Indians: Imperial Tribesmen of Old Oregon (Norman, 1972)
Ferryboats on the Columbia River (Seattle, 1974)
The Chinook Indians, Traders of the Lower Columbia River (Norman, 1976)
Myron Eells and the Puget Sound Indians (Seattle, 1976)
Indians of the Pacific Northwest: A History (Norman, 1981)
A Guide to the Indian Tribes of the Pacific Northwest (Norman, 1986,1992)
Dreamer-Prophets of the Columbia Plateau: Smohalla and Skolaskin
   (Norman, 1989)
John Brown Bibliography (1989)
Indian Slavery in the Pacific Northwest (Spokane, 1993)
John Slocum and the Indian Shaker Church (Norman, 1996)

This book is published with the generous assistance of the McCasland
Foundation, Duncan, Oklahoma.

Library of Congress Cataloging-in-Publicaton Data

Ruby, Robert H.
    John Slocum and the Indian Shaker Church / by Robert H. Ruby and
John A. Brown; forword by Richard A. Gould,
        p. cm.
    Includes bibliographical references and index.
    ISBN 978-0-8061-6043-6
    1. Slocum, John 1841–1897. 2. Indian Shaker Church—History.
3. Indians of North America—Missions—Northwest, Pacific.
4. Missionaries—Northwest, Pacific—Biography. 5. Indians of North
America—Northwest, Pacific—Religion. 6. Nativistic movements—
Northwest, Pacific—History. I. Brown, John Arthur. II. Title.
E78.N77S567   1996
289.9—dc20   95-52252
                                                                 CIP

Text typeface is New Century.

The paper in this book meets the guidelines for permanence and durability
of the Committee on Production Guidelines for Book Longevity of the
Council on Library Resources, Inc. ∞

To the Shakers

Contents

Illustrations

Foreword

This book about John Slocum and the Indian Shaker Church is a welcome contribution to the literature on Native American religious movements and their ability to adapt to conditions imposed by Euro-American culture. The book chronicles the history of the Shaker movement from its beginnings with the charismatic figure of John Slocum and his vision of 1882 following a near-death experience to the schisms and political pressures of the late twentieth century. The authors provide a carefully researched historical account that is, at the same time, clearly written and evocative of the central themes of Shakerism: healing through God's power by individual actions (but also by uniquely Shaker means) and intensely focused community support for both the healer and the patient.

I discovered the Shakers in 1962 in the tiny community of Smith River in northwestern California. Ruth Roberts, then the head of the Del Norte County Historical Society and a close friend of the Yurok and Tolowa Indians of that region, had urged me to visit the Shaker congregation. She rightly saw them as a core element for social and cultural cohesion in the region and pointed to their excellent record of drawing Indians away from alcohol. What began as a somewhat perfunctory visit soon turned into a sustained and rewarding involvement with this remarkable group of people.

For me, a graduate student of anthropology at the University of California, the contrast with the situation then at Berkeley could not have been greater. Dissension on campus over the growing U.S. involvement in Vietnam was on the rise, as were the Free Speech Movement and other highly publicized protest activities. The Berkeley campus was divided in a manner that presaged larger divisions that were soon to appear throughout American society. Yet, while all of this protest was taking place four hundred miles to the south, here was a community of Indians carrying on with a coherent religious tradition that provided a focal point for their lives despite important differences in tribal background and religious viewpoints. In the early to mid 1960s it was important to me to know that there were places in the world where communities were not being ripped apart by military politics.

As I came to know the Shakers of Smith River better, I realized that there was dissension there as well, with local disagreements, personality clashes, and even political disputes (some of which are referred to briefly in this book). Yet somehow the center held. As my knowledge of the Shaker community at Smith River increased, I became concerned with the question of what kind of "social glue" held the congregation together. At times it seemed that the Shaker congregation was either flying apart or lapsing into torpor. My student and friend, Dale Valory, pointed out after one visit that he thought it was all over at Smith River, that nothing could revive the Shaker movement there. Yet on my next visit, there they all were with their bells, songs, and candles, shaking and curing as if nothing had ever been wrong. Revisits during 1974, 1976, and 1981 confirmed the durability of Shakerism and the keen sense of belonging to a community that Shaker beliefs and practices imparted. But the unanswered (and perhaps unanswerable) questions about social glue remained. What held this group together despite individual and factional differences, external political pressures, and institutional schisms?

As the authors point out, curing has been the focus of Shaker belief and behavior ever since John Slocum and the first wave of Shaker leaders including Slocum's wife, Mary Thompson, and other early figures like Mud Bay Louis. Faith healing is a feature of many Christian sects, but Shaker beliefs and practices relating to curing are exceptional. Although presented honestly as Christian in principle, Shakerism retains a unique combination of Native American styles of singing, body movement, and verbal declarations. Even individuals who are not known as healers themselves participate directly in curing and are regarded as essential to the curing process. This, in turn, leads to a high level of emotional support by the Shaker community for anyone perceived to be in need of its ministrations.

Shaker congregations are not closed communities. Despite a long history of opposition from government officials and leaders of different mainstream Christian denominations, the Shakers continue to welcome outsiders and to tolerate slippage from within. Schism within the Shaker Church, especially between Bible-reading Shakers and traditional Shakers, has not produced the kind of sectarian bitterness seen so often with other Christian sects. In the Smith River–Crescent City area of California, the Shakers were well known to local whites, who, without exception among those I spoke to, regarded them with respect. These whites were quick to point out the success of the Shakers in combating alcoholic excess among Indians, and some were impressed by their healing successes as well. One medical doctor, Bertrand Vipond (then at Seaside Hospital in Cresent City), indicated that he admired the Shakers and believed that if, after first seeking medical help from conventional sources, an individual still needed assistance, he or she should be encouraged to visit the Shakers. This was at least thirty years before the term "holistic medicine" became a household word! Not surprisingly, Dr. Vipond was highly regarded by the Smith River Shakers, who were not in any way opposed to white medicine. As several of them said to me, "Try Vipond first—if it don't work, try the Shakin'."

As an anthropologist, I was schooled in "participant observation," that is, the way an outside observer learns to understand and appreciate another culture from the insider's point of view. With the Smith River Shakers, it was hard to remain an outsider for long. I soon encountered the force of a truly charismatic personality in Charlie Bighead, who was then at the height of his powers as a leader and healer; I saw some of the most devious factional politics one could imagine in relation to the Shaker Church's land claims on the old Smith River Rancheria; and I was shaken over by Charlie and Mary Bighead in 1973. (For the record, I was in good health but found the intense involvement in the process inspirational at the very least.) But did this participant observation lead to a better understanding of the social glue that binds the Shakers today and has throughout their history?

The value of Ruby and Brown's book is that it gives historical perspective to the kind of local snapshot provided by my observations and experiences at Smith River. In reading this book, I was encouraged to think about the Smith River Shakers in relation to the long-term trajectory of their historical experience as a movement and was reminded that Smith River was, and still is, a marginal community in the overall context of the Indian Shaker movement. Yet that marginality was also an important factor in the preservation of traditional values by the Smith River Shakers. Their remoteness from the dissension and power struggles in the major congregations farther north seems also to have aided in producing a tolerance for differences of opinion and style that avoids acrimony or alienation.

Perhaps one can extend the metaphor introduced by anthropologist Homer Barnett, during his studies in northwestern California in the 1940s and 1950s, of "the marginal man." This was the idea that Indians who had retained much of their traditional background but were also strongly influenced by Euro-American culture were, in a sense, marginal to both. They were neither fully Indian nor white in their cultural outlook or in their social relationships. But that same quasi-outsider's status meant that their influence on the course of culture change among the Indians was greater than that of most of the more traditionally oriented Indians, and they were sometimes important sources of cultural innovation. Perhaps groups as well as individuals can function in a similar manner to produce unique combinations of cultural values and behavior. The notion of innovative and adaptive responses to the pressures of Euro-American cultural encroachment since the late 1800s suggest a sort of creative marginality by the Shakers that continues to the present and may, in part, account for the durability of the Indian Shaker religion, at least in northwestern California.

Another explanation of the social glue that binds and preserves the Shakers as a community can be found in a classic socio-

logical study by Max Weber. In his widely read essay on the
"routinization of charisma," Weber defines charisma as a "certain quality of an individual personality by virtue of which he
is set apart from ordinary men and treated as endowed with
supernatural, superhuman, or at least specifically exceptional
powers or qualities."* What makes Weber's analysis special is
his recognition of the equal importance of a legitimizing community of followers or believers who are "called" to a charismatic
mission—and thereby incur the duty of recognizing and subjecting
themselves to charismatic authority—and the continuation of that
charismatic authority through stable social and administrative
institutions—in other words, routinization.

The history of the Indian Shakers is replete with both charisma
and routinization. The authors have described the experiences of
John Slocum, which fit closely with Weber's definition of charisma.
Their account of the later struggles by the Shakers to establish
formal, official recognition for their church within the various
states and provinces where they are located represents what Weber meant by routinization. According to Weber, as charismatic
communities become routinized, with formal charters, established
leaders and administrators, and more routine procedures, they
increasingly run counter to the original charismatic impulse that
inspired the community in the first place. The historical continuity
of a charismatic community rests upon a contradiction that Weber saw as a general principle in the structure of human societies.
Charismatic communities can decline and become extinct as the
original charismatic impulse is lost in the process of routinization,
or they can fail because no one in the community of believers organized the group sufficiently well to assure its survival after the
death or decline of the original charismatic founder.

The point, of course, is that, unlike many Native American religious movements since the arrival of Euro-American culture,
the Indian Shakers have not failed. As the authors point out, the
central role of healing as an activity that replicates and renews
John Slocum's original vision keeps the charismatic credibility of

---

* A. M. Henderson and Talcott Parsons, eds., *Max Weber: The Theory of
Social and Economic Organization* (New York: Oxford University Press,
1947), 358.

their religion alive in the minds and hearts of followers. At the same time, the necessity of evolving administrative institutions to meet challenges imposed by Euro-American governments and competing religions forced the Shakers to adapt ιo the requirements of the larger society. Would routinization ever have come to the Shaker religion without these outside pressures? The Shakers organized themselves well enough to maintain their religion without allowing the process of routinization to overwhelm or displace the original charismatic impulse. As a result, the Shakers have a history to look back on and a future to anticipate.

Weber's ideas may not be quite the social glue I was seeking but they help explain the structural contradictions that occur in religious groups of this kind. The historical longevity of the Indian Shaker religion is proof that, in spite of difficulties, the Shakers have resolved these contradictions well enough to keep the faith alive over many generations. In short, the Indian Shakers are not a cult. This book provides a richly detailed and well-documented account of the historical development of the Shakers. It extends from their charismatic beginnings through their struggles to adapt to white institutions and create a durable structure for their religion to their present condition as a viable community of believers still deeply in touch with the original impulses that inspired their founder.

RICHARD A. GOULD

Brown University
Providence

Preface

Having lived in two strongholds of American Indian Shakerism, Washington's Skagit and Yakima Valleys, we developed years ago an interest in this religion that culminates in this study. In the 1920s in the Skagit Valley of western Washington one of us lived a mere forty feet from the house of a devout Shaker family, easily within earshot of their ringing bells and earnest prayers. From this vantage point he had ample opportunity to observe not only their ceremonials but also the moral conduct of their lives. These same Shaker hallmarks were observed in the Yakima Valley of eastern Washington by the other of us, and in his memory is etched a graveled country road above which, on an eminence commanding a view of Satus Flat, stood a small, weathered Shaker church house, its belfry uniquely positioned to the rear of the building.

Also helping to stimulate our interest in Shakerism was the renewed interest in Native American spiritualism formerly suppressed by observer writers in accounts primarily concerned with military exploits and material culture. This renewed interest led us to contact prominent Shakers, especially the late Bishop Harris Teo of White Swan in the Yakima Valley, who, with his wife, Lorraine, requested us to record the history of their church. We are grateful for their care of the church records, which involved returning them from long storage in Canada to safekeeping in the Washington State Historical Society archives in Tacoma. We are also grateful that records of the Bible-use Shakers have been deposited in archives of the Washington State Library in Olympia.

We are grateful to the many scholars whose work we have used in preparing this study. By the same token, we acknowledge the help of the Shaker community. Nor can we overlook the efforts of certain members of the white community, especially those who chronicled Shakerism's formative years. Perhaps the most rewarding by-product of our efforts is an awareness of the sincerity and Christian morality of our subjects. We have also been impressed with the adaptability of their founders who, from a native background, adjusted to the requirements of the dominant white culture.

We trust that this text will make one further contribution. Now over a century old and extending from Washington state northward into British Columbia and southward into Oregon and northern California, western American Indian Shakerism is still easily confused by some with the Shakerism of eastern America. If we can make western Shakerism better known, perhaps people will no longer say, "Oh, they're the ones who make all that beautiful furniture."

ROBERT H. RUBY

Moses Lake, Washington

JOHN A. BROWN

Wenatchee, Washington

John Slocum
and the
Indian Shaker Church

Tribes with members active in the Indian Shaker Church.

CHAPTER ONE

John Slocum
and the Beginnings of
the Indian Shaker Church

In November 1882, John Slocum (Squ-sacht-un) lay near death on Skookum Bay, located on Hammersley Inlet on upper Puget Sound. The bad spirits invading the body of the forty-year-old Sahewamish logger had rendered him weak and sickly. Five native doctors, their incantations accompanied by the rhythmic cacophonies of rattles and charms, had failed to cure him. Now Slocum "journeyed to heaven and returned." Judge James Wickersham, a Tacoma attorney for the Sahewamishes to whom Slocum told his story, used the Indian's own words to describe his experience: "All at once I saw a shining light—great light—trying my soul. I looked and saw my body had no soul—looked at my own body—it was dead. . . . Angels told me to look back and see my body. I did, and saw it lying down. When I saw it, it was pretty poor. My soul left my body and went up to [the] judgement place of God."[1] Soon after "returning" to his body, Slocum created what would become the Indian Shaker Church (ISC).

Slocum's relatives and others present at his death eagerly told of his miraculous experience. One account told how Slocum's last breath left his body and how his soul, ascending with a great light into heaven, was met by angels.[2] The *Mason County Journal*, published in Shelton, Washington, near the Skokomish

Reservation and Slocum's home, reported that angels—calling his name, John—informed him of something of which he was well aware: "You've been a pretty bad Indian."[3]

In 1900, Charles D. Rakestraw, who had been supervisor of an Indian school on the nearby Chehalis Indian Reservation since 1883, published an account of Slocum's experience. According to Rakestraw's sources, in Slocum's "journey to heaven" he had entered a fenced yard in which stood a house. The front door of the house opened, and he entered to find it empty. Although aware of a "presence," he saw no one. Another door opened for him to enter, and inside this other room he was greeted by an unidentified, well-dressed man who asked if he believed in God. He was then led into yet another room, where he saw a large photograph of himself. "This picture revealed to John all of the bad deeds of his life," Rakestraw wrote, "and he saw that he had been a very wicked man." Slocum was next escorted down to a room where men whom he recognized were burning in a furnace. Then, wrote Rakestraw, Slocum talked with God. (Other accounts, including Slocum's, report that he talked with angels.)

According to Rakestraw, Slocum pleaded with the angels for deliverance from a netherworld doom, begging permission to return to earth and promising to do everything possible to escape the blazing furnace. The angels offered him a chance to return to earth on condition that he preach the word of God and live a moral life. Before returning to assume his earthly body, Rakestraw wrote, Slocum was led to an upper room and then to the rooftop, where he looked out on a bright land of beauty and comfort and experienced a sense of deep tranquility.[4]

When Slocum related his experience to Judge Wickersham, he reported that he was ushered back to earth to preach the Christian life of sober and upright morality. "I have understood all Christ wants us to do," he said. "Before I came alive I saw I was a sinner. Angel in heaven said to me, 'You must go back and turn alive again on earth.' I learned that I must be a good Christian man on earth, or will be punished." Slocum's message was simple: "There is a God—there is a Christian people. My good friends, be Christian."[5]

During Slocum's transfiguration, Mary Thompson (Whe-Bul-eht-sah) had sat at her husband's side in silence, while her niece, Nancy George, the only other person in the room, sat off to one corner. A fragment of red suspender had been wrapped around Slocum's face to hold up his chin, and both women believed Slocum was dead.[6] Then Nancy George noticed a sudden movement in his toes. Though Mary Thompson admonished her not to look at the body, George continued to do so. Next, she saw Slocum's hand move and then his head. When Slocum sat up, George left the room to announce the exciting news to those outside, inviting them to enter the room.[7]

Mary Thompson later reported that when Slocum had "regained consciousness" from what she said was a broken neck, he sat up and asked for water to cleanse his body. Thompson said that when she brought the water, Slocum rejected it because the vessel in which she carried it belonged "to the Sin." Then he said, "You must build a church."[8] Still weak, Slocum was first helped into the bed in his home, where shamans had earlier tried to cure him, but then asked to be placed in another bed so he could begin with all things new—things not associated with sin and evil. He also wanted a white robe to wear to symbolize his new morality and mission. Soon, according to one source, he was speaking "in an inspired, educated fashion although he had been unable to read and had no talent for speaking."[9]

Slocum wasted little time carrying out his heavenly mandate. "In the beginning of your Christian life," he exhorted friends and relatives who had kept his death watch, "you must confess your sins, before you expect to make your home in heaven to be accepted by God and make everything right, where you make your mistakes."[10] After an unidentified "good Christian man" prayed with him for four days, Slocum heard a voice saying, "You shall live on earth four weeks." Slocum interpreted this as a command, reporting that his "soul was told that they [his followers?] must build a church for me in four weeks," after which people would come to it to worship God. With help from others, Slocum soon commenced building a church house.[11]

Christian missionaries had been in the upper Puget Sound region for nearly a half century, and their influence was clearly at work here. Slocum's exhortative words were those of Protestant clergy, and Roman Catholics provided the symbols the Shaker Church would adopt: bells, candles, crosses, flags, albs, and holy pictures. Secular influences from white culture were also evident, from the sheet placed over Slocum in death to the coffin that his brother Tom sought in Olympia.[12] Many northwest Indians who had become associated with Christian churches believed that initiation into Christianity meant salvation from physical harm rather than assurance of spiritual preservation. Some had welcomed the missionaries, believing that power from the mysterious sources of Christianity would enhance the power Indians already had from native beliefs. But others, according to one missionary, believed that not enough had been done for them by Christian clergy, that they had become "the prey of degenerate and vile white men."[13]

Undeniably, there were negative consequences from the meeting of two such different cultures—Christian and Indian—on the rough-hewn Puget Sound frontier of the midnineteenth century. Although missionaries taught love and forgiveness, the Indians soon became aware of conflict between Roman Catholic and Protestant clergy in their quest for Indian souls. This divisive conflict was unsettling for many Pacific Northwest Indians, and it helped bring Slocum to the point of his experience.

Slocum's revelation was probably also a result of his own dissipations. He had spent much of his woodsman's earnings on whiskey, tincture of Jamaica ginger, and gambling. Mud Bay Louis Yowaluch who later led the Shaker Church, would express a similar disorientation: "We all felt blind those times. We lost by drowning—our friends drank whisky and the canoes turn over—we died out in the bay."[14] Slocum's experience provided a new spiritual dimension in responding to these conditions—one that embraced both Christian and native beliefs and addressed some of the Indians' social and health problems.

John Slocum was not the only Indian religious leader in the Pacific Northwest to emerge during the late nineteenth century in response to the presence of whites. Force of arms had failed to dislodge the whites in the Puget Sound during skirmishes between Indians and U.S. troops in 1855 and 1856, and Indian visionaries related their heavenly sojourns to inspire hope in people caught in an agonizingly disruptive period of change. Smohalla, a Columbia River Wanapam Indian, predicted his people's eventual reinheritance of the earth. Skolaskin, a Sanpoil, sought to effect his people's escape from earth to a common meeting place in heaven. John Slocum sought neither the removal nor the destruction of whites—nor yet an escape from earth. Like some other visionaries, however, he advocated a moral code, accompanied by beliefs and ceremonies, to ensure his people's survival in a world dominated by white Christianity.

The foundation of that code rested on Slocum's death experience. Often scholars are more concerned with the causes and consequences of events than with the events themselves, but such should not be the case in Slocum's death. The nature of that experience seems to have eluded both students and followers of Slocum. Some anthropologists have explained what happened to Slocum as a vision or a trance. There is even a pervasive opinion that Slocum was "playing possum." Others attribute Slocum's experience to a stupor or to phantasms resulting from a drunken seizure or to a coma resulting from tuberculosis or a broken neck. One version claims that Slocum was trying to extricate himself from the evil designs of a scheming shaman who had induced the illness in order to receive a large remuneration for his healing services.[15]

Whatever the claim, Slocum's death symptoms fit a well-established syndrome.[16] The name most commonly applied by clinical psychologists and psychiatrists is "near-death experience" (NDE), but it is also known as "life after life," "life after death," and "out-of-body experience." The reports of NDEs follow a common pattern, although individual expressions and interpretations vary in degree and detail and not all contain every phase. First, the subject having reached the point of death through illness, trauma, or attempted suicide, there is bodily separation in which the self ascends and looks down on what it recognizes as its own lifeless body. Present-day students of the NDE make no attempt to identify the self as mind, soul, spirit, or life. Slocum, who described his bodily separation in terms as precise as those used by modern-day NDE subjects, called his self the "soul."[17]

A bright light, such as that reported by Slocum, is described by almost everyone who has reported experiencing an NDE. Many NDE subjects have also described a darkness, which they compare with being in or looking into a tunnel. Seattle physician Melvin Morse, who conducted a study of children who experienced NDEs, wrote that the children told of going up or down stairs or through a hall, which he concluded is a substitute for the tunnel experience. Slocum's movement through the series of rooms may represent such a passage. In NDE journeys, subjects have reported seeing or speaking to those they have known or to whom they were related, much as Slocum recognized people in the furnace room. Typically, those experiencing out-of-body "life view" phenomena report looking in a mirror and seeing a collage of images of themselves and being reminded of the bad things they had done. For Slocum and many others, this phase of the experience leads to self-evaluation.[18]

During his NDE, Slocum reportedly did not hesitate to express a wish to return to earth, promising to turn his life around and to preach the saving power of Christ. As he was taken to the roof to view a serene landscape where "everything was beautiful," he confirmed—as do other NDE subjects—a sense of transcendence that created in him a life-changing spirituality. NDE subjects also have described an awareness of a being with whom they communicate. In some instances, the "presence" has been interpreted as an awareness of God, with whom they talked but could not see. Most persons experiencing similar "deaths" have reported seeing angels instead of a supreme deity. Likely because he had been baptized by Roman Catholic missionaries and had attended Protestant missionary services on the Skokomish Reservation, Slocum saw representations of angels in human form with wings, flowing white robes, and perhaps halos. After his experience, he vividly reported having met angelic beings who guided him and gave him the option of returning to his body.[19]

The NDE syndrome is ages old, and is a worldwide phenomenon. In Sanskrit, it is called *kundalini* and represents an enlightenment induced by energy released from storage at the base of the spine. At the moment of transcendence, recipients are thought to be geniuses "of high order." From such experiences, researcher Raymond A. Moody reported that he had found no subjects of NDE who had not undergone "a very deep and positive transformation." Kenneth Ring confirmed that these persons have "direct personal realization of a higher spiritual reality." The essentially spiritual experience, Ring concluded, serves to catalyze spiritual awakening and development. Inherent in the transformation is the resolve to take up a crusade.[20] It was in this mode that Slocum not only resolved to abandon his former excesses to preach the word of God, but also to give tangible evidence of his life change

A sketch of John Slocum
from a photograph in the
Smithsonian Institution.
This sketch appeared in the
Mason County (Shelton,
Wash.) *Journal*, December
10, 1897.

by founding a new church.

Ring also reported that NDE subjects were "ecstatic" and experienced "noetic illumination."[21] This fits well with Slocum's utterances after his "death," which contrasted sharply with the obscene language he had used before his illness. Slocum attributed to divine intervention his ability to communicate the urgency of fulfilling his heavenly calling by persuading others to follow his teachings. His new words, cleansed of profanity, were proof of his desire to follow his heavenly calling; he even admonished his people to foreswear profanity themselves. Slocum fits the NDE profile so well that Ring could have used him as a subject for his study. That Slocum experienced the classic NDE symptoms without ever having heard of the syndrome only validates his near-death.

In any event, this one event in John Slocum's life gave rise to the Indian Shaker Church (ISC). Word of Slocum's new religion spread among natives of southern Puget Sound and subsequently to other places in the Pacific Northwest. The enthusiasm for the new church, although much less extensive than other religions that took root during the nineteenth century, is reminiscent of George Fox's Society of Friends (Quakers), John Wesley's Methodism, and Joseph Smith's Church of Jesus Christ of Latter-day Saints (Mormons). There was also precedent in Native American communities of spiritual persons who had reported their transcendence of the material world. They included Handsome Lake, a Seneca; Tenskwatawa, a Shawnee; and Smohalla, who influenced Wovoka, the Paiute who began the Ghost Dance movement. Interestingly, all of these men fused elements from one or more religious sources to create their own set of beliefs and practices.

John Slocum began his spiritual journey with influences gathered from both his native heritage and Christian teachings. Had he more fully heeded the teachings of those traditions and had he not so easily succumbed to the destructive practices of whites, he might not have taken his journey at all. But all of these conditions combined to produce Slocum's transformation, which formed the life-changing legacy he sought to bequeath to others.

CHAPTER TWO

Pacific Northwest
Native Religion and
Early Christian Missionaries

T ime and tide from an aeonic past formed Puget Sound and the
fingerlike extensions that stretch from its southern extremities,
among which is John Slocum's homeland. Sweeping inland from
the Pacific Ocean, strong westerly winds pelt the sound with heavy
rains, helping to create a forested panoply of cedar, fir, spruce,
and hemlock. To the northwest is the Olympic Peninsula, with its
wild, rugged, concentric mountains. Only occasionally did native
peoples enter the Olympics, and then cautiously to hunt game and
gather roots and berries. According to native oral tradition, in "the
days long gone by," people came to a small place in the heart of the
mountains called the Valley of Peace. For some unknown reason,
the powerful god Seatco became angry with those in the valley and
caused the ground to shake, burying them beneath earth and water. Only a few escaped to tell of the catastrophe, and they never
went to the mountains again.

To the south lay the Willapa Hills, nature's first continental
line of defense from the battering of Pacific storms. Unlike the
Olympics, these hills offer less leeside protection from the ele-
ments, and storms sweep eastward to the Cascade Mountains.
Impeding their progress is majestic, perpetually snow-capped
Mount Rainier—known as Almost to Heaven, or Tacoma, "the

nourishing (or mothering) breast," whose glacial milk nourishes valleys below.

There are many stories about the creation of the Puget Sound area. According to one story from native oral tradition, parched inhabitants of the desert on the lee side of the Cascade Mountains asked Ocean for water. Ocean sent two daughters, Clouds and Rain, to create a land of flourishing vegetation. Thirsty for even more water, the desert people dug deep holes in which to store it. But Ocean was lonely and grieved for his daughters, and he sent messengers to escort them home to the sea. The selfish desert people refused to let them go and sent the messengers back alone. The vengeful Great Spirit retaliated by scooping out Puget Sound to form the Cascade Mountains, blocking the rain from the sea and causing lands to the east to revert once more to desert.[1]

The Sahewamish-Squaxins, Slocum's people, lived in the Puget Sound basin, along with neighboring Skokomishes and other native peoples. They appropriated natural gifts with remarkable resourcefulness, fashioning canoes from the sacred cedar to skim the waters of Puget Sound and stripping tree fibers from the cedar's inner bark to weave floor coverings, hats, shawls, and skirts. With ingeniously devised tools, they took a variety of fish and other foods from along the shores of Puget Sound. In nearby hills, they hunted game and gathered roots and berries. They also took advantage of ancient trails and much-traversed sea lanes to establish complex trade patterns that long antedated the coming of whites. They formed close ties with other villages, not only for trade and socializing but also for protection from enemies. Slaves from distant places came to them through trade or capture. Subsistence patterns and life ways among Squaxins and their neighbors changed during the early nineteenth century as they acquired goods and technologies from Euro-Americans. From aboard ships and later from land-based trading posts, the Squaxins and other native peoples were introduced to sugar and molasses, metal tools and utensils, calicos and other fabrics, guns, beads and baubles, liquor, and diseases.

Traditionally, natives of the region implored Tamahnous—a guardian spirit, a power assumed in youth—to provide their needs. They also believed the Changer, a deity figure called Dokibatt by the Skokomishes, could effect a change in the sources and types

NATIVE RELIGION AND CHRISTIAN MISSIONARIES

of their provisions. Reverend Myron Eells, a Congregational minister who came among Skokomishes, Squaxins, and Clallams in 1874, wrote ten years later: "Whether this [Dokibatt] is a dim tradition of the coming of Christ or not, I have never been able to satisfy myself. I can only record it as I have learned it from the Indians. But it is certain that in their first learning of our Savior, they have connected the two together."[2]

Puget Sound natives regarded religious activity as sentient and personal, ranging outward to the cosmological and forward to the eschatological.[3] Important in the religious practice was the belief in a life soul, an inherent spiritual entity present from birth (and different from Tamahnous). If people lose their life souls, their bodies become ill. Such a loss could occur when a ghost came from the land of death, belowground, to snatch the life soul of a person on earth (usually a relative) and return to the netherworld with it. The theft of a life soul could also originate with an angry person who wanted to visit illness on someone for revenge. The angered person might hire a shaman who had the power to induce a ghost to steal the life soul of the victim. In either instance, it took a good shaman with a power stronger than the thieving ghost to recover the lost soul.[4]

The Skokomishes believed that ghosts existed for a time after death, hovering over and around villagers, awaiting summons from powerful shamans to steal life souls. Reputable shamans were hired to diagnose illnesses and to cure sicknesses of the soul. Shamans were also hired to "shoot" pieces of bone, wood, pebbles, and the like into disliked persons. In order to cure victims and recover lost or stolen souls or to exorcise foreign bodies, participants sang, chanted, and beat sticks on boards. Shamans made incantations and "awful contortions" and in some instances shook rattles and scooped foreign intrusions from the bodies of sufferers.[5]

Lacking understanding, if not tolerance, of such native practices, Reverend Eells described their ceremonies in the late nineteenth century as a "howling and praying" over victims. One practice Eells knew little about was the secretive "black *Tamahnous*" ritual in which individuals in "their savage days" went through "disgusting ceremonies" conducted by black-faced shamans. In 1916, believing the society was moribund, a Clallam Indian felt safe enough to relate how candidates for the society were selected for membership. The initiation, he recalled, included a few days' isolation to instruct candidates how they should conduct themselves at the ceremony. Unaware of the initiates' welfare, he said, were those on the outside who feared their child had died, which was indeed the fate of some of them. Death could also befall those who divulged the society's secrets.[6] Many years later, and with more understanding than Eells had, T. T. Waterman described the Spirit Canoe ceremony, an important religious ritual for healing the sick. When shamans returned with strayed souls, replacing them in bodies of wanderers, the restored person fell into what he termed a "shaking fit." Shamans believed that this power entered poles that were drummed on roof boards, throwing their drummers into a tremulous state.[7] In another type of soul recovery, power planks or boards held at participants' sides quivered and moved about, throwing their holders into tremors and even drawing persons around the room and through fires.

In early postcontact times, the Power Sing, a ceremony derived from both curing and noncuring shamanic rituals, was conducted by persons who had no shamanistic powers. In the ceremonial demonstration of fire tricks, nonshamans gave life to inanimate objects and pierced and cut portions of people's bodies. The Power Sing was used by natives who sought protection against hostile warriors and shamans from other groups. Although participants could become extremely aggressive and cause death, the demonstrations were socially sanctioned and there were no reprisals from relatives of those killed. With white contact, these activities declined, but they would find expression in a different venue—the Indian Shaker Church.[8]

There is no question that Christian missionaries played an important role in the suppression of shamanism. What some have generously called the first "exposure" to Christianity in the region occurred on August 1, 1790, when Spanish explorer Alfred Manuel Quimper, commanding the *Princess Real*, landed at Neah Bay on the southwestern shores of the Strait of Juan de Fuca at its confluence with the Pacific Ocean. On landing, sailors carried a cross ashore, chanted a litany, and named the place Nunez Gaona. On May 1, 1792, Lt. Salvador Fidalgo, commanding the *Princess*, established a village on the site. There Fidalgo and his men stayed a few months. Records make no mention of a chapel or chaplain there, but one Catholic historian recorded that Makah natives "were converted," implying the presence of a priest and a place of worship.[9] The short-lived Spanish presence evoked little enthusiasm among the native peoples in the region. Mitigating what might have been a more pleasant meeting was the natives' wariness of the strangers, especially since instances of physical conflict between maritimers and natives had occurred all along the northwest coast. Word of such troubles could easily have reached the village at Neah Bay, for it lay at the crossroads of maritime trade.

After Spain lost its hold on the region at the end of the eighteenth century, Britain controlled it through the Hudson's Bay Company (HBC), a large fur-trading enterprise. Influenced by evangelical movements in the wake of the Napoleonic wars, officials of the London-based company kept the idea of Christianity alive among the Indians by charging HBC traders with instilling Christian principles among natives at its posts. The post with the most religious influence on John Slocum's predecessors was Fort Nisqually, established in 1833 in southern Puget Sound near present-day Olympia, Washington. The post attracted natives from the region around Puget Sound and the Strait of Juan de Fuca who came to exchange furs for company goods.

Records of one HBC trader reveal early efforts to impart Christian teachings and traditions to the natives. On Sunday, December 22, 1833, the trader claimed to have altered the natives' "savage natures." A week later, on December 29, natives gathered "for edification," and on Sunday, January 12, 1834, there were "a good many Indians about the place beginning to think seriously on religious subjects." Two weeks later, on January 26, the trader spent the Sabbath performing his religious duties, "in which they [the Indians] have become very punctual." While exposing the native population to Christian teachings, the HBC trader also recognized the importance of harmonizing Christian teachings with native dance. Without such, the man admitted that the Indians would "think very little of what we say to them."[10]

The Methodists also brought their religion to the frontier. They were the first missionaries to respond to the "Macedonian Call" of a Flathead–Nez Percé delegation to St. Louis in 1831, which sought the whites' "Book of Heaven." The Indians who made the journey to St. Louis had come under the influence of Iroquois Indians who had come among the Flatheads and neighboring natives in the early nineteenth century. The Iroquois had taught the Flatheads and others an elementary form of Catholic doctrine. One student of the Flatheads reported that an Iroquois, Shining Shirt, had prophesied the coming of white-skinned, black-robed men to teach them a new religion and give them new names. The "black robes," according to the prophecy, would change the Indians' lives both spiritually and materially. Shining Shirt predicted that wars would cease and a flood of white men would follow. Anthropologist Leslie Spier cited Iroquois Christian teachings as influential in the formation of the Prophet Dance phenomenon. He traced the spread of that dance from the Flatheads to other native groups east of the Cascade Mountains. There is evidence that its spread, or at least its influence, reached natives of the Puget Sound area several years before Christian missionaries did.[11]

In 1838, Catholic priests Francis N. Blanchet and Modeste Demers reached the lower Columbia River at Fort Vancouver. They had come from eastern Canada to effect spiritual repairs among Hudson's Bay Company employees and to minister to the region's native peoples. Appointed vicar-general of the Jesuit order soon after arriving at Vancouver, Blanchet went north roughly fifty miles to the Cowlitz Prairie to minister to company employees and their families. In Simon Plomondon's home, he established the first Roman Catholic mission in what is now the state of Washington and also ministered to the natives who gathered there. The Indians' response was lukewarm, although some of them had already visited Fort Vancouver in search of religious instruction. At Cowlitz, Demers also baptized native children and taught their parents canticles and how to make the sign of the cross.

Aware of the Methodist intent to establish a mission at Fort Nisqually, about fifty miles north of the Cowlitz mission, Blanchet dispatched Demers there to compete against Protestant teachings. Word of his coming must have spread, for when Demers arrived on April 21, 1839, he found Indians from twenty-two groups at the fort. Demers's mission at Fort Nisqually became the fountainhead of Christian religion in the upper sound.

Demers was aware of the challenge facing him. He judged that the natives' morals were bad but, with an optimism typical of other Catholic missionaries, noted that "their humane and docile char-

This sketch, by J. R. Blackwood, was made from a historical sketch of Fort Nisqually, a Hudson's Bay Company post established in 1833 in John Slocum's home territory on the southern reaches of Puget Sound. The fort was both a trading and a religious center for the Indians of Puget Sound and its environs. John Slocum may have been influenced by the Roman Catholics and Methodists who at one time or another ministered to the native traders at the fort. (*J. R. Blackwood, Moses Lake, Wash.*)

acter gives hope that God will deign presently to receive them into His church." Wary of having so many Indians within the fort, post trader William Kittson obliged Demers to move with them outside the walls, where he could explain "the dogmatic and moral truths of the religion." Because the older Indians declined to receive baptism, Demers administered to their children that initial sacrament of the church's "seven medicines."[12]

Late August 1839 found Blanchet—"the great French chief," as he called himself—explaining to natives at Fort Nisqually the principles of his faith. His words were conveyed through an interpreter speaking the Chinook jargon—the only communication available to Catholic priests in the early days of their mission. In his own small house, perhaps not unlike those of natives who lived near the fort, Blanchet answered his neophytes' questions about the creation of the world, the fall of the angels and Adam, and redemption through the Savior. Like Demers, he stressed the importance of baptism to remove "the spiritual stain which comes to us from our first father [Adam]."[13]

Blanchet reinforced his teachings with pictures and "the ladder" (to the Indians, the *saghalie* stick), which he had devised to depict the great events of Catholic history. On the lower rungs of the ladder, the fiery hell of the netherworld, destination of nonbelievers and Protestants, was illustrated. In a nightly service, Blanchet led the Indians in prayers and the rosary, followed by incantations. Upon leaving the mission on September 12, just weeks after having arrived, he distributed images and crosses "of differing values according to the quality of persons receiving them." He spoke about the kingdom of God, shook hands with about three hundred natives, and went on his way south to the Cowlitz mission.[14]

The secular department of the Methodist mission, an outpost of Jason Lee's Willamette station, had been established before Blanchet arrived at Nisqually. In 1840, Dr. John P. Richmond, a Methodist minister, arrived at the fort with his family, but they would stay for only two years, leaving shortly before their home was burned by what some believed was a vengeful Indian. When Navy Lt. Charles Wilkes visited Richmond at Nisqually in 1841, he reported that prospects for the mission were "not very flattering," since the mission was "doing nothing with the Indian tribes."[15] Richmond said he was leaving Nisqually because of the "inevitable doom" of the natives." They were "fast sinking into the grave," he concluded, from habits that prevented them from hearing the gospel.[16] Richmond would also have been aware of the intermittent and devastating diseases that had hit the area in the 1830s and ravaged large numbers of natives, especially those who lived along the lower Columbia. Undoubtedly, Richmond would also have been discomfited by the Catholic missionary presence at Nisqually.

To reinforce that presence, Blanchet had left the Willamette Valley on May 4, 1840, returning to Nisqually on May 16. Among the many natives at Nisqually was a Sahewamish chief from an island (perhaps Squaxin Island) located near the southwestern extremity of Puget Sound, in John Slocum's homeland. At Nisqually, Blanchet followed the ministerial routine that he and Demers had used on their previous visits. Sometimes wearing an alb, he made the sign of the cross, rang a bell summoning the natives to mass, taught canticles, and baptized children. The missionaries at Nisqually reported that the natives were able to "memorize words very readily" while gaining foreign ideas "rather slowly." But what some clerics termed "innate dullness of the Indian mind" was simply their difficulty in understanding English and, possibly, the Chinook jargon. More readily understandable and appealing were the missionaries' bells. Blanchet was convinced that the natives believed his words and understood the significance of the cross and bell, noting that on one occasion they "hurried forward at the first sound of the bell."[17]

Although four decades would elapse before John Slocum's revelation, the 1840 visit of the Sahewamish chief to Nisqually could have set in motion a chain of events that would link Slocum and his people to the missionaries' teachings.[18] Important links in that chain were such elements of Catholic worship as bells, crosses, and baptisms, all very observable and dramatic symbols and practices in Catholic worship. The Indians appear to have been ambivalent about the rite of baptism, which was Blanchet's most immediate concern if he was to rescue them from the flames of hell. Although older natives did not submit to baptism, they allowed their children to receive it. Those adults apparently believed there was efficacy in baptism as there was in other practices and symbols of the Catholic Church and may have thought it gave their children physical and spiritual protection. Considering the heavy loss of life Indians had experienced from alien diseases, they may also have believed that baptism offered immunity from death.[19]

Lieutenant Wilkes observed the fruits of Blanchet's and others' labors in 1841 near Port Discovery on Discovery Bay, a small arm of the Strait of Juan de Fuca. There he met an Indian who showed him a cross and repeated his "ave" with "great readiness and apparent devotion." North of Port Orchard, Wilkes also saw a strong Catholic influence on Whidbey Island. He noted a large cross and a building, 172 feet by 72 feet, in which there were "rude images" and natives "telling their beads" and singing Catholic hymns in their own language.[20]

Following the spiritual path blazed by Jesuits Blanchet and Demers, secular priest Jean Bolduc spent the winter of 1842–1843 at Cowlitz and then journeyed to Puget Sound to establish a mission. At Nisqually he found a small encampment of natives, "the remnant of a tribe formerly rather numerous, but today destroyed partly by the syphilitic diseases the white man has given them."

On Sunday, March 18, 1843, he was in the vicinity of lower Vancouver Island, "for so many years the theater of hell's abominations," meeting with Clallams, Samishes, and Cowichans who had threatened to kill "the priest" (probably Blanchet) about a year earlier.[21] After waiting in vain for a ship to take him to trading posts to the north, Bolduc returned to Whidbey Island, where he shook hands with over 600 Indians and baptized 130 of their children. Chief Netlum's son told him that his father had said mass every Sunday and acted as the natives' confessor, for which services he collected payment.[22]

Because of the missionary efforts of Blanchet and Demers, in 1850 Pope Pius IX created the diocese of the District of Nisqually, which included the settlement of Olympia. But the missionaries were less successful than they had hoped, and some oblates (following secular priest Auguste Veyret) would later differ with Blanchet and leave the diocese for Canada. One of the secular priests, Father Louis J. D'Herbomez, wrote, "Experience has proved only too clearly that all the good we can hope to do among the Indians of the Oregon and Washington territories can be reduced to this—to care for the Indians who are still benevolent toward us (and their number decreases every day), to baptize the children, the sick and the agonizing."[23]

In 1853, a smallpox epidemic devastated Pacific Northwest Indians, spreading from the Chinooks of the lower Columbia River to Puget Sound tribes and then to the Makahs, who lost half their people to the disease.[24] It is likely that the deaths contributed to a continued pace of Catholic baptisms. The Indian wars in the Northwest did little to ingratiate Catholic priests to the Squaxins. In 1854, the Medicine Creek Treaty set aside the nearly fifteen-hundred-acre Squaxin Island (Kla-che-min) in the south sound for the Sahewamishes and Squaxins, and the two peoples were designated "Squaxin." A June 30, 1856, letter from J. W. Nesmith, superintendent of Indian affairs for Oregon and Washington territories, relayed word to the secretary of the interior that Squaxins did not encourage visits from Catholic missionaries.[25] The center of continuing Catholic efforts among Puget Sound Indians was the Tulalip Reservation (in Snohomish Indian homelands), where Rev. Eugene Casimir Chirouse, O.M.J., was appointed its agent and was authorized to serve Indians in the northern sound. So important was his influence that Indians reckoned time by "before Father Chirouse came" (1857) and "after Father Chirouse left" (1878). His position and that of his church would be strengthened by Pres. Ulysses S. Grant's Peace Policy of the 1870s, which assigned agency governance to church bodies.[26]

Although having gleaned a large harvest of juveniles through baptism, the clergy, especially Blanchet and Demers, must have felt a deep sense of loss for not having reaped a full harvest of native souls. Nevertheless, they helped lay a reoriented spiritual groundwork among the Indians upon which John Slocum and his followers—carrying vestiges of native traditions—could build their church.

The World of
John Slocum

John Slocum's world was one of traumatic change for him and his people. In December 1854, Puget Sound Indians and the U.S. government signed a treaty at Medicine Creek. The following year, Indians on the sound signed additional treaties at Point No Point, Neah Bay, and Quinault River. Across the Cascade Mountains to the east, in the Walla Walla Valley, Columbia River Plateau tribes also signed treaties with the government. The Indians' disgruntlement with the reservations established under these agreements was a major cause of the ensuing Puget Sound phase of the Yakama Indian War. It was during this conflict that the primarily neutral Squaxins and other Puget Sound tribes were moved about to keep them safe from Indian "hostiles."[1]

After the Indian wars were concluded in 1858, whites continued to move into the Puget Sound area, taking up land that had formerly belonged to native tribes. From 1874, when the government allotted lands on the Puyallup Indian Reservation, non-Indian populations burgeoned in such Puget Sound cities as Olympia, Tacoma, and Seattle. The Indians were overwhelmed, not only by such encroachment but also by the need to further accommodate the newcomers' demands for land. Between 1860 and 1890, the year after Washington achieved statehood, the non-Indian population of Washington grew from something over a thousand to 348,390.[2]

The lethal by-products of decades of white encroachment on native lands were drink, disease, and death, intensifying Indian anguish as their culture underwent severe change. New kinds of food, clothing, and shelter were superimposed on native traditions, resulting in what has been termed "half-civilization." The norm for coastal tribes at contact had been a society stratified into an aristocracy based on wealth and lineage, free commoners, and slaves acquired through war or inheritance. This traditional social structure crumbled as Euro-American traders imposed new trade practices and products on natives. The resultant changes in native economic patterns reduced the wealth and status of the aristocracy and eliminated slavery through attrition.

At about the time of Slocum's birth, in 1838 or 1839, native cultural traditions were being eroded under the influence of the missionaries who appeared at Fort Nisqually. The decade and a half after clerics came to the area was one of relative calm before conflict between whites and Indians broke out in reaction to economic interruptions and federal land-taking policies. Old mores were challenged by new religious standards amidst the Catholic-Protestant contest for Indian souls. New concepts of time, work, and wages were imposed on Indians, who took up logging, oystering, and other jobs. Formal education threatened traditional native learning customs, and many Indians resisted the government's schools. In 1857 a government school on Squaxin Island reported only five boys and three girls in attendance. Over the next several years, the Indians began picking up the debris strewn by the storm of cultural change.[3]

It was during this time that John Slocum (sometimes called S'dup by his people) came on the scene. He had been raised at Church Point on Skookum Bay on Hammersley Inlet near present-day Shelton, Washington. Slocum was a lineal descendant of Old Chouse, who reportedly lived to be over a hundred years old and was "Hyas Tyee" or "big chief" of all Indians in the southern sound before whites came to the area.[4] Old Chouse's son, John's father, was a hunter and trapper. He bore the moniker "Old Slocum," perhaps to distinguish him from John and John's half-brothers, Tom and Jack. Old Slocum's first wife, John's mother (probably a

Suquamish), was said to be crippled. After her death, Old Slocum took two more wives, a common practice among the native nobility. Under a government decree to keep but one wife, however, Old Slocum chose the older of the two and abandoned "Auntie" Slocum, the Skokomish mother of Tom and Jack.[5]

In his declining years, Old Slocum went blind and returned to live with Auntie Slocum in a float house anchored on Oakland Bay near Shelton. The two canoed to various places where Auntie Slocum worked for whites and also did business for herself, gathering and shucking oysters and selling them from house to house. She found recreation at horse races, especially during Fourth of July celebrations, when she would leave her husband in the care of a white family who fed him and kept him from straying by securing him with a rope.[6]

Little is known of John Slocum's early years. As an adult, he was described as being about five feet eight inches tall and weighing 160 pounds; he reportedly had a sparse beard and thick, long black hair. If this description is accurate, Slocum was of average height and build for a Puget Sound native male. As early as 1857, Slocum wore clothing like that worn by white loggers. In addition to his native language, according to one source, he spoke reasonably good English, even though he never attended school. Judge James Wickersham of Tacoma, Slocum's contemporary and legal counsel, recorded that Slocum had a "fashionably flat" head, produced by pressure applied to his head when he was an infant. The cranial disfigurement, although allowed for all free people, was the special hallmark of upper-class natives. As to Slocum's mental traits, Wickersham described him as "modest and rather retiring . . . [with] unquestioned confidence in himself and his mission."[7]

By the time John Slocum was an adult, it appears that the two most important things in his earthly world were logs and liquor. With an abundance of timber, Puget Sound mills, eastern capital, western markets, and a large Indian labor force, the region's magnificent coniferous forests were literally attacked by whites seeking quick profits. The first sawmill in the area was built in the upper reaches of the sound in 1847, and by 1856 sixteen sawmills operated around the sound. In the 1850s most of the region's lumber was shipped to places such as San Francisco, where the 1852 fire had created a high demand for it.

The industry continued to grow, with mills being built near Slocum's home, such as the Willey Mill built in 1871 at the head of Big Skookum Bay. Lacking adequate lumber for an expanding market, this and other Puget Sound mills continued to depend on local Indians to supply their logs. In 1878, Washington Superintendent of Indian Affairs R. H. Milroy reported that Indians were responsible for two-thirds of timber cutting west of the Cascade Mountains. At about that same time, logging operators received from five to seven dollars for every thousand board feet of timber delivered.[8]

Slocum became a "boss logger" who owned his own logging outfit and hired and paid his own crew. His crew felled huge trees with crosscut saws and debarked sections of logs, which they slid over eight-foot skids placed crosswise at ten-foot intervals. The skids were greased by constant applications of dogfish oil. The men built corduroy roads and bridges over saltwater marshes and muddy bays. Slocum was part of this effort both before and after his 1882 "death." In 1887, the March 11 *Mason County Journal* reported that Slocum—with a fourteen-man crew and six oxen— was planning to open a road a mile from the railroad near Shelton, Washington. When booms were full at Hammersley Inlet, where Slocum and others sledded their logs, steamers boomed them to other mills around the sound. In addition to the Port Blakely mill on the southern end of Bainbridge Island (west of present-day Seattle), logs were shipped to the Port Gamble mill on the upper Kitsap Peninsula.

Slocum spent some time on the Skokomish Indian Reservation, and there is the strong possibility that he was either involved in or influenced by a plan that Indian agent Edwin Eells (Reverend Eells's brother) devised for the Indians. In his 1882 report, Agent Eells wrote that logging was the main business on Puget Sound but that Indians were not allowed to cut and haul from their reservation. He wished that unemployed Indians did not have to leave the Skokomish Reservation to work where they were exposed to "vice and drunkenness" and "the lower classes of civilization." Presumably before he knew of restrictions on harvesting reservation timber, Eells had tried to organize timber sales for the benefit of Indians by establishing several camps with from a dozen to twenty Indian men and white teamsters. He also got the Indians to use two yokes, of oxen instead of one to haul logs to Hood Canal for booming to Seabeck, about thirty miles distant on the canal's eastern shore. He then accompanied the Indians to see that the logs were properly scaled. After the sales were made, the workers sat in a circle where silver dollars were thrown to each until the money boxes were empty. Eells withdrew fifty cents from the proceeds from each thousand feet of lumber sold so those who were weak and sick in the tribe could purchase flour, blankets, and other goods. Despite carefully reporting all transactions to the Indian Office, Eells was subsequently sued by the federal government for allowing timber cutting on the reservation.[9]

Liquor was the other important element in Slocum's world. In 1864, an Indian agent reported the Squaxin Island Indian Reservation was "surrounded by logging camps, which are occupied by men of very loose and immoral habits, who are continually taking the Indian women and furnishing the men with whiskey."[10]

On the Skokomish Reservation in 1865, Subagent John T. Knox requested five to ten soldiers from Fort Steilacoom to prevent the Indians from trading annuity goods for whiskey. Knox claimed one small victory by purchasing the claim of a peddler, "the Dutchman," to keep liquor out of the hands of "those devils, who live on the Indians." Nevertheless, because there was no governmental control, the whiskey peddlers got off to a fast start, even recording early bans on sales as a "big joke."[11] In 1874, Agent Eells admitted that "trying to prevent the Indians from drinking and fighting the whiskey ring was one of my most difficult undertakings. It was uphill work and I lost more often than I won."[12]

The same year, Eells reported a "gleam of light" with the appointment of a new U.S. district judge, a U.S. marshal, and a prosecuting attorney, which he claimed "struck terror into the hearts of those who had fearlessly broken the laws for many years."[13] Securing convictions of the whiskey peddlers was difficult, however, as they threatened to kill Indians who revealed the sources of their liquor. The situation was so bad, especially in such remote areas as Dungeness on the Strait of Juan de Fuca, that Reverend Eells went there in 1878 to try to protect the Indians from the whiskey sellers. Eells noted that Indians who lived off the reservation—as Slocum did for a time—were more tempted to drink and had less fear of punishment by government officials.[14]

The Skokomish Indian Reservation was also in spiritual turmoil during the 1870s, with native, Roman Catholic, and Protestant religions in ferment. John Slocum witnessed or heard of these conflicts and knew many of the people involved. He was also involved in the ferment himself. He had been baptized by a Catholic priest and over the years had come under the influence of both Presbyterians and Congregationalists.[15]

Reverend Myron Eells and his agent brother, Edwin, provide the earliest information about developments in this religious swirl. Both men stood at its vortex, not as impartial observers but as participants. As agent of the U.S. government, Edwin sought to carry out the government's 1871 mandate to stamp out Indian doctoring. For his part, Reverend Eells was wary of a possible Catholic influence among Indians on the reservation, despite Grant's Peace Policy, which had awarded Skokomish Agency management to the Congregational Church.[16] Eells's hopes for a Catholic-free agency, however, were shattered on August 22, 1875, when he noted what he termed a "Catholic nest" in the Indian camp on the Skokomish. Among the practitioners were Quilcene George and Billy Waterman, both of whom would become prominent in John Slocum's church.[17]

The possibility of Catholic influence seems to have stimulated Reverend Eells to renewed missionary and investigatory effort. On June 18, 1877, he reported success in teaching rote prayers to Big Bill, a Skokomish Indian, and to others who had received instruction and baptism from Catholic priests. When Eells had visited logging camps in 1875 to hold prayer meetings, Big Bill had emerged as the leading exponent of Christianity. He learned from Eells how to pray sentence by sentence, for which ability his people selected him as the one most suitable to pray.[18] Big Bill and others took Eells's teachings and created a religion that combined Protestant and Catholic beliefs with traditional native practices. Because many of the Indians had been Catholics, a number of whom Father Eugene Chirouse had baptized and trained as catechists and termed "Indian priests," Reverend Eells applied the label "half Catholic" (the other half, native) not only to Big Bill but later to John Slocum's followers as well.[19]

Indian resistance to the Congregationalists came from what Reverend Eells called the "Catholic sett [sic]," which included Big

Bill and others who would later convert to Slocum's religion. The group, wrote Eells, made "some fun of our religion" while leaning "rather strongly toward the Catholics and talked that way." He claimed that by advice, reason, and command he resisted the Indians' intent to invite Father Chirouse to return among them to preach, especially since the priest could communicate with them in their own language. As Eells recorded it, a greater threat would have been for Chirouse to have sent an Indian "priest" or catechist to work with them.[20]

Trying to expunge Catholic teachings and practices from his charges' minds, Eells discovered a formidable obstacle in Big Bill's ministrations. In the mid-1870s, both Eells and Skokomish head man Dick Lewis had recorded that Big Bill experienced visions. Lewis later remembered that Big Bill had been sick for about five years and his hand was turning black. When his hand "was loosened," Big Bill received help from God, at which time an angel was so close to him that he began to shake, relating strange things to the people. One of those revelations, said Lewis, was that the Lord would take speech away from an elderly woman. "And it was done," Lewis recalled. Later, Shaker Head Elder Tenas Pete recalled that Big Bill had said that God would send a sickness on logger Chehalis Jack for laughing at him. "So all happened true," according to Tenas Pete.[21]

Reverend Eells balked at Big Bill's attempt to give as much validity to native teachings as he did to the Bible. Eells told Big Bill that his revelations were not as valid as those found in the Bible and attributed some of Big Bill's communications with the divine to an infection of his nervous system. The spiritualism of Big Bill and his followers was more than Eells could stand, he complained, and their "music is horrid."[22] Ill from tuberculosis, Big Bill wavered in his faith, turning to God and Catholicism and sometimes to native doctors and his own Tamahnous. But during his rift with Eells, he reverted more to his own religious beliefs and held services. Nevertheless, Eells received him into the Congregational Church on May 9, 1880, and allowed him and his people to sing their songs as they listened to Eells preach. Big Bill requested baptism in Eells's church and Eells agreed. When he was too ill to attend church, Big Bill held services in his own house, twice on Sundays and on Thursday evenings to imitate Congregational practices. Big Bill died thirteen months after his baptism by Eells.[23]

According to reports from Eells and Big Bill's brother, some weeks before Big Bill died he had an unusual experience. After he had tried to hang himself, Big Bill hallucinated.[24] He saw a light coming up the road and heard a voice that sounded like his grandfather's. Someone by his side said, "I am the one that called you. I am Sandyalla, your brother." (Sandyalla may have been an old friend of Big Bill's who had died a few years before.) According to accounts, Sandyalla's coat buttons shone with light as he handed Big Bill a cup and told him to drink from it. "You have done wrong today," said Sandyalla, "and I am going to arrest you."[25] Sandyalla then put handcuffs on the sick man. One woman later claimed to have seen smoke (representing evil) coming from every joint of Big Bill's fingers. Sandyalla reportedly put one end of a string into Big Bill's mouth; the other end reached to heaven. Then Sandyalla put the string in his mouth and talked to God. Something like a ball with sharp things fell from heaven. That ball, said Sandyalla, is like bad words Indians say to others, which are like taking a pin from the ball and throwing it at someone—bad words are a bad thing. He told Bill, "I have been trying very hard to plead for you, so that you can enter Heaven. You have been sick five years now, and every year I have said to God, O let him live a little longer. Because you wanted to hang yourself is the reason I arrest you. Only six of us, your relations are in Heaven. The place is far off from this place. We six feel sad that all of you on earth do not turn to God. When daybreak comes I am going to fix you some way."[26]

Shifting from punishing to promising words, Sandyalla said that a place was prepared for Big Bill above and there was no reason why he should wish to remain in this wicked world. Sandyalla judged that God did not like it when shamans had told Big Bill they were going to "draw out the sickness." It was God, said Sandyalla, who made people sick and no Indian doctor had the right to take care of Big Bill. An Indian doctor should first pray to God to do the healing, said Sandyalla, since God tested people with sickness to make them think of him. Rather than malicious shamans assaulting people and making them ill, Sandyalla told Big Bill that God gave sickness to those he liked so they would contemplate him in songs and prayers so they could be taken to heaven. To Sandyalla,

Wade Le Roy, engineer and long-time counselor and organizer for the 1910 Shaker Church. Following service in World War I, Le Roy, a white, became a Shaker convert and traveled to various Shaker churches by means as varied as motorcycle and airplane to conduct business. (*Robert H. Ruby and John A. Brown*)

Big Bill later reported, bad words were like throwing a pin at another, a practice reminiscent of native cures in which illness was believed to enter people through evil darts. In Sandyalla's credo, all persons were not lost, for "when Jesus was here on earth the people speared him, and the blood flowed down; so when Jesus sees anyone here cut or shot, he has pitty [*sic*] on him, good or bad and takes him to heaven."[27]

Sandyalla equated wealth with evil. He told Big Bill that rich whites and Indians do not think about God. Adam and Eve were poor because they chose evil over good. He went on to tell Bill that children do not belong to parents, but are on loan from God, who claims them until they are old enough to know the difference between good and evil. After that, they are on their own. In disciplining, switches are to be balanced with supplications, Sandyalla reportedly said, since God takes children's lives after they suffer corporal punishment at the hands of their parents.

In Sandyalla's exposition, according to Big Bill, unseen angels from both God and Satan came together in this world on God's

Leotah Bustillo of the Indian Full Gospel Church, who functions as a minister in that body, photographed on the Tulalip Indian Reservation. In keeping with the strong tradition of shaking and healing, Bustillo conducts services among the ill of her race. (*Robert H. Ruby and John A. Brown*)

Sabbath. The good angels come to assess and record people's good thoughts and deeds. The bad angels come to record and assess evil deeds, The bad angels come to record and assess evil deeds, such as cursing, stealing, and drinking.[28]

Near morning, Sandyalla reportedly told Big Bill that the world would turn upside down and Indians would be transformed into nonhuman objects if they did not turn to God. They were to thank God like songbirds each morning. There were other directions as well. Because all cedar was good in God's sight, it must not be kept under water. When people get sick they should light candles; In fact, Big Bill was to burn candles on both sides of him to light the world from sin and to do good. The apparition also told Big Bill that he would die on a Sabbath day but would not suffer harm since guardian angels would keep watch over him. Writing Big Bill's name in a book to take to heaven so it would be there when his soul arrived, Sandyalla urged the dying man not to have his people change their names, since God would have the names of the good people written in his book. In heaven Big Bill would have everything he wanted. Departing, Sandyalla sang a song: "By and by I will go to that happy land, by and by I will reach that happy land. There my heavenly father dwells. Holy land is the name of that place where I shall soon go."[29]

On awaking, Big Bill told his people to kneel and pray for an hour and a half, after which an angel would come down. The women who were there at the time, along with Dick Lewis, Big Bill's brother-in-law, and Joe Dan, Big Bill's brother, shook the sick man's hands. After his meeting with Sandyalla, Big Bill reportedly repudiated shamans.[30]

Big Bill finally succumbed to tuberculosis in mid-June 1881. Reverend Eells preached the funeral sermon, being less resistant to the idea since Big Bill's repudiation of shamans fourteen weeks earlier. He believed Big Bill's death represented his final shedding of Tamahnous. In the funeral service, Eells deferred to the use of such elements of Catholic worship as candles, spoken prayers, and signs of the cross; even so, Big Bill's followers held their own service for him, singing the songs he had told them to sing.[31]

Big Bill left behind what he believed were Sandyalla's teachings, which were kept alive by Billy Clams, who had shared religious leadership with Big Bill on the Skokomish Reservation, and Big Bill's brother, David. Big Bill's followers regarded his last words and songs as precious, and they combined them with those of Billy Clams. Reverend Eells did not approve of the new leadership: Billy Clams was "one of the worst Indians," he said, because he and his followers had confessed to being part Catholic. "Part full of Mary," Clams was now the most troublesome Indian on the reservation, according to Myron Eells.[32]

Agent Edwin Eells may have had even more hostility toward Clams than his brother did. He had had Clams arrested in early 1876 for disobeying an order to return to the reservation, give up the woman with whom he had eloped, and return to his wife. In about mid-July of that year Clams abandoned his wife a second time and eloped with another woman in a stolen canoe. In September, Eells appealed to Gen. O. O. Howard, who commanded the Department of the Columbia at Portland, for soldiers from Port Townsend to arrest Clams and return him to the Skokomish Indian Reservation. Early the next year, Agent Eells had Clams delivered, arrested, and jailed in the Port Townsend guardhouse, seeking to impress upon the Indians that Clams was being punished for disobedience more than for adultery and theft. Eells reported Clams's first episode as causing a revolt among Skokomishes and the second as stirring up more seeds of discontent among them. Billy Clams was eventually disenfranchised, and his rights to receive annuity goods were withdrawn. But the Eells brothers had not heard the last of him.[33]

Big Bill's spiritual journey was an important preview of John Slocum's, and there are interesting comparisons to be made between the two men's experiences. Both suffered life-threatening illness, and both were unconscious sometime during their illnesses. Both were influenced by Catholic, Protestant, and native teachings, and both had violated the moral standards of all three religions. Both Big Bill and John Slocum received redemptive heavenly messages, and finally, both were determined to save the souls of their people.

For his part, Slocum resolved to rescue his people from the chasm between shamanism and his new religion. The theological foundation of his new religion was Christianity. "I received the power from God to give you understanding that we must obey God the maker of mankind with all our strength," he exhorted his followers. "Obey one God, that is, God and his son Jesus Christ, and obey the spirit which God given to you."[34] He asked his people to follow him in order to be saved through the power of God and to prepare for their heavenly home. The alternative, he said, was hellfire and damnation. Slocum followed an important Christian mandate: Avoid things of the past; put aside the bad and become a good person if you would have a happy future, he said. Typical of this good-bad dualism was Slocum's injunction to trust the good spirit rather than the evil spirit. Once believers were purged of the worldly bad spirit and their bodies were surrounded by the protective power of the good spirit, they need pay no attention to harm. Their good spirit, according to Slocum, would take care of them and see that no evil spirit harmed them.[35]

The influence of Christianity on Slocum was also apparent in his wish and command to build a church house. According to one source, he ordered the structure built during the month after his "death." Reverend Eells reported that Slocum announced that a church house was needed on Skookum Bay, but he had to rely on

others to build it. Using lumber from a sawmill at the head of the
bay, his followers were apparently unable to complete the church
in the mandated four weeks, and part of the roof of the flimsily
built church was covered with matting. At one end was a wooden
cross; another cross, with candles on each wing, stood atop the
altar, or prayer table. The building was apparently windowless,
as other early frame Shaker church houses would be. Slocum requested a bell, which his followers obtained in nearby Olympia.
Upon completion of the building, about fifty converts "filled the
house and began to worship God."[36]

The practice of exhortation was important in John Slocum's
church, but even more important was the practice of healing. Evidence of that appeared in Slocum's first prayer after returning
from "death": "Our God is in heaven," he prayed. "If we die He will
take our life to heaven. Help us so that we shall not die. Wherever
we are, help us not to die. Our Father, who is there, always have
a good mind on us."[37] To his followers, this was as much a man-
ifestation of power as it was of faith. Charles Rakestraw of the
Indian school on the nearby Chehalis Reservation quoted Slocum
as saying;

> When people are sick we pray to God to cure them. We pray that he
> take away the evil and leave the good. When our body and heart feel
> warm we do good and sing songs. We learn good while we pray—
> voice says *"Do good."* We learn to help ourselves when sick [rather
> than receiving help from Indian doctors]—for help to cure him. We
> learn something once in a while to cure him. If we *don't care to help
> him we generally lose him.*[38]

Slocum emerged as a rescuer of bodies and souls. Most important for his credibility was his near-death experience, word of
which spread among the Indians, especially those of upper Puget
Sound. That he had survived to relate his celestial experience gave
strong impact to his words. Even more important was a second
experience—one in which he was rescued from the brink of death
by his own wife—an experience that would give Slocum and his
religion new life.

CHAPTER FOUR

Reviving
a Struggling Church

Less than a year following his "death" experience, John Slocum met with a second catastrophe. The event would revive the struggling church and bring about dramatic changes in the lives of many of its people. Slocum had been delivering vignette-like, lackluster messages to his followers, perhaps indicating his own backsliding, and it appeared that the excitement over his "death" had begun to wane. Slocum himself had in some ways foresaken his heavenly mission to race horses and canoes, gambling on the outcome. It was his wife, Mary Thompson, who now brought about a dramatic change in the course of the Shaker faith.[1]

According to one version of the story, on the day following a large and lengthy meeting on Squaxin Island, Slocum began hemorrhaging from the nose.[2] He attributed his condition to having had too much fun the previous day, when he had returned to Enetai at the mouth of the Skokomish River after burying a child at Bald Point. Slocum had caught a ride as a passenger in a canoe race. When the canoe fell behind, the paddlers asked him to help. Slocum obliged by taking up a paddle. Suddenly, he was stricken with pain and told Mary, "No matter if I am dying, don't let me go to those Indian doctors any more."[3] Slocum had already rejected shamanism. After his "death", he had told his father to tear the

clothes off Doctor Cush, a Skokomish shaman, and an unidentified
Squaxin shaman, possibly to symbolize rejection of shamanism.
He had even gone so far as to forbid shamans entry to his church
unless they repented, joined the new church, and promised to cure
without charging for their services.[4]

Mary Thompson was apparently sympathetic to Slocum's request, for she and her family believed that a shaman, Doctor Jim,
had been responsible for Slocum's earlier "death." She was also involved in a bitter, longstanding family feud over shamans. Several
years previously, Thompson's brother, Isaac (Henry) Thompson,
had allegedly contracted with a shaman to kill John Kittle, a
Slocum relative, because he coveted Kittle's wife. There were also
some who believed that John Slocum's father, Old Slocum, had arranged for the death of Thompson's father. Old Slocum believed
that his son's illness and "death" were the work of shamans whom
the Thompson family had hired.

When John Slocum began hemorrhaging at the Squaxin Island
meeting the day after the canoe race and it appeared that Mary
was not going to call for a shaman, the suspicious Old Slocum took
matters into his own hands and called in a female shaman to attend the sick man. In one version of the story, the shaman said she
could return John's straying soul to his body. With this assurance,
Old Slocum had John's brothers, Jack and Tom, take John to the
shaman's house, despite Mary's efforts to dissuade him from doing
so.

Some time later, Thompson went down a trail through the woods
to a beach at Church Point (in some accounts, to a stream) not far
from where the shaman was treating her husband. She may have
gone out of grief and worry as well as out of anger at John's family.[5]
At that point, from whatever cause, Thompson lost consciousness;
regaining it, she began to tremble all over. Her fellow religionists
explained Thompson's loss of consciousness as the power of God
and the Holy Spirit. Others claimed that on nearing the beach
Thompson heard Christ in heaven telling her not to weep but to
go home because her husband was still alive. When some of her relatives tried to restrain her, she reportedly broke away from them
and went home, where she found that Slocum had been carried
from the shaman's hut and placed on a bed.

Thompson had Slocum taken from his bed and laid on the floor

Mary Thompson, wife of the Shaker founder, John Slocum. Through her shaking she revived her husband after a severe illness in 1883. More than anyone else she put the imprint of shaking on his religion. She opposed those who would add practices such as Bible reading in church services. As in other churches of the time, however, men played the dominant roles in the Indian Shaker Church. Although at this writing no Shaker woman has served as bishop, women have been elders, ministers, and missionaries. From early times to the present they have actively participated in shaking and healing services. (*Indian Shaker Church Archives*)

in the middle of the room. According to reports, she ordered someone to place a wooden cross on the floor near him. Intermittently crossing herself, assured now of her power, she handed a bell that Slocum had used in services to her brother Isaac, whom she positioned at the right side of Slocum's head. She then ordered Isaac to ring the bell.[6] She reportedly ordered more handbells brought in and asked some of the group to come forward to witness what was about to happen.

In one account, Thompson began to sing a spirit song, which she might have composed. When the others could not keep time with the rhythm of the bells, she grabbed them and gave instructions to have the bells synchronized with her singing. She had covered Slocum with every woolen object she could find and positioned people around him. She placed her daughter Maggie, who was menstruating, at his head so he would not have to face her, a gesture reminiscent of the isolation of native women during menses. Placing her mother at Slocum's left shoulder and her sister-in-law at his left side, Thompson then positioned herself at his right shoulder. All held candles except Isaac, who rang his bell in rhythm with Thompson's singing. Now Thompson began to shake over Slocum, a condition that would eventually give Slocum's religion the name "Shaker." Soon Isaac and Thompson's mother and sister-in-law began twitching and jumping as well. When Isaac waved his arms and spoke of God, four persons, said to be under the power, shook, a sign of redemption and salvation. Thompson was said to have sung songs "direct from God" and danced around the room as she went through the process of restoring her husband to life. When those she touched began shaking, too, Thompson's relatives believed it a sign of blessing from the "Big Father" in heaven.[7]

According to Slocum's followers, the sick man's hands soon began trembling under the power of God and control of the Spirit. He then rose to his feet, and within a day his body and flesh returned to normal; he had gained back the weight lost immediately before his healing. This supposedly fulfilled Thompson's prediction that Slocum's face would fill out rapidly, as though bitten by a horsefly. Slocum's recovery was rapid, and he soon returned to logging and exhorting.

Slocum's people now interpreted the use of shaking as a God-given power to cure illness. They also believed that he had received the gift of prophecy.[8] This acquisition of the shaking power naturally caused a great stir among Indians, who went in large numbers to Mud Bay, about six miles west of Olympia, to see Slocum.

Joe Young gave testimony to the revival, and Thompson's role in it, thirty years later::

> I was with John Slocum when he come to life again. I know the year and the month not the day. Now the people from good many tribes gathered to that place, but they did not believe him when he preached to them. And he got sick again. I was there. I was there across the Bay just a little ways. . . . No one was a Christian at that [time]. Now the people said now let us pray for him. So we went to him and took him to the Church and he got up and he said, God's work is not that way. He did not mention the Shake. And soon his wife got . . . [it] as

a gift to her from God and, I believe she was the lady that the shake was given to.[9]

Dick Lewis also verified that Mary Thompson received the shake and that it was distributed from her to all "like a big tree."[10]

Thompson's role in creating the basic beliefs and premises of the Indian Shaker Church should never be minimized. Native people were accustomed to seeing power demonstrations, but Thompson showed them that the gift of power was no longer the sole province of medicine men and women. Others like her could also open the door to healing through newly found powers.[11] According to one researcher,

> Mary [Thompson] Slocum instituted the Spirit, the "shake" ritual, with two important doctrinal components that of "gifts" or specific abilities conferred by the Spirit and that of "a help" or power. Certainly the concept of the Spirit, the verity of it and the continued sources of power whether new or re-interpreted by the Shakers makes this Christian religion attractive to Indian people who are vitally interested as well in practicing the power concept.[12]

The practice of shaking did not originate with Mary Thompson but had deep roots in native tradition. One precursor was the Spirit Canoe, a primary religious ceremonial for healing the sick. Anthropologist T. T. Waterman saw in the ceremony's shaking "the exact counterpart of the modern Shaker exercise. The Spirit Canoe ceremony was an important link between the old and new religions. It was no coincidence, wrote Waterman, that Puget Sound natives formed the nucleus of Shakerism, because "for generations there . . . [had] been 'shaking' phenomena connected with the [Spirit Canoe] performances."[13]

Waterman also reported that the shaking associated with soul recovery occurred in ceremonies in which shamans sought help from a certain spirit power.

> The power is accompanied by certain peculiar motor disturbances. The Indians . . . quiver, jump about, and drag around the people who try to hold them. The psychological explanation [for the seizures] undoubtedly is that there is an expectancy of a certain definite pattern in the minds of the performers, who get the shaking visitation and contribute the resultant quivering and jerking to the objects which they hold . . . [while] certain appointed men accompany the songs

by pounding against the roof with the long drum-poles [which] "of themselves" then begin to shake. The men can scarcely hold them.[14]

Another belief transferred from precontact times was that spirit powers could possess individuals and cause shaking seizures. Thus empowered, those who were possessed were able to tell when the powers would enter the poles that healers' helpers beat against roofs, causing the poles to tremble. Those who used cedar boards, in the canoe ceremony, for example, also possessed the power to recover lost souls. According to Waterman,

> The Indians say that the wooden object became "possessed" and shook the performer, while we would, of course, assume that the performer fell into a shaking seizure, such as occurs in many religious exercises among other races and in other parts of the world, his shaking agitating, in turn, the objects he carried. It seems to me that in these old performances and these ancient objects we have the background upon which the present day motor disturbances developed, which give the Shaker group its name. I know educated Indians who have seen these old spirit-objects come to life and cause the person holding them to tremble like a leaf.[15]

Jay Miller, a student of the Spirit Canoe ceremony, wrote more recently that "trembling is a sign of possession or contact with power throughout the world. Quivering hands are still a notable feature among modern shamans during cures. The hands of Lushootseed speaking religious leaders with power boards or poles tremble when these gifts are in use."[16] Anthropologist Marian W. Smith confirmed that features of the Power Sing were also carried over into Shaker ritual.[17]

In many ways the Shaker ceremony was the equivalent of shamans wrestling with spirit boards in canoe ceremonies. Although Shakers moved away from the belief that souls were spirited from evil persons, for a time they believed in the concept of soul loss. On the Skokomish Reservation, for example, an elderly woman reportedly captured the wandering soul of Dora Peterson. After binding it with her handkerchief, she took it to the Shaker church house where Dora's mother shook over the soul to restore it to her daughter. Among northern Shakers who feared soul loss, a shaman or medium was called in to examine victims to determine if their souls were gone. Nooksack Shakers supposedly had "eyes" to see the soul, described as a tiny doll, and believed they could persuade ghosts to return stolen souls.[18]

Another important element that made conversion to Shakerism easier was the native belief in the guardian-spirit doctrine. According to anthropologist June McCormick Collins, this belief provided continuity between the old spirits and the new Shaker source of supernatural power. When a person joined the Shaker Church, Collins wrote, his or her guardian spirits went away for a while and returned under a new guise as a Shaker spirit, "the spirit of God." According to this interpretation, a person did not have to give up his or her supernatural guardians when becoming a Shaker but simply retained them in a new form, eliminating a primary reason for not joining the new church.[19]

Not only did shaking and other early practices have native origins, but so did the anglicized name. As found in church records, the phonetic English equivalent of the Puget Sound Salish word for "shaking" evolved as Chaddon. Another English name for shaking is Tschaddam, a term said to have been given in jest to Slocum's followers by other Indians. The name "Slocum tum-tum," from the Chinook jargon for "heart," was applied to Slocum's followers because it sounded somewhat like Tschaddam. In March 1884, Edwin Chalcraft, schoolmaster on the Chehalis Reservation, called Shakerism the "new Mud Bay religion" since that place had become the center of Slocum's church. The new religion was also known for a time as "John Slocum's church." Chalcraft took credit for the word "Shaker," stating that in his conversation and correspondence with Agent Eells they had used that name. He added that it was not long before Slocum's followers adopted the name, calling themselves the "Shaker Church."[20]

Over the years the native elements of Shakerism diminished as the church came under the influence of an increasingly predominant white culture. White pressure against Shakerism was personified by Edwin and Myron Eells, who Shaker advocates believed were attempting to destroy Indian culture. It should not be assumed, however, that John Slocum and his followers were engaged in an attempt to lessen the importance of native society. They were not political, except possibly on a few occasions when they were urged to be so by white politicians. They did proselytize in their zeal, but never for profit. Among other things, Shakerism played a role in Indians' shedding the restrictive aboriginal class structure for an egalitarian, nonauthoritarian system. Shakers also broke down the wall between native and Christian beliefs, learning and adapting, often with more grace than those who opposed them. But the church might never have reached such prominence if Mary Thompson had not given it a strong second breath by advancing the shake as a healing mechanism. News of her experience infused the struggling church with new life and power. Nowhere was this more evident than in August 1883 on Skookum Bay, where the "Big Meeting" took place.

Billy Clams, the successor to Big Bill, had caught the enthusiasm generated by Mary Thompson's shaking. Clams and Slocum shared the same religious interests and were both caught up in the fervor, which might explain why the Big Meeting was held at Slocum's place. When Clams began seeing visions and angels, he induced Big Bill's brother David to quit work to attend the meeting. In various logging camps, including David's and Tenas Charley's, Clams told workers that they had to attend the Big Meeting to ensure their salvation. His motive appears to have been not so much a pull toward Slocum as a push against Reverend Eells, whose baptisms Clams said were ineffectual. Clams's prophecy that, within days, the world would be consumed by fire helped persuade the Indians to close the camps and assured that thirty to thirty-five workers would journey the short distance from the Skokomish Reservation to the Big Meeting on Skookum Bay.[21]

According to Reverend Eells, who received reports from those who attended the Skookum Bay gathering, Skokomish Reservation Indians were told that they would be lost through sin if they did not attend the meeting. It was reported that four women would be turned into angels at the meeting and that other wonderful things would happen, just as they had to John Slocum. Nearly half the Skokomish Indians under the leadership of David and Dick Lewis were said to have "entered heartily" into the meeting.[22]

At the Big Meeting, according to what Indians and agency personnel later told Reverend Eells, women tried to fly like angels and four would-be angels "died" in the belief that they had powers like those that had enabled Slocum to revive. The dead were then brought to life, it was believed, in direct, visible, and dramatic fashion in emulation of the miracles of Jesus. There was no shortage of visions, and one person prophesied the end of the world.[23] According to Eells,

> The followers of this new religion dreamed dreams, saw visions, went through some disgusting ceremonies a la mode the black *tamahnous*, and were taken with a kind of shaking. With their arms at full length, their hands and arms would shake so fast that a common person not under the excitement could hardly shake half as fast. Gazing into the heavens, their heads would also shake very fast, sometimes for a few minutes and sometimes for hours, or half the night. They would also brush each other with their hands, as they said, to brush off their sins, for they said they were much worse than white people, the latter being bad only in their hearts, while the Indians were so bad that their badness came to the surface of their bodies and the ends of their finger nails, so that it could be picked off. They sometimes brushed each other lightly, and sometimes so roughly that the person brushed was made black for a week, or even sick.[24]

In his report, Reverend Eells was careful to note that it was a government employee, agency schoolteacher B. F. Laughlin, who believed the meeting should have been stopped. Unlike Laughlin and the two Indian police and interpreters who went to Skookum Bay, Reverend Eells had no legal authority in the matter. As Eells recorded it, Laughlin "talked to them so plainly" that the Indians returned to their homes the next day. Reverend Eells also recorded some of the unfortunate legacies of the meeting. Because of a "horseback ride and maneuvers" (possibly from shaking and brushing off sins), Big Bill's sister-in-law, David's wife, lay near death, having given premature birth to a child who lived less than a day. On his return from the meeting, Dick Lewis lay ill for a week. Eells also noted the economic consequences of closing the camps during the normally productive period in good August weather.[25]

Most likely, the Big Meeting had ended simply because the excitement and hysteria generated there could hardly be sustained for long and because it was difficult to feed so many people. Although the Indians may have departed Skookum Bay in hunger, they feasted on certain beliefs and practices either introduced or strengthened there. Meetings were held in homes from six o'clock in the evening until midnight, with some Shakers balancing lighted candles on their heads. Reverend Eells described them as "acting like Indian doctors" while using a little Catholicism in efforts to rid themselves of their sins. To Eells, their behavior appeared to be an attempt by chiefs Dick Lewis, Jackson, and Tumstum to revive the old Tamahnous. Agency physician J. T. Martin feared that lengthy and vigorous shaking would drive the participants crazy. He believed their actions were detrimental not only to themselves but also to other Indians, who were frightened by their behavior.[26]

After the Big Meeting, Eells discussed its consequences with his agent brother. Agent Eells suggested banishing Billy Clams to Port Madison. He was aware that Clams had successfully drawn Indians to his religion, but in October 1883, just two months after the Big Meeting, Reverend Eells reported that the former gambler and his people had given up their shaking and their Catholicism, a position they maintained into February 1884.[27] Nevertheless, Reverend Eells reported that Clams and his wife continued to have "shaking troubles" into April. Eells succeeded in bringing Clams into the Congregational Church in November, but the shaking continued. Monitoring the situation on the Skokomish Reservation, Agent Eells believed that the shaking in Shakerism (which his brother termed "the new religion") violated an April 10, 1883, ban against Indian doctoring. He apparently believed that Shakerism was merely an extension of previous doctoring in opposition to a ban of 1871 that sought to stamp out such native practices. Reverend Eells believed that "a respectable number of the Indians declared against the old style of curing the sick" and observed that many medicine men had joined Slocum's religion because its style was more nearly in accordance with the native religion than with Christianity.[28]

Reverend Eells could not have overlooked the fact that there were redeeming features of the Skookum Bay meeting—the attendees' resolve to avoid drinking, gambling, swearing, and other bad practices, for instance. This was not enough, however, to prevent him from casting a wary eye on the new leaders who emerged from the Big Meeting. Among them was Mowitch Man, whose religion was founded mostly on dreams and songs. Mowitch Man was energized by the belief that the Creator had told him to teach the Indians "to have strong hearts and get ready for me [God]." Like Billy Clams, he attended Congregationalist services, but he also held services in his home on Thursday and Saturday evenings.

Nevertheless, some native religionists judged Mowitch Man to be too much into dreams. He also had two wives, which violated the Christian teaching to which they had been exposed. At Reverend Eells's insistence, Mowitch Man became monogamous and took the younger of his two wives, though he subsequently divorced her in 1888 because she refused to perform domestic chores.[29] Reverend Eells wrote that some Indians "said they saw Mowitch Man [and] myself in hell. That I was kept here [on the reservation] to get the Indians land from them and that I told them lies in my church preaching."[30] After only a year, Mowitch Man's religion died out.

Big John, a Skokomish married to a Squaxin woman, also left the Big Meeting with a newfound mission. He had been so enthusiastic at the meeting that he was "attacked with shaking as badly as anyone." Returning to the Skokomish Reservation, he began his own version of the new religion and held shaking services at Mud Bay. His religion did not last, however, mainly because of an incident that occurred two months after the Big Meeting. On a Sunday afternoon, after Big John had received "a startling revelation to the effect that he was Christ Incarnate and his wife was the Virgin Mary," he and his people marched through the streets of Olympia to a local church.[31] A minister sympathetic with their cause had invited the group to hold services there, believing the Indians had been hampered by missionaries. He may have had in mind Reverend Eells, who showed little tolerance toward clerics of other Protestant faiths. Agent Eells described the Olympia episode:

> There was a minister living in Olympia, who felt as though the missionaries were not treating them [the Indians] fairly, and he induced the Presbyterian church to invite them to come up and hold services. A few members objected, as they did not think the Indians clean enough. About Christmas time they were invited, and they camped on the outskirts of the city. Sunday afternoon they formed a procession and marched about one and one-half miles through the streets from their camp to the church. One of them [Big John] rode on a horse, which was led. He had his arms extended in the shape of a cross, and his head was a little to one side to imitate Christ on the Cross. Immediately behind him walked his squaw, whom they claimed was "Eve," and all the rest of the Indians walked in a line behind her with their heads extended up to heaven, symbolic to get

help from God. As they camped in fish cabins, the scent from their
clothes was very strong. The Indians who joined this church were
very moral. They stopped drinking, quit using tobacco, gambling,
swearing, etc., and in most respects were very much improved. How
Big John who claims to be the priest could hold his arms extended
as he did the whole distance was a marvel.[32]

After singing, chanting, and praying, Eells added, they left "behind them such a perfume that the minister who had invited them
failed to get the sympathy for them from his people that he had
desired."[33]

Big John's ministrations were cut short by ridicule and regulation. The ridicule came not only from the white community but
also from the Indians themselves. The regulation came in the form
of the 1883 ban against Indian "medicine men" leading various
forms of dancing. Big John's ride through Olympia was considered
a violation of the ban, and he was arrested and jailed for holding
forbidden meetings on the Skokomish Reservation. Believing God
would open the jail and release him, his followers stood around expecting the building to fall to pieces. After the Olympia fiasco, Big
John changed his claim; rather than a heavenly figure, he said, he
was a mere prophet.[34]

Excesses at the Big Meeting and tragedies in its aftermath dis-
illusioned many followers of Mowitch Man, Big John, and other
would-be religious leaders. Although Big John suffered persecution, which in itself tends to draw adherents to a cause, his
excesses and failed prophecies were disillusioning. Billy Clams's
indecision, wavering from shaking to nonshaking, and his troubles with agency officials did little to help him retain the loyalty
of Big Bill's followers. Mowitch Man failed not only because he had
two wives but also, in the Indians' words, because he was "rather
dreamy" and "partly dying for want of real life."[35]

But John Slocum's religion survived. Most important for the
survival of Slocum's faith was the simple fact that its shaking
provided a physical means for imparting power to practitioners
in their healing and other ministrations. Other circumstances,
of course, also set the church's course and allowed it to thrive.
Government bans against Tamahnous practices helped furnish
the impetus that prompted non-shaking Indians to turn to shaking. Shaker curing sessions gave members a combined ritual

and mechanical mastery over their environment such as they had achieved in the days of the guardian spirit complex. Shakerism might also not have fared so well had Slocum not left organizational matters to others while he supplied its spirituality. And finally, buttressed by strong opposition to licentiousness and liquor and by its withdrawal from shamanism, John Slocum's Shaker Church remained within the bounds of propriety under the sheltering arm of the Christian faith.

CHAPTER FIVE

The Formative Years
of the Church

In the years following John Slocum's vision in 1882, Shakers called their church "Slocum tum-tum." From its tenuous beginnings, a decade of maturation brought Shakerism to its formal organization in 1892 and laid the foundation for its incorporation in 1910. Those whites who knew about the new religion knew about the Shakers' emphasis on moral behavior, but many were still uncertain about the extent to which the church had abandoned traditional native practices to become Christianized. Lida W. Quimby, field matron on the Puyallup Reservation, was among the minority when she wrote in 1902: "Superstition if you will, hypnotism, spiritualism, Christian Science, or whatever dogma permeates their belief, there is a God-fearing, Christ-loving piety that makes for better living; a germ of Christian God-likeness planted in simple hearts choked with weeds of superstition and oppressed by injustice and persecution, and dense ignorance."[1]

Into the twentieth century, non-Shakers may have been unaware of Shakerism's continuing spiritual status, but some would surely have been aware of its physical growth—if for no other reason than the increasing number of Shaker church houses being built and the numbers of people attending services there.

The early statistics on the official membership of the church were gathered by whites and were rarely accurate. Like many other Indians, Shakers may have been reluctant to give government officials accurate numbers for fear that their children would be sent to distant boarding schools. They were also unaccustomed to keeping track of figures or of making lists of members. In 1892–1893, according to Rev. Myron Eells, there were six hundred Shakers in the church; Judge James Wickersham put the number at five hundred in 1893. In 1894, Daniel L. Dawley of Tacoma placed membership in the Shaker Church at three hundred. The first available lists of members kept by the Shakers themselves cover the years 1912 through 1915, undoubtedly a response to requirements for incorporation of the church. In 1915, Head Elder Alex Teio claimed a membership of three thousand with "the increase right along"; three hundred of those members were on the Yakama Reservation. But because many Indians attended more than one church, compilation of membership statistics was difficult at best. Even now Shaker membership fluctuates not only over the years, but also over months, growing during winters, especially between Christmas and New Year's, when faltering members return to the Shaker fold.[2]

Unlike native societies with strong class distinctions, the Shakers developed a spirit of community in which members not only administer "helps" to believers in local churches but also help establish other congregations and support members of those communities. Shakers demonstrate an uncommon respect for each other, openly receiving backsliders and advocating no form of excommunication. New members are admitted to the church after receiving spirit powers that enable them to shake. Because the door to Shaker membership is more easily opened through revelation than through the Bible, Reverend Eells speculated that the ability to read and write was not a qualification for Shaker membership and that once the majority on the Skokomish Reservation became educated the "Shaker religion will go much as the tamahnous went."[3] But missionary Sarah Ober believed that

only the moral class of uneducated but intelligent Indians accepted this new religion, while the more superstitious and ignorant still clung to their old beliefs and practices, the Tamahnous.... But when the paternal Government forbade the ancient religious rites, these

turned to Shakerism, and under its name continued the old practices. Now but few of these, however, are clinging to the old religion,
but have come out into Shakerism.[4]

Shaker membership is made up almost exclusively of Indians.
There is no formal prohibition against non-Indian membership,
but it has been very unusual for any whites to become members.
Perhaps the first white to become a member was a Swedish im-
migrant, Otto Strom, who married a Hoh Indian Shaker in 1896
and converted. It was not until after the 1910 incorporation of
the church that whites were permitted to shake, and the earliest
recorded mention of a white member appears on a December 1917
list of eighty-seven Klamath Shakers. Shakers generally have not
looked askance at the half dozen or so whites who have joined
their church since its founding, but an abundance of white members would threaten the "Indianness" of the church, as sought
by Shaker founders and revealed in the constitution and bylaws.
Some church documents included more racially exclusive provisions than others did. Harold Patterson, a non-Indian convert to
Shakerism, concluded that Shaker homogeneity was a reaction to
the missionaries' insistence that Indians "slavishly reject the cultural expressions which are the basic orientation of their lives and
become white people."[5]
The formative years of the Shaker Church coincided with a
growing public awareness of the church. Many whites accepted
the Shakers' strong moral principles, but some were suspicious
of their shaking and gyrations. The ambivalence is indicated
in anthropologist Marian W. Smith's characterization of Shakerism as "avowedly Christian" and fellow anthropologist Leslie
Spier's assessment that it was "pseudo Christian." Sadly, the lack
of Indian writings in those formative pre-1910 years leaves the
record less clear than one would wish, and one must rely heav-
ily on non-Indian observers. It was curiosity as well as fear that
attracted so much comment from missionaries, government employees, schoolteachers, journalists, and other travelers to the
Pacific Northwest. Not surprisingly, most criticism of Shakers
seems to have come from whites who were most closely associated
with them, especially government agents and physicians.[6]
Some response to Shakerism was patronizing, such as Edwin

Pictured here are Harold Patterson and his wife, Shirley. For a long time, up until 1972, Patterson was an educator on the Quinault Reservation. A white Indian Shaker Church member, he served as treasurer of the Shaker church at Taholah. (*Robert H. Ruby and John A. Brown*)

Chalcraft's qualified judgment that "The beliefs and ceremonies of the Shakers vary in different groups of Indians, and are more nearly in harmony with the Christian religion where the missionaries have had the most influence, which seems to bear out the thought that these people are still seeking the truth and may be ready for help when it comes to them in a way they can understand."[7] Obviously, Chalcraft, schoolmaster on the Chehalis Reservation, believed the Shakers had some distance to go to reach religious maturity. Others were harsher. Reverend M. G. Mann, a Presbyterian, asked Reverend Eells in 1891 to stop the Shakers' "unChristian" and "unbiblical" shaking.[8]

Charles Buchanan, who arrived at the Tulalip Reservation in 1894 as agency physician, had few positive reactions to the Shakerism introduced there in 1896 by Johnny Steve and his wife. He feared that what he considered a compromise with the old "pagan" religion and a "hodge podge" of barbarism injected into it along

Reverend Myron Eells,
Congregationalist
missionary among the
Skokomish and Clallam
Indians. Although modern
anthropologists question
some of his observations,
many of those observations
retain their value since he
was an eyewitness to many
events of early Shakerism.
(*Northwest and Whitman
College Archives*)

with elements of Catholicism and Protestantism would be the un-
doing of Indians in general. He predicted that the dozen Shakers
on the Tulalip would contaminate the other 450 Indians on the
reservation. As proof of Shaker illiteracy, he cited its adherents'
failure to cultivate allotments and make material improvements.
He also alleged that two Shaker ministers, professing abstinence,
had died of delirium tremens. Others who had become Shakers,
he claimed, had deserted wives, abused children, and engaged in
"orgies" that rendered them unproductive. Later, while serving as
superintendent of the Tulalip Agency, Buchanan complained to the
commissioner of Indian affairs about meddling Shakers coming on
the Tulalip Reservation to infect its Indians with their religion.[9]

   William Whitfield, a local historian and contemporary of Buchanan, may have helped influence his opinion of Shakers. In his
History of Snohomish County, Washington, in which jurisdiction
the Tulalip lay, Whitfield described Shakerism as the "greatest and
most far-reaching of the substitute tamanamus creations, and the
most effective, adroitly and cunningly devised."[10]

A Shaker service on the Quileute Reservation from a sketch entitled "The Shake Dance of the Quilente Indians," drawn by an Indian pupil at the Quileute Day School. The sketch appears in an article by Albert B. Reagan in *Proceedings of the Indian Academy of Science*, 1908.

In 1908 Albert Reagan, the teacher at the Indian school at La Push on the Quileute Reservation, described a Shaker service where faces were "hideously distorted" and where he observed "quivering, trembling, twisting, writhing hands wave, whirl, gyrate in all directions till the scene reminds one much of the demons in the 'inferno' dancing over a lost soul." The "simple-hearted Indians," he wrote, "believe that in this performance they are worshipping the most high God."[11]

After attending a February 16, 1909, Shaker meeting in which a Quileute Indian stood for an hour, arms outstretched, seeking power, Reagan was convinced that the major propellant in Shakerism was self-induced hypnotism. After witnessing one man who acquired the "power" and then spent forty minutes in a "spell," Reagan concluded that Shakerism was but "a step in advance of the worship of the old time; but . . . a very short step" in which "the most 'skookum' Shakers are often the least moral."[12]

It was the Shakers' advocacy of temperance, perhaps more than anything else, that finally helped Shakers achieve legitimacy in the eyes of the government and the public. From the founding of the Slocum's church in 1882 until its incorporation as the Indian Shaker Church in 1910, Washington was a battleground between temperance and nontemperance forces, with Protestant churches and other groups often at the forefront of the antiliquor movement. The Shaker Church fought against the use of liquor, but its support of temperance has always had a different emphasis from that given by non-Shakers. The Shakers' efforts have been geared more to protecting Indians from alcoholism than to protecting all people from that destructive disease. Still, no other church or temperance group has more adamantly opposed liquor and tobacco use than has the Shaker Church. In his 1896 report from the Puyallup Reservation, Agent R. E. L. Newberne optimistically reported that Shakerism had done much to discourage intemperance among the Indians. "It is the only religion, so far as I know," he wrote, "that will keep an Indian of western Washington sober if he is inclined to get drunk."[13]

It was DeKoven Brown who told the nation of Shaker temperance efforts. In his widely read article in *Colliers* on September 3, 1910, Brown wrote that through John Slocum the "Great Spirit is directing the work of saving the red men from their greatest curse—whisky." He quoted Head Elder Alex Teio's succinct description of the damage wrought by liquor. "Whisky," Teio declaimed, "is the cause, more than anything else, of the decay of Indian manhood in this country." "Working quietly but steadily," Brown wrote in the *Colliers* article,

a little band of Indian Shakers . . . [is] doing more to stamp out intemperance in the Northwest than any other factor. Asking no help from whites or from the Indians themselves, but believing that they are directed by the spirit of their departed leader and founder of the sect, John Slocum, the priests of the belief are found in nearly all the Indian villages of Washington and Oregon. They teach one doctrine—temperance—cry continually against the evils of the liquor habit, and expound crudely the teachings of the Bible.[14]

The editor of the *Mason County Journal* in Shelton, near John Slocum's home, reported on March 11, 1887, that Shakers had risen from being the "lowest of vagabonds" to a sober, industrious, and well-behaved group. Some of the Shakers, according to the *Journal*, owned lands and draft horses and subsisted on their own. In the April 1, 1887, edition of the *Journal*, "V E X" wondered if the whites were so far gone that "they would not heed to a message, even though it was sent from Heaven." On May 25, 1888, however, the editor wondered if the reverence with which Slocum's followers held him was not greater than that given the "Hyas Tyee [God]," of whom he claimed to be an apostle.

In the October 1894 issue of *The Northwest*, Daniel L. Dawley wrote, "In spite of . . . [a] feeling of distrust in the bosom of Jew and Gentile, some good thing does occasionally come out of Nazareth, and a real, live Indian sometimes imitates the white men so closely that it is extremely difficult to prevent him from proving that the white man has no monopoly of goodness. . . . The religion of John Slocum is one of strict morality."[15] In addition to the prohibition against liquor—along with censures against those who stole, lied, smoked, gambled, quarreled, and raced horses—Dawley reported that Shakers also washed themselves with soap and water. Furthermore, he complimented them when he observed that even a Presbyterian minister on the Puyallup Reservation (possibly the Reverend Mann) wanted his elders to mingle with Shakers in hopes some of their temperance would rub off.[16]

After the turn of the century, reporting took a sensationalist turn similar to that in William Randolph Hearst's papers. The July 19, 1908, *Seattle Post-Intelligencer*—soon to be a Hearst paper—carried an account of a Shaker service under the headline "Strange Rites and Ceremonies Of Redman's New Religion." The article carried sketches of Shakers violently contorting and described Shaker services as a "religious orgy," with participants "whirling like dervishes," "shaking their sins away," "thudding feet," and singing in a "rhythmic chant." The reporter judged that Shakerism was a "step upward" but was no substitute for Christianity to elevate Shakers from "savagery and superstition."

Shakers did not escape criticism from other Indians either. Traditionalists believed that Shakers were upsetting the old forms of worship, while progressives believed they had not sufficiently distanced themselves from it. There were those who believed that some Shakers had sold out to whites by taking advantage of

Sketch appearing in the July 19, 1908, issue of the *Seattle Post-Intelligencer*. Showing a sensationalist bent, this newspaper, like those of William Randolph Hearst, depicted Shakers as wild dancing, shrieking maniacs. The illustrator appears to have difficulty depicting the faces of these Indian dancers.

provisions for receiving allotments, as on the Puyallup Reservation. Some of the most outspoken critics were those who had not defected from Catholicism to join them. There was a strong Catholic presence on the Swinomish Reservation, where a Catholic Indian "of sorts" denigrated Shakers. Anthropologist Erna Gunther quoted, the critic as saying,

> Now we could get most of the membership away from the Shaker church if we'd only let them preach. They all want to preach, be the whole show. That's why they are Shakers and that's why they are singers. They want to do all the talking there is to do themselves, be the center. They don't want anybody to tell them anything. If we'd let them all be priests, we'd have the Catholic church here so full they'd be falling out of the windows.[17]

John Slocum (*left*) and his successor, Louis Yowaluch (Mud Bay Louis). (*Smithsonian Institution, Washington, D.C., neg. 3021*)

Farther north, in Canada, the Comox Indians of Vancouver Island, influenced by Catholic missionaries, went to Nanaimo "to laugh" at the Shakers. According to Gunther, their action meant that "a well-developed Catholic mission will stop the spread of the Shakers more readily than the presence of any Protestant denomination."[18]

During those years, as the Shaker Church continued to solidify its practices and beliefs, a most important change occurred—the shifting of the Shaker nidus from Skookum Bay to Mud Bay. Closely associated with the move was the shift in Shaker leadership from John Slocum to Mud Bay Louis Yowaluch (Aiyal) and his younger brother, Mud Bay Sam. Where Slocum had been influenced by Catholics and Congregationalists, the Mud Bay brothers had come under stronger Presbyterian influence. Louis had been a Presbyterian elder at the time he became a Shaker and was said to have been most responsible for Protestant elements entering Shakerism.

Mud Bay Sam, brother of
Mad Bay Louis Yowaluch,
first bishop of the Indian
Shaker Church. Sam
received his name because
his home was on Mud Bay,
six miles west of Olympia,
the capital of Washington.
It was at his home that
leading Shakers met in
1910 to reorganize their
church. (*Indian Shaker
Church Archives*)

Louis stood in contrast to Slocum in both physical and mental attributes. Slocum's was a five-feet-eight-inch, mildly stooped frame; Louis was six feet tall, raw-boned and muscular. Slocum was described as "modest and rather retiring," which might also help explain his deference to Louis. He was also, according to one source, "dull and unimaginative," which caused his congregation to lose "almost all momentum." The two men did have some things in common: Before their conversions they had traveled the same path, gambling, drinking, and swearing; more importantly, both were committed to advancing their church.[19]

According to Peter Heck, later a Shaker bishop, Louis first got the shake when traveling home in a canoe after hearing Slocum preach. He gained the respect of his followers because of his change of lifestyle and his newly found honesty, fearlessness, and "love of right." His people approved of his vigor in establishing new churches. To use his own words, they knew that his "heart is upside down." Further, Louis's appointment satisfied Slocum, who acknowledged his leadership.[20] The loss of leadership, however,

This image of John Slocum hangs
in the Shaker church house on the
Skokomish Reservation, which was an
important place in the formation of
his religion. (*Indian Shaker Church
Archives*)

did little to diminish Slocum's influence. He continued preaching to his people, who held him in semireverence until his death.
Shakers did not carry their adulation so far as to consider Slocum
a messiah, but they did regard him as a witness sent from God.

Mud Bay Louis became the leader of the church, and Mud Bay
Sam was placed at the head of the church's healing branch. Sam
claimed to have performed "wonderful cures" on both whites and
Indians, an ability he said he had acquired from a vision-inspired
promise that he would become a "medicine man." Like his brother,
he had been not only dissolute but ignorant, "just like an animal. No doctoring, no medicine—no good." "My soul was sick,"
he confessed.[21] Summing up the Shaker credo at this time of
transition, he declaimed:

No, we do not believe the Bible. We believe in God, and in Jesus Christ as the Son of God, and we believe in a hell. In these matters we believe the same as the Presbyterians. We think fully of God today. A good Christian man is a good medicine-man. A good Christian man in the dark sees a light toward God [possibly an allusion to that experienced by John Slocum or possibly to some native belief regarding light and darkness]. . . . I believe this religion. It helps poor people. Bad man can't see good—bad man can't get to heaven—can't find his way. We were sent to jail for this religion, but we will never give up. We all believe that John Slocum died and went to heaven, and was sent back to preach to the people. We all talk about that and believe it.[22]

Sam's reference to Presbyterian influence on Shakers is instructive. There is no question that there were important shared elements in the two churches. Yet, Shaker relations with Presbyterians, especially on the Chehalis Reservation, were scarcely those of a love feast.

The Chehalis and Squaxins had traditionally engaged in trade and communication, with each other; the Chehalis Reservation was, after all, only a short distance south of the Squaxin. Edwin Chalcraft reported that shortly after he had arrived on the Chehalis in October 1883, Shakers were sent there and to the Skokomish Reservation "to secretly investigate" the possibility of establishing missions. He also wrote that the Chehalis Indians had given little indication that they were paying any attention to the new religion. This was apparently despite the Shakers' warning that the Chehalis who did not join their ranks would be transformed into birds and other animals. Because of such threats, Chalcraft and others who worked for missions and the government saw Slocum's religion as threatening their own work. In 1884, Rev. Myron Eells recorded that Shakerism had spread not only to the Chehalis but also to the Nisqually Reservation. In the Indians' words, according to Eells, it was seemingly "as catching . . . as the measles."[23]

On January 19, 1884, the Court of Indian Offenses on the Chehalis Reservation addressed the problem of the religious excitement at Mud Bay and its effect on the Chehalis Indians. The court decided not to allow a Chehalis Shaker leader, John Smith, to attend a meeting of Shakers at Mud Bay, and Chalcraft refused to sign a pass permitting him to go. Defying the order, Smith went anyway. He met with John Slocum, Mud Bay Louis, and Mud Bay Sam, who told him that a flood would come as in the "time of Noah," at which time God would provide a big canoe that would allow only the Shakers to survive. Convinced of the truth of the prophecy, Smith returned to the Chehalis with word of the flood and armed with Shaker teachings, which he passed on to Peter Heck and others. Heck's wife was reportedly converted at Mud Bay in 1884, and her husband became a Shaker convert shortly thereafter.[24]

Heck described his conversion to Chalcraft on March 19, 1884: "Last Saturday night my hands began to shake, and then they crossed each other and shook two hours. I was sitting on a pile of rails. Then I knelt down and shook two hours; then stood shaking three hours; then stood with my arms stretched out straight, one-half hour; then I took hold of a rope that reached to heaven, with both hands." When Chalcraft asked if Heck could see or feel the rope in his hands, Heck replied,

> No, I could not see or feel the rope, but I know it was there. Next, I heard a voice in heaven say, "Pull the rope and ring the bell in heaven." I did so. Then I crossed myself three times and commenced to walk but stayed in the same place; then to run but did not go any. I heard the voice of God saying, "He come to see me." Then I talk English, I say, "I am glad." God wanted me to preach to everybody what he tell me. He said, "Nobody can destroy me. I am God. I am going to destroy the world a second time, one and one-half days from now." This means one and one-half years.

Chalcraft then asked, "How do you know God means one and one-half years?"

> Something in my breast tells me He means that time. God said, "Go to Oakville and preach there next Sunday, to Mud Bay week after next, and preach there; and in three months go to the Quinauilt [sic] and tell them there what to do." There is something wrong there so God cannot send his voice. That is the reason He wants me to go there. The voice said, "Come back and stop at your home. Take back that wagon where you got it from Perry Eu-cha-tan, you never pay for it; and take back that lumber to Joe Mormon, you buy it and never pay him." The last God said was, "All who believe on you and what you do, will be saved." The shakes make our sins fall to the ground,

that is all they are for. In seven months, the shaking will stop as all our sins will then be gone. The world itself, will shake next July 4th all day.

In a note to Heck's story, the skeptical Chalcraft wrote, "This is Peter's story, written as he was telling it, and had he been a good prophet, the world would have come to an end about September 16, 1885."[25]

A month after John Smith got the shake, some Chehalis Indians went to Squaxin Island to meet with Mud Bay Shakers at Old Bob's (Chief Gogoyaskad's) place. At a meeting there Marvin Davis and James ("Jim") Walker both got the shake. By this time, the Shakers had been so successful in converting Chehalis Indians that Peter Stanup, Reverend Mann, and Rev. John Thompson, the general missionary of the Presbyterian Church, held a meeting in the Olympia Presbyterian church to discourage Shakers from proselytizing. Also in attendance were John Smith, Peter Heck, Charles ("Charlie") Walker, the same Jim Walker, Marvin Davis, Harry Alo-wa-het, Mud Bay Louis, and John Slocum. The Presbyterians in attendance wanted the Chehalis delegation to have its Indians stop their shaking. They hoped to accomplish this by having the Mud Bay group build its own church. But the Chehalis delegation wanted to retain some of the shake and proposed a formula by which they would remain "about one-fourth shake and three-fourths Bible, and to put the Bible first and the shake last." This proposal appeared unsatisfactory to the Presbyterian administration, which sought to keep Chehalis Indians from visiting both Mud Bay, and Old Bob's place on Squaxin Island.[26]

Chalcraft reported that strange things had happened on the Chehalis Reservation after Smith returned from Mud Bay. The first occurred on March 3, 1884. After girls in the school dormitory should have been sleeping, George Mills's wife, their matron, heard strange stirrings upstairs. She found fifteen of the older girls standing in a circle waving their arms, their bodies trembling in apparent emulation of the new religious group. The next day, Nancy Smith, an "intelligent" nineteen-year-old, complained that a Mud Bay Indian man visiting the Chehalis had decided she was to marry Cap Carson, an Indian bachelor. When she refused to do so, she was threatened with imprisonment. She was also forced to stand with outstretched arms in the form of a cross, holding candles until they burned out.[27]

Shortly thereafter, on Friday, March 7, Reverend Mann, the Presbyterian minister, arrived on the Chehalis Reservation to conduct his monthly church service. He apprised Chalcraft of the new Mud Bay religion and the Shaker method of curing the sick, which, in Chalcraft's words, "so closely resembled the old Indian Ta-mah-nous practice, prohibited in Rule 6 of the official Rules Governing the Court of Indian Offenses, that special attention should be given it."[28]

The next day Chalcraft received word that since agency physicians had failed to cure Bruce Ben of consumption, he would be doctored in a Shaker meeting. After dark, Chalcraft went to investigate the meeting, taking care to rationalize his presence to the Indians: "When we have a prayer meeting at the school house, you folks come and take part, so we have come to yours." John Smith, who was in charge of the meeting, admitted that Bruce Ben was present but denied they had any intention of treating him. The skeptical Chalcraft pretended to leave the meeting but instead hid in the grass and discovered that the meeting was indeed being held to cure Bruce Ben. Chalcraft described what happened next:

> The bell ringing continued in a peculiar manner, slowly and softly, then rapidly and harshly. There was some singing and chanting in a guttural tone, which the boys said had been used by the Indian doctors in earlier days. There were sounds like people jumping up and down on the floor, and others like striking the bare body with the palm of the hand. In the midst of the confusion we heard Pike Ben's voice saying "I've got the sin, I've got the sin." A moment later, the door opened and there was Pike with hands clasped as though there was something in them, which he threw out of the door and at the same time blowing his breath after it. When the door opened we could see Bruce Ben, the sick man, sitting on a chair stripped to the waist, with others prancing around him. A little later we heard some one say, "he could not doctor well because there was too much sin left in the house by the white man [Chalcraft]." . . . Several of them went to work purifying the room by "catching" the sin and throwing it out the door.[29]

The next Sunday, March 16, Mann prohibited the Indians' customary postsermon discussions, presumably to give Shakers no opportunity to rebut his sermon. That afternoon, Marvin Davis told Chalcraft that Mud Bay Indians had been at Smith's house, trying to induce Chehalis Indians to become Shakers. Davis told Chalcraft that God appeared at Mud Bay and that when Mud Bay Louis came to Smith's place he had persuaded the Chehalis to believe that such a visitation had occurred.[30]

Accompanied by head chief and associate judge Jim Walker, Chalcraft went to Oakville on April 12 to see a woman who he claimed "was still sick from the Shaker excitement at John Smith's house when her child was born." On the way, he stopped at Smith's house to inquire about a truant schoolgirl. Hearing bells ringing, he burst into the house, where he found associate judge Charlie Walker, who was also a policeman, sitting barefoot in a chair, his trousers pushed as high as possible on his legs, while Smith doctored him for rheumatic feet. On a wall was a large picture of a cross; lighted candles were on a table. At Chalcraft's entrance, all but the principal Shakers slunk down in their seats. When Jim Walker ordered the Shakers to cease their shaking and bell-ringing, according to Chalcraft, they "stopped their performances so suddenly that their theory of not being able to stop *until all sin is out* is exploded."[31]

The following day, John Smith and Peter Heck were at the Presbyterian services of Reverend Mann, who had been informed of Chalcraft's intervention. Mann took the occasion to tell the two "misguided" Shakers that not only had they lost "the true faith" but they were also "leading their people astray." After the service, he turned a cold shoulder to the Shakers in attendance. Coming out of the church, Heck was overheard to make an insulting remark about Reverend Mann, prompting George W. Mills, the industrial teacher, to shake him by the collar. That same day, Chalcraft hurried to Heck's father's place with interpreter George Quinotle to threaten Doctor Jim, a prominent Mud Bay Shaker, with imprisonment in the "skukum house" should he not leave the reservation in two hours. If he and his friends returned, Chalcraft threatened, they would be jailed and put on a diet of bread and water. Doctor Jim was reportedly gone within ten minutes.[32]

At one o'clock on Monday afternoon, April 14, Chalcraft, acting as presiding officer, called the tribal police court to order. Associate judges Jim Walker, Charlie Walker, and Pike Ben sat on the rostrum, with Mills, Mann, and many Shakers and non-Shakers in attendance. Chalcraft discussed Shaker curing sessions and reaffirmed that aboriginal shaman practices were prohibited under "Rules Governing Courts of Indian Offenses." Silence greeted his words. Chalcraft called on Smith to speak, but Smith said that no one would believe him even if he were to speak. Chalcraft responded that white men would believe Smith if his words were true. Seeking to achieve some legitimacy with his critics, Smith said he read the Bible, as had John Slocum, and that Slocum had brought a message from God for poor illiterate Indians to do good and cure Indians for no pay. Peter Heck told how Indians had listened to white preachers for a long time without changing their bad habits, but they had put all the bad behind them when they had become Shakers. He reiterated the importance of his own vision. Mumblings in the audience indicated a divided opinion about healings.[33]

Chalcraft and the three-judge tribunal, which had taken no part in the deliberations, retired to an adjoining room with Mann and Mills. Judge Charlie Walker said Mann was doing good in teaching white people how to live, just as Slocum had done good in teaching the Indians. Chalcraft broke in, stating that Walker's words were irrelevant because Mann and the church had nothing to do with the question at hand, namely, the doctoring of the ill. George Ben Pike said that it was God's will when Indians began to shake, and they could not stop until the sin was gone. If that was true, Chalcraft responded, then it was wrong to punish them. Jim Walker said that there would be less trouble if Indians went to Mud Bay less frequently, and Chalcraft suggested that such travel henceforth require passes authorized under government regulations. With that, the discussion ended. Chalcraft and Walker were given authority to enforce the court's action. Chalcraft considered the arrangement a safe move, since "Jim was loyal to me, and anyway he could not write his name to a pass." Under the order of the court, the judges signed with their thumbmarks.[34]

On May 9, Agent Eells was on the Chehalis for three days to congratulate Chalcraft for opposing Shaker curing services. He warned that as agent he would make no compromise with those who practiced the cure and told them to "do as Mr. Chalcraft says to do." But, despite Chalcraft's efforts, shaking and healing continued on the reservation. At the school on June 11, for example, Smith's wife was attempting to pull or shake rheumatism from a girl's arm when they heard Matron Mills approach and they made a hurried exit.[35]

Prohibiting Shakers from leaving the Chehalis, however, did not keep Shakers from other reservations from visiting the Chehalis. After one such visit, Bill James's wife returned to the Skokomish to begin disseminating Shakerism among the Indians there. She said that she had received her religious beliefs from Jim Walker—(the very man whom Chalcraft believed was "safe" from shaking)—and Smith and his brother Ed. Shakerism continued to spread from the Chehalis, ironically helped along by Chalcraft's liberal issuance of passes to traveling Indians.[36]

By October 1, 1884, according to Chalcraft, shaking "had lost enough of its vigor [on the Chehalis Reservation] to permit discarding the Pass Order."[37] During the lull in Shaker activity, he and Reverend Mann continued to preach in the reservation's Presbyterian church with some Shakers in attendance. Chalcraft believed that a visit from Presbyterian minister Peter Stanup and two elders in the Puyallup Presbyterian Church—all Chehalis Indians—"had a good effect which was felt for a long time." But on the night of February 27, 1887, the long-lasting "good effect" of their sermons apparently ended when a number of Shakers gathered at George Walker's place to cure Puyallup Bill of spitting blood. Placing Puyallup Bill in the middle of the room, his healers rubbed his arms and legs, brushed him, rang bells, and held candles. Their efforts had no effect, however, which they explained as Bill's failure to receive the gift of healing. They then shook over Clara Walker, who also failed to get the shake. They were all seated when the police broke in on them. Puyallup Bill and four of his healers, including John Smith, were convicted by the tribal court and sentenced to ten days' farmwork. George Walker and Hyas Pete were sentenced to a day's labor for contempt of court.[38]

Failing to make headway with older Chehalis Shakers, who clung tenaciously to their faith, Reverend Mann saw a ray of hope in working with their youth. This strategy was not new. Clerics of various denominations had shifted their efforts from adults to the young, who were generally less affected by tradition. One Sunday in March 1887, Mann judged the time right and gave the youngsters "good talk." They should honor their parents, he said, but not follow the "evil things they do," such as ringing bells, crossing themselves, and shaking.[39]

Over the next two years, Chalcraft began to alter his view of the Shakers. In March 1889, for example, he expressed doubts about a Chehalis police court verdict that found Jim Walker guilty of shaking. He also included in his narrative the testimony of Pike Ben, who had spoken of the strong Shaker resolve to advance Slocum's religion and whose shaking a few years earlier had concerned him so much. Chalcraft completed his official duties on the Chehalis Reservation in 1889. A quarter century later, long after the Shaker Church had been recognized as a legal entity, he wrote an account of his relationship with Shakers on the Chehalis. The narrative reveals that while he initially may have held the Shakers in low esteem, he could attest not only to the legitimacy of the Shaker Church but also to the persistence of its adherents in advancing the tenets of John Slocum.[40]

The role of the Indian Shaker Church and the participation of its members in native society were delineated during this seminal period. Both the white Christian community and federal officials saw in Shakerism too much of what they believed to be paganism. In time, however, the position of church and state relaxed because of the Shaker Church's position on moral issues, especially temperance. As early as 1885, the Presbyterian Church made a study of Shakerism, apprising congregations of the principles of the Native American religion.

Ironically, acceptance of at least the Christian aspects of Shakerism by the white community was indirectly responsible for divisiveness within the Shaker Church itself. The difference in belief and practice grew out of an increasing literacy among its members and their advocacy of use of the Bible in Shaker services. Opposed to them were those who sought to retain the fundamentalist beliefs of John Slocum, holding that power came not from the written word but through inspiration. Slocum's principles remained strong among his followers, but the growth of his church required leaders other than he, who, despite their rejection of Bible use, had to follow requirements and standards of the white culture in which they found themselves. During this period, membership in the church grew and the faith spread, while at the same time Shakers fine-tuned their beliefs and identified the character of their religion.

CHAPTER SIX

Healing
the Sick

The Shaker Church came to define its purpose through its moral and religious principles. The Quileute Shaker creed, which largely described the beliefs of the Indian Shaker Church in general, appeared in Webster H. Hudson's *Quileute Independent*, at that time the only newspaper published by an Indian in Washington state. The principles and purposes were copied in two articles by Albert B. Reagan, the teacher of the Quileutes from 1905 to 1909. Reagan wrote that the church's "watchword" was "Do good to those who do good to you" and that its "guiding prayer" was "Our God is in heaven. If we die He will take our life to heaven. Help us that we shall not die. Wherever we are, help us not to die. Our Father who is there, always have a good mind to us." The objective of the church, according to Reagan, was "to teach the Gospel of Jesus Christ, and to forward His Kingdom among the Indian race; to fight against the evils of intemperance, which we believe to be [a] detriment to the advancement of our race, all of us pledging ourselves to abstain from using intoxicating liquor in any form; and to further the pursuits of civilization and Christian living." To this day, the "articles of faith" comprise a belief in "God the Father, Jesus Christ the Son, and the Holy Spirit, the Three in One" and in the Shaker movement, "a dispensation of Almighty God to His

Indian children, to the end that they may see, with spiritual eyes, their evil ways, and to point our way to salvation through Jesus Christ the Son." The Shakers believe that "Jesus Christ has the power to forgive sins on earth" and that "God hears our prayers for the sick, and that if we pray and believe He will heal us of our physical ailments."[1]

Although Shakers sanction Jesus Christ in their credo, the figures of the diety receiving the most attention appear to be God and the Holy Spirit. The three beings apparently are recognized as separate persons or manifestations of the trinity at different times and places.[2] The Shaker creed thus bears similarity to that of orthodox Christianity, with the addition of the new elements of healing, temperance, and race. For Shakers, this does not mean that they are separated from Christianity, but that they have a dispensation from God.

To implement the goals, purposes, and functions of the church, the Shakers adopted various accoutrements of Christian churches, such as candles, bells, crosses, and gowns. During the revival of shaking after Slocum's second healing and the Big Meeting, those who established new churches made many calls on Rev. Myron Eells for "large Bible pictures."[3] The symbols adopted by John Slocum were chosen for their sensory qualities, with sights and sounds that were similar to dominant traditional native symbols. Mary Thompson then took those symbols into curing and consoling rituals. "Most significant," wrote anthropologist Pamela Amoss, "the symbols originating with John were reinterpreted and given new significance by Mary."[4]

The experiences of both Slocum and Thompson developed in Shakerism a ministering to the sick, especially in the form of what Shakers call "help" or "helps." Helps have been described as logically infinite, expanding in both kind and number, and embellished with the power that enlivens them. Helps are extended to regular church members as well as to joiners and backsliders, with backsliders being treated as though they are ill. Shakers believe God creates "spirit" as both power and gift, enabling believers to achieve personal helps and giving them the ability to extend helps to others. Shakers believe they are vessels who acquire and hold the power that enables themselves and others to receive helps. According to anthropologist Erna Gunther, "The most important function of the church from the Shaker's point of view is the 'help' they can give."[5]

The concept of helps originated in native ceremonies. In his research on aboriginal Duwamish ceremonies, T. T. Waterman identified nineteen helps, observing that several "medicines" or "powers" appeared to have had similar purposes—for example, giving men wealth or success in hunting—with each type of help having its own proper name, song, paraphernalia, and ceremonial performance. Shaking, quivering, and jerking were involved in seeking helps, as was the quivering of objects within a room.[6]

Acquiring the power as a joiner of the church is comparable to acquiring a guardian spirit. When joiners first receive the spirit, they receive power and truth in belief and action. A person's specific ability is also a gift believed to be a spirit power from God, and possession of the Holy Spirit is evidence of genuine contact with God. Shakers also believe the gift of power is manifested in involuntary shaking, which comes under the power of God and control of the Holy Spirit. Some Shakers use a handkerchief to impart power helps. These powers include the right to hold candles in ceremonies, "light up" patients or joiners, ring bells, "give shake," receive songs, heal, preach, dedicate or bless ritual objects and places, officiate, baptize, interpret illness, and prophesy.[7]

It might appear that the strong connection between sickness and sin in the Shaker Church would cause believers to assume that even the common cold was evidence of the presence of some evil. When one Shaker accused another of being full of sin because he was sick all the time, the accused responded, "But we can't help it when we catch cold and get sick." Anthropologist Dale Valory judged that "sickness is almost a way of life with Shakers, and their behavior suggests a deep-rooted paranoia and neurosis." Dealing with it more broadly, Pamela Amoss wrote, "Health is the chief area of concern where religion functions prominently." A family who strayed from the faith, lack of support for a church's officers, or a selfish will ("getting ahead of God") could result in someone's falling ill. One Shaker official said that part of a healer's success in helping those who did fall ill was that patients were more receptive to cures because they knew that their healer understood their illness. By understanding the nature of illness, this official asserted, the healer could effect the cure.[8]

Helps are also extended to smokers, drinkers, gamblers, adulterers, and other wrongdoers. One disease not usually contracted by devout Shakers is alcoholism, which has plagued some backsliders and new members. According to Helen Clark, a missionary on the Makah Reservation, it was a Makah Shaker, believing it better to shake than to stagger, who exuberantly invited, "Come and shake; it's as good as getting drunk. You tingle all over." Clark reasoned that those who shook had no desire to drink. She quoted one missionary who said, "Take alcohol out of whisky and the dance out of Shakerism, and the Indians would not care for either."[9]

The burden and removal of these ills, however, is in a different context from that of traditional Christianity. Those who are treated are buttressed by members "brushing" and "burning" the evil from them. Responses to treatment in such services occur spontaneously as candidates seek one type of helps or another. Often ceremonies are repeated nightly (as many as six consecutive nights is not unusual) until Shaker healers receive the power to fill needs or remove from subjects those things that hinder their receiving helps. All members are eligible to heal, although a few Shakers are considered to have stronger healing powers than others. Charlie Bighead, a Cherokee Seminole and leader of the northern California Smith River church, explained it this way: "When the Lord shuts their [healers'] eyes, this means they are in His power and He would lead them. If there was a sick person present, the Lord would lead them in this way to the pain. For the person being cured, the hands of the healer felt red hot, right through the body. But you must believe in order to be cured."[10]

In the early days of the church, candidates for healing were caught in a dilemma when Tamahnous treatment became increasingly difficult to obtain. Even when treatment was available, many were apprehensive of the power and purpose of native healers who exacted heavy fees for their services. These fears and uncertainties worked in favor of Shakers, not only because Shaker healers demanded no pay but also because they "advertised" the church's most important services. And for many, according to Edwin Chalcraft, John Slocum's religion was a "program [that] was substituted for that of the old Ta-mah-nous program, with which it seemed a twin brother."[11] Shaker curing ceremonies were more accessible than traditional methods. The healers in Shakerism were simply members of congregations, in essence representing a measure of emancipation from shamanistic domination. This is not to imply that shamans healed in isolation, for they received support from others in their efforts, but most shamans were from and were working with a more selective group than the Shakers were. In evaluating the functions of shaman and Shaker groups, it must be said that the more diversified Shaker groups played a greater role in the healing process.

There may also have been comfort in the Shakers' traditional belief in the origins of some illnesses. Erna Gunther found that the Shakers' belief that illness stemmed from spirit possession had been carried over from earlier traditions. Natives of southern Puget Sound, for example, had one or more guardian spirits, most of them good but some bad. It was the bad ones that were believed to cause illness, although good ones could cause it if they became contrary for one reason or another. If one did not demonstrate guardian spirit power then spirit possession, which rendered persons ill, was to be feared. In Shakerism, the ringing of bells that accompanied shaking replaced the old sounds of pounding sticks and shaking rattles.[12]

There remains in Shakerism more than a trace of power contests, reminiscent of early times when healers in one area were considered more or less powerful than those in another. Bodily intrusions were successfully extracted by good shamans exercising power greater than that of the shamans who had induced the illness. "Cures formed the bases for all shamans' claims to power," wrote anthropologist Marian W. Smith, "and there is little wonder that a cure is involved in the one incident which found local acceptance"—the curing of John Slocum.[13]

The Shaker Church has moved away from the pernicious blood feuds in which rival shamans competed in struggles that often resulted in death by poisoning or other means.[14] At the turn of the twentieth century, Helen Clark told of a medicine man whose followers believed he had something behind his ear that he could "throw" at anyone to hurt or even kill them. At about the same time, Albert Reagan told how more than half of the Quileutes had begged him to prevent Doctor Lester, a medicine man, from killing them with his Tamahnous.[15]

The shamanistic practice of curing intrusive illnesses found in Shakerism a new identity and nomenclature. Traditional native belief held that illness was invisible to all but the shamans who exorcised it. The shamans would curette the illness from patients into their cupped hands or suck it out into their mouths, after which it could be released or killed. The Shakers substituted this technique with brushing and burning. One Shaker explained that his people rid the body of uncleanliness "by their spiritual discernment." They "objectify spiritual elements through their prayer and their manipulations and. . . . have control of it in that way and sometimes they actually see something like a garment or a cloth or something, a monster."[16]

In the curing part of their ceremonies, Shakers do not produce physical objects, as shamans do, but pantomime the disposal of pain and sin by brushing it out, throwing it away, burying it, or drowning it. With eyes closed, the healers approach the subjects without groping, divining the needs of those seeking to be healed and helped, "seeing" and touching critical areas of the patients' bodies. Those with the spirit to heal claim to see the sin of the illness or the problem as a shadow. Shakers may also burn the sin or pain out by passing a burning candle along the sufferer's limbs. This technique also had roots in pre-Shaker times, when shamans extracted and burned hard substances or threw them some distance, exclaiming "Go away, evil spirit."[17] The Shaker adaptation of this old practice was not too far removed from the Christian practice of exorcism, especially in the twentieth century. "Shakerism in the beginning was and still is an expression of conscience," wrote anthropologist Homer G. Barnett. "Slocum and those who followed him were oppressed by a sense of guilt greatly abetted by the Christian concept of sin."[18] In Shaker healings, such sin is believed to be in the air where it can pervade a room.

There are many descriptions of curing ceremonies. On the Skokomish Reservation during the 1940s, Joe Dan's daughter, Irene, reportedly went out of her head after a man had become angry at being asked to give up his seat in church to some visiting Shakers. After several shakings over her, the faithful effected a cure when the visiting Rev. William Hall of the Jamestown Shaker church brushed out the malevolent intrusion. To dispose of it, he buried it in a baking powder can. A day or so later, the man who had become angry was caught digging down to recover the intrusion, which he claimed was his power, but he reportedly died on reaching the receptacle. According to Reverend Eells, the Jamestown Shakers used a handkerchief to catch a "bad ghost" that they then blew away after emerging from their church house. The Quinaults used a can with a lighted candle on its top to hold sin. Taken to the forest, the can and candle gave the purveyors time to escape the malevolence of the sin.[19]

Some Shakers practice a blowing technique, which T. T. Waterman claimed originated with the Blowers, a Yakama Shaker sect. Before becoming Shakers, the Blowers practiced shamanist "medicine" in the Medicine Valley of the Yakama Reservation. Instead of curetting or sucking pain from sick bodies, however, they used an expiratory procedure to cure, and they blew on other Shakers when they met them.[20]

Deaths that occurred during the early years of Shakerism, like those in aboriginal times, were regarded as consequential evidence of shamanistic power struggles. Shaker deaths during such struggles came to be regarded as substitutionary losses. Anthropologist June M. Collins found that when persons became Shakers they believed that their guardian spirits enabled them to obtain the power to shake as well as to capture the guardian spirits of non-Shakers and force them to convert. Non-Shakers pitted their powers against those of Shakers, who claimed they could see the non-Shakers' spirit powers. If they were strong enough, Shakers believed, they could capture and refuse to return the spirits of non-Shakers, bringing illness to those who refused to join the church. When the non-Shakers capitulated and joined, their spirits were returned so they could be healed. This recruitment strategy was so common that nonmembers often boasted that their spirits were able to resist capture.[21]

Such beliefs persist in the church. In the mid-1960s, Wade Le Roy, the Shaker secretary-organizer, addressed a Shaker group in the White Swan church house. In the audience were two Yakama shamans whose purpose was to use a "power play" to weaken the Shakers' power by intimidating them. "I felt their gaze on me," reported Le Roy, "just like a serpent fixes his eyes on a bird to assure its capture." He said he avoided their gaze while speaking and then impaled them with his own, rendering them helpless as they fell to the floor and crept from the church house. Shakers believe that Le Roy would have become ill if the shamans had stolen his power.[22] Shakers have become less secretive about their use of power than they were early in their history, but there remains a residue of secrecy lest someone outwit them. Power plays also involve persons struggling against less visible forces. One such "play" is the recurring, spontaneous, and uncontrolled shaking that requires the help of others to stop. Whatever the form that shaking takes, reports of successful healing strengthens not only the patient's faith but also the position and reputation of the healers and their church.

Not every Shaker receives satisfactory healing, and some leave the church and go to white physicians to be cured. But some claim that white physicians cannot heal "Indian sickness," and Karen Bighead, a Smith River Shaker, characterized those who sought white doctors as lacking in faith. Interestingly, non-Shakers who are unhappy with white doctors often go to Shakers to be healed. In the late 1920s, on the Klamath Reservation, Mrs. Boyd Jackson, affectionately known as Grandma Jackson, spent several months in a hospital. Unable to cure her paralysis, her doctors discharged her and sent her home to die. She sought help from Shakers, who reportedly cured her after working over her for three nights. When she could eat and walk again, she said, "I've been healed. . . . They [at the hospital] gave me some heart pills once. I gave them to the birds. Now the birds all have strong hearts."[23] There are also reports of whites seeking healing in the church. One such sufferer was said to have been cured of chest pains by Harry Moses, the minister at Concrete Washington, who made surgical-like brushing motions and removed handfuls of worms from the victim.[24]

There are many reports of Shakers being disappointed in the power of those who tried to help them—including both Shaker healers and white doctors. On March 23, 1916, for example, Sammy Hoh's son died on the Quinault Reservation after both Indian doctors and Shakers had failed to cure him. But Shakers appear to be as charitable to non-Shaker healers who fail to cure as they are to their own people who fail. Shakers in northern California no doubt welcomed the several young women who had failed to become traditional native doctors and became Shaker healers instead, saying that Shakerism required no "secret 'magic' or hidden gimmicks for regurgitation; and it . . . [had] no association with payment, coming from Divine inspiration."[25]

Shakers cling doggedly to the belief that they can work miracles with their helps to those with particular needs and that they succeed where non-Shaker healers fail. In looking for help, patients go to Shaker homes and church houses, whose centers are vital places of healing. Up to a dozen chairs are placed in the centers of church houses for the ambulatory ill and for those who have other needs. In a Shaker church house at Nespelem on the Colville Reservation in March 1992, the authors observed eight chairs that the ill were invited to occupy. Among those accepting the invitation were the very young, including a boy of ten or eleven years, and the very elderly. Young mothers also sat in the chairs, their eyes closed, holding small children. There appeared to be no formal procedure among the healers, who moved rapidly from one person to the next. The ill were brushed on arms, legs, sides, or abdomens, depending on the location of the illness. Women fanned the ill with heat from their candles as others stomped around the room in traditional fashion, ringing bells and uttering the familiar "hai hais" of their chants. These syllables, uttered by shamans in pre-Shaker times, have taken on a new meaning for Shakers. One woman said they mean "holy" and "beautiful." In traditional fashion, the sin that was drawn from the ill was carried to the prayer table or cast into the air for its release.[26]

Early descriptions of healing ceremonies suggest that little has changed over the decades. In 1913, Edwin Chalcraft reported that in one of the "more Christian-like" churches—where the decorations consisted of "cheap religious pictures" and a cross and candlestick behind the pulpit—a large space had been left open down the center of the room. There, he wrote, the more devout worshippers remained on their knees during the service, crossing themselves occasionally. Chalcraft also reported that a gospel hymn, translated "into Indian" (perhaps Coast Salish or Chinook jargon), was sung and sin was "thrown" outside the room "with a blow of the breath."[27]

Shaker curing services into the early twentieth century were described by missionaries, government personnel, reporters, and informant-descendants of participants. Of what appears to have been a typical pretwentieth century healing service, one observer wrote,

> . . . while it is a religion for use at all times, yet it is practiced especially over the sick, and in this way takes the place of the medicine-men and their methods. Unlike the system of the medicine-men, it has no single performer. Though often they select for leader one who can pray the best, yet in his absence another may take the lead. Like the old system, it has much noise. Especially do they use bells, which are rung over the person where the sickness is supposed to be. The others present use their influence to help in curing the sick one, and so imitate the attendants on an Indian doctor, getting down upon their knees on the floor and holding up their hands, with a candle in each hand, sometimes for an hour. They believe that by so holding up their hands the man who is ringing the bell will get the sickness out more easily than he otherwise would. They use candles both when they attempt to cure the sick and in their general service, eschewing lamps for fear of being easily tempted, as they believe coal-oil lights to be from Satan.[28]

Anthropologist Leslie Spier, who believed there was a link between Shakerism and the Prophet Dance, gave an eyewitness account of a "performance" for a sick man on the Skokomish Reservation in 1922. He prefaced his description by stating that Shaker emphasis was on curing the sick rather than on relatively impersonal church services. In curings, he wrote, the participants became "suffused with religious emotion, and ringing the bells in a perfect fury, and not seldom losing their senses." In one prayer service—like those routinely held on Friday or Saturday evenings—a sick man was seated in a chair in the middle of the room facing the alter table. According to Spier, the rite began with praying and singing accompanied by the ringing of several pairs of bells. From time to time, individuals cried "hai, hai" in long, drawn-out, quivering, descending tones, after which they began shaking and standing in place. They then jumped up and down, placing both hands, palms toward the body, in front of the chest, moving their hands rapidly back and forth. Standing with arms extended to their sides—or, less frequently, in front—they fluttered their hands. Their movements began slowly, increasing to a "hysterical rapidity," according to Spier, at which point they began circling the room, some with eyes closed, jumping and fluttering as they went.[29]

After an interval, Spier reported, several people gathered a-round the sick man and slowly brushed him with their hands from head to foot and from foot to head. They passed their hands close to his body without touching, a noticeable departure from the intense rubbing of earlier times. A sharp exclamation announced that one of them had caught the "disease" in his cupped hands above the patient's head. The malady then appeared to drag its captor into a corner near the alter table, despite others' efforts to hold the cap-tor around the waist. One of the group went outside for a crock of water, into which they put the captured illness. They screwed the lid onto the crock, carried it outside, and buried it. Praying and singing resumed until the performance ended. In similar healing services, the bell ringing, circling, singing, and chanting can last from a few minutes to several hours, depending on the needs of the occasion.[30]

The motions used to treat the ill vary little throughout Shak-erism. All Shakers use the same manipulation to extract the pain of sin, which is seen as a dark spot in the sick person and is "thrown away." Healers from British Columbia to California pantomime the struggle to extract pain and evil as they move to door, win-dow, or prayer table to rid victims of malevolent intrusions. In a process that anthropologists call transference, healers release the captured sickness with arms raised in a sudden jerking motion, opening the closed fist in which it is held. At Smith River, heal-ers nearly always clap their hands softly three times in trinitarian fashion toward the prayer table, where they make left turns, cross themselves, and return for further healing. Sometimes animal spirits have been blamed for illness, such as when a serpent's spirit wrapped itself around a young girl's neck and caused her to have choking spells. It was reported that Shakers at Taholah cured her of this malady.[31]

At the Smith River church house, according to anthropologist Dale Valory, healers, bell ringers, and "motivated wanderers" en-deavored to "get up the shake," some maneuvering with eyes closed. Others turned and whirled around, while yet others reeled about almost to the point of falling down from the power received,

as "eyes remained closed but for the slightest crack which the light
of their candles betrays." This, Valory concluded, allowed "most
to navigate fairly accurately while giving the impression of clairvoyance." Some, he reported, stared blankly ahead in a catatonic
mode. All were expected to participate, although some stood in
place, stomping or shifting from side to side.[32]

The dancing and bell chiming, the observer noted, was done to
a four-four beat. Dancing, Valory wrote,

> comprises two types, one with two subtypes. Each foot stamps either
> one count, feet alternating, or two counts, feet alternating. The sec-
> ond type has special features, however. In all cases the entire foot
> is used to strike the floor, but a subtype of the second type involves
> alternating heel and toe, of first one then the other foot, so that four
> counts are measured: heel-toe/heel-toe. This subtype can be utilized
> while sitting on a bench, as it is not necessary to lift the entire foot.
> Alternatives may be employed: heel-toe/toe-heel. The other subtype
> of the second type involves two counts per foot: right-right/left-left.
> It is certain that the first type, with one count per footfall, becomes
> most dramatic—and noisy.[33]

There have been some variations in curing ceremonies, sometimes in the intensity of physical activity involved. In a 1966 Smith
River healing service, for example, five Yakama men working together joined cupped hands to extract a patient's pain, which they
took to the prayer table and "threw" the extracted pain toward the
cross. If Smith River Shakers were familiar with this practice, they
never adopted it. They claim that their practices are less severe
than those of the Washington Shakers. In their curings, Smith
River Shakers nevertheless often use strong enough movements
that subjects are "toppled from their seats." Sometimes even the
healers appear to faint when sin is extracted from their patient,
reportedly from accidentally consuming the evil.[34]

Gesturing is important in Shaker healings. According to anthropologists Richard A. Gould and Theodore P. Furukawa, there is "a
greater degree of referential exactness in the gestures used in curing among the Shakers than there is in the use of languages or
the Bible." In services such as those at Smith River, healers with
their eyes closed are directed to the victim's pain or sickness, which
they locate with their hands while brushing patients' backs, necks,
and shoulders. Using considerable pressure, healers then slowly

draw their hands down to the patients' waist level and in some instances even to the floor. Clapping their hands three times and raising their arms toward the alter table, they utter such words as "Praise Jesus" and "Praise the Lord." Sometimes they return to the table to cleanse themselves from the "evil thing." The climax comes when the healers, their hands clasped and often shaking, are directed by the "power" to where the pain is located. Their hands are then drawn off in a pulling motion.

Shakers claim to have cured many medical problems, ranging from arthritis to infections and trauma and including respiratory ailments, fevers, cramps, and weakness. In the early Shaker credo, healing was directed toward patients without distinguishing between physical and psychosomatic illnesses, since the differences were not understood. In time, healings were directed at those who suffered from "feeling bad" in the realization that such "feeling" stemmed from a "crisis situation" induced by sorrowing and mental suffering.[35]

Shaking ceremonies require physical endurance, so relative good health is important in the Shaker Church. A newspaper correspondent attending a Shaker service in the early twentieth century observed the stamina of its participants. It was remarkable, she reported, how the Shakers she observed—most of whom were past middle age—were able to sustain the violent exercising hour after hour, even the whole night long. Perspiration streamed from their bodies, yet they showed no exhaustion and the next day were none the worse for their exertions and ready to shake the next night.[36] That the elderly could engage in vigorous shaking and stomping while suffering arthritis and other infirmities suggests that they functioned on bodily endorphins.[37] According to Helen Clark, however, some of the most infirm and weak did not last past the initial shaking and dropped out of the church. She also cited a high attrition rate among younger people, who, although buoyed up in their initial shaking, later found themselves too weak to participate. Clark gave no explanation for this reaction, but the response may have been attitudinal.[38]

Those who remained in the church believe strongly in the preeminence and inseparability of shaking and curing. As John Smith told Edwin Chalcraft early in the history of the church and after Mud Bay Shakers had cured his son by shaking, God had given

them the power to cure illness. That is why God did not want
his Indian believers to receive money or blankets for services,
as white physicians required. Because the power is God-given,
Shakers believe that no hint of venality should defile shaking and
curing ceremonies, so gambling, drinking, and other bad habits
are strongly discouraged. Shakers regard shaking and healing as
not only vital to the survival of their members who fall ill, but also
to the health of the church itself.

CHAPTER SEVEN

Worship
and Ritual

While shaking and curing are at the center of the Indian Shaker Church, other elements have also been incorporated. Much of what would become Shaker tradition—including church rituals and ceremonies as well as day-to-day practices and religious accoutrements—came from a mix of native tradition and familiar elements of orthodox Christian churches. Early in the twentieth century, missionary Sarah Ober described the Shaker Church as a "curious intermixture of the old heathen religion and Christianity" in which "the warp of ancient superstitions was interwoven [with] the woof of Christianity, all intermixed with the wild phantasms of those to whom were vouchsafed visions." But all of that, she claimed, was changing yearly as the church acquired more Christian precepts.[1]

Ceremonies take place in Shaker church houses and sometimes—this was especially true during the early years of the church—in members' homes. Early church houses were built with donated labor and money—and often on donated land, some of it from tribal councils. They were painted white and had only one room, entered by means of several steps at the rear (which to non-Shakers would appear to be the front). A belfry, situated at the front of the church, enabled a minister in the main room to pull the bell cord during services. Backless benches lined white, painted walls, and a white prayer table at the front of the room was covered with a white cloth that often had a crocheted lace border. Early churches had no windows. A California Shaker once explained to anthropologist Richard A. Gould that any attempts to open windows during a shake, no matter how warm the weather, would break down the separation of activities "*inside* the building and the world *outside*." Missionary Helen Clark wrote that the Makahs had a similar belief. "When the windows are open," she wrote, "they [Shakers] do not so readily get into a frenzy, so they prefer a tight room."[2] The only light in the room during services came from inexpensive white candles. Simple wooden sconces with tapers hung on the walls, and wooden chandeliers with candles hung from the ceiling.

Like Big Bill before him, John Slocum did not allow the use of coal-oil lamps in the church, believing they were of the devil. In the late 1880s, participants in Shaker services wore candles and sometimes garlands of flowers on top of their heads.[3] This practice was soon abandoned, however, as was the earlier practice of passing hands through candle flame, although the symbolism of candle burning to remove sin or evil has been retained. Like Catholics, Shakers set candles around the living and the dead. In the Shaker church houses of the late twentieth century, electric lights are turned off, and candles are used during services, burning in simple, white, wood-framed chandeliers, in wall sconces, and on the altar table.

The simple cloth-covered tables or altars, where worshippers are controlled by the spirit, are the focal point in Shaker church houses. One Shaker rule, which ministers and elders explain to joiners, is that they or their household must have a "prayer table with bells and candle which shall be used when helping the sick."[4] The prayer tables occasionally hold vases of artificial flowers, religious pictures, and Bibles.[5] The customary entrance into Shaker church houses is from the west. Prayer tables are positioned toward the east, the direction for prayer and the direction in which souls travel at death.

The earliest meetings were held to treat illness and occurred whenever a need arose, but there soon developed the practice of holding these meetings to fill spiritual and physical needs as well.

Much symbolism in Shakerism is seen on this prayer table of Bishop Harris Teo. Such symbolism was borrowed from Roman Catholicism, which first appeared in 1838 along southern Puget Sound in the general homeland area (near present-day Shelton, Wash.) of John Slocum. Bishop Teo, who died in 1991, lived near White Swan in the Yakima Valley. (*Robert H. Ruby and John A. Brown*)

Early on, restrictions were often placed on these meetings. On the Quinault Reservation at the turn of the century, even though Shakers were ordered to end nightly sessions by ten o'clock in summer and nine o'clock in winter, they often violated the rule because shaking and curing were so vital to their religion. Later, when government officials became less attentive to Shaker practices, church members were emboldened to extend shaking and curing times well past the ten o'clock curfew, even into the small hours of the morning. In 1915, the commissioner of Indian affairs complained to Klamath Shakers that their meetings were lasting as long as six days and nights and that the meetings "are very similar to those of the old medicine men."[6]

By the time the Shaker church was formally organized a decade after John Slocum's experience, services were being held not only on what had become the traditional Thursday nights but on Saturday nights and Sundays as well. In time, services were held regularly on Wednesday nights.[7] In later years, the church decided to hold Friday and Saturday night shaking sessions, which better accommodated the schedules of workers. Curing sessions are often referred to as "night work," which is conducted with more shaking, stomping, and other maneuvering than occur during daytime services. Giving helps rarely occurs on Sundays, and then only in response to special requests. Sunday services are given over to praying, singing, brief exhortations, and admonitions, rarely to shaking.

Entering the center rear of a church house, members walk single file around the room, sometimes turning around counterclockwise on entering and again as they approach the alter table. This circling motion unwinds the self and leaves all troubles behind. Directions have significance in many aspects of Shaker teachings. One old Shaker saying has it that the trail to the west is big and easy to find, and if it is taken one does "bad." The reverse holds true for one doing "good" along the narrow road going toward the east. While the physical circuit of Shaker ritual is important, likewise a good journey traveled in thought guides one on a "straight line." Mud Bay Sam explained that "a good Christian man in the dark sees a light toward God. God makes a fog—good Christian man goes straight through it to the end, like good medicine."[8]

During Sunday services—the most ritualistic of all Shaker services—members entering from the back of the church house turn three times, bless themselves, make the sign of the cross, and intone, "In the name of the Father, the Son, and the Holy Ghost." Walking straight to the alter table, they raise their arms, offer a silent prayer, and usually ring a bell and bless themselves. They align themselves across the front of the room, and each sings a song or offers a prayer. Turning to their left, they pass along the men's side counterclockwise to where the men sit. The women, in a continuing counterclockwise direction, pass along to the right side before sitting down. A leader, or "floor manager," begins the worship and opens the floor for messages and testimony. Speakers tell what God has to say through them; others sometimes follow with a ritual cleansing of hands passed near a candle flame on the prayer table. Some speakers testify to the "regenerative and heal-

ing powers" of their religion. Any distinguished visitors are then
called on to speak.[9]

Regularly scheduled weekly meetings—referred to as "opening
the church" (or "prayer meetings" by whites)—are held in the
evening and sometimes last late into the night.[10] After entering
the church house for these meetings, the men and women move
to their customary sides of the church. A leader—and then others
from the congregation—testifies and exhorts. Those with spirit
power use candle heat and power brushing to treat the ill and
those who have special requests for helps. This is accompanied by
bell ringing, singing, stomping, and shaking.[11]

Over time, the general format for services has remained constant, but there is local and generalized diversity of rituals. Some
worshippers, for example, do not go straight to the altar and bless
themselves. Instead, they turn around three times in place, bless
themselves, and pass along the women's side of the church and
over to the alter. They then raise their arms and pray as tradition dictates, ring a bell, and bless themselves before continuing
counterclockwise.

There is no sermonizing as done in Protestant churches; instead,
speakers and singers voice their spiritual sensitivities. That is
how joiners, newcomers, and young people learn Shaker beliefs.
In his study of the Musqueams on the fringes of Vancouver, British
Columbia, anthropologist John Edward Michael Kew wrote, "It is
my view that this lack of concern for dogma stems directly from the
fundamental postulate of the traditional cosmology that defined
the supernatural as variable in form, motive and power, and the
relationship of the individual human with the supernatural as personal and organic rather than detached and mechanical."[12] Shaker
indoctrination, then, primarily involves introducing joiners to the
physical maneuvers involved in the services.

As in Protestant services, there are exclamations, however. As
important as the "hai hais" is the word "massey" or "massee"
(pronounced mossy), which means "thank you [God]." This is the
equivalent of "hallelujah," "praise the Lord," and "amen." The
word is derived from Chinook jargon, "mah'-side," and from the
French "merci," which means "thank you." Bodily movements ac-
company exhortations; the exhorters' eyes are closed as though
to shut out the material world. The same people who voice the

sounds of shaking and curing occasionally sing some of the songs
and chants that are important in Christian churches.[13] Shaker advocate and attorney James Wickersham recorded two songs and
translated them into English:

> Stalib Gwuch Kwe (Song of Heaven)
>
> When we get warning from heaven;
> Then the angels will come;
> Then the wonderful bells will ring:
> Then our souls will be ready;
> Then they will go up to heaven;
> Then we will sing with Jesus;
> Then we will be happy with Jesus.

and "Qua-da-tsits Stalib (Preacher's Song)

> Then we shall sing;
> Then we shall sing;
> Then we shall sing;
> Up in heaven's house.
> Then we'll be happy;
> Then we'll be happy;
> Then we'll be happy;
> Up in heaven's house.
> Then we'll be happy;
> Then we'll be happy;
> Then we'll be happy,
> Up with Jesus.[14]

Erna Gunther reported that a California woman attending a
Shaker meeting sang the following song to the approval of local
Shakers:

> How can you meet Jesus
> If you are not true?
> How can you meet Jesus?

At Jamestown, Gunther heard this song:

> Lead me, oh lead me,
> Lead me, oh Jesus,
> Lead me, oh lead me,
> Oh Jesus.

In subsequent verses the word "lead" was replaced by "guide," "help," and "love."[15]

As one Quileute Shaker put it at about midtwentieth century, everyone wanted to sing his or her own song "just like a hit-tune craze or a fad in fashions." During evening meetings, the uniformity of singing that is characteristic of morning meetings breaks down, and individual snatches are heard in an aura of increasing tempos. The tempo reaches an apex when bell-ringing leaders set a slower beat, taking from twenty to thirty minutes to return to the original beat. When new songs are introduced, good singers often compete with each other. Individuality in traditional Shaker singing precludes the use of hymnals, because songs are not sung in English. Some songs belong to individuals and are sung only when their owners are present. The words of many songs come from dreams or are heard during shaking.[16]

Most scholars group traditional Shaker songs with Christian hymns, especially hymns sung by Pentecostals who have broken from traditionalists. Gunther told how some Shakers remembered songs from early mission school days and concluded that their revival would have been as much through recall as revelation. Loran Olsen, an authority on Indian music, wrote that "old Shaker tunes represent Protestant hymns, Catholic chants, popular tunes and old Indian songs in various combinations." Willard Rhodes, another authority on Indian music, stressed the syncretic character of Shaker songs in which elements of the old guardian spirit songs are combined "with rhythmic and melodic fragments of gospel hymns of evangelical sects that have been elaborated according to native principles and techniques of melodic development." Traceable to Shaker guardian spirit songs, Rhodes wrote, were the "emotional involvement and absorption of the singer, and the singing style with its relatively clear intonation, refined and expressive vibrato, the employment of the diminuendo at the close of a song, and the deep, heavy, audible inhalations which punctuate the phrases."[17]

Loran Olsen described Shaker singing as having "great power and rhythmic enthusiasm," pointing out the considerable sliding between pitches and a mixture of the text with "vocables," or melody-carrying syllables. The variety of Shaker music, he wrote, reflected several sources as well as "modal" scales. The music is also pentatonic (five tones) and monophonic (one line), with much improvisation.[18]

Shaker prayers, much like Shaker songs, were regarded by believers as special gifts from God. At the Memorial Meeting on the Skokomish Reservation in August 1913, Chehalis minister John Smith uttered such a prayer:

> Oh our heavenly Father
> Oh our heavenly Father
> To our Soul heavenly Father
> To our Soul Secret Father in heaven
> Oh Father in Heaven Bless this place
> Help us all, I am praying to you
> Send your angel of Peace
> And help us keep all evil away from us.
> Have mercy on us
> Save us our Dear Savior
> Bless all the People here at this place
> Through Christ our Savior, and Amen.[19]

This and other prayers are rendered with inflections and modulations. Of the many prayers Albert Reagan recorded at the turn of the century, he labeled one a "guiding" prayer:

> Our God is in heaven.
> If we die He will take our life to heaven.
> Help us that we shall not die.
> Wherever we are, help us not to die.
> Our Father who is there,
> Always have a good mind to us.[20]

This nondeath theme is especially strong in Shaker prayers. Like other Indians, the Shakers have suffered high mortality rates, not only from native illnesses but also from diseases introduced by non-Indians. In addition, the number of accidental deaths increased with employment in dangerous work such as logging and with the consumption of liquor.

What has been termed Shaker "prayer" involves total congregational participation. Rather than directing their thoughts to God in prayer, worshippers utter intercessory words that they believe God directs to them. They offer prayers at the opening and closing of services and at the beginning and end of meals. Prayers are offered not only for those present in meetings but also for those who are absent. During the Vietnam War, for example, prayers were offered for the safety of people in the service in that conflict. Near the beginning of the service held by a Shaker Bible-use group in a home at Taholah on the Quinault Reservation, for example, a man in a trance reportedly held the spirit of a soldier and passed it among the worshippers. As it passed from one to another, each worshipper prayed for the soldier. A calm but intense dance followed, and the soldier's spirit was returned to him.[21]

During early times, Shakers prayed in several native languages at once, producing sounds that, to white ears, were more cacophonous than choral. Chinook jargon helped congregations adjust to the problem of linguistic diversity. Eventually, English became the dominant language spoken in services, although the intonations of prayer, with words in crescendos and diminuendos trailing off to a whisper, can be unintelligible to strangers. One observer noted that the older members of the Smith River church used native languages that were incomprehensible to younger members. The young people believed that it took a special "power" to use such language.[22]

To strangers a most unintelligible language is that of glossalalia which, according to Pamela Amoss, signifies entrancement. In the manner of Christian apostles receiving the Holy Spirit at Pentecost, Leotah Bustillo, an Indian Full Gospel Church minister on the Tulalip Reservation, claims that words spoken in her church can be understood in the various languages of her parishioners. Tongues were also heard in the ISC Smith River church house and some others. One Shaker leader believes that words spoken in ISC services have meaning for Germans, Japanese, and other nationals.[23]

Crosses, symbolizing the suffering and death of Christ, are very important to the Shakers and are found in Shaker church houses and homes. The first rule that ministers and elders pass on to Shaker joiners is the importance of making the sign of the cross, a practice reminiscent of Big John's ride through Olympia, his arms outstretched to form the bar of a cross. Crosses are so important that on one occasion, when Shakers were involved in an internal dispute on the Quileute at La Push in 1911–1912, the Rev. Robert E. Lee and Elder Jerry Jones removed the cross from the church,

Ordination service at Nespelem, Washington, 1992, for Steven Iukes, Sr. (*left*), a minister in the Indian Shaker Church; Fred Manual (*center*), assistant minister; and Steven Iukes, Jr. (*right*), secretary. (*Robert H. Ruby and John A. Brown*)

causing a number of its members to move to "a separate building." In a later incident, an elder of the Taholah church reportedly became so angry with the management of church affairs that he erected a cross at his home and smashed it into splinters in front of visitors. Landes Kallapa, a leader of the Makah Shakers, went so far as to abandon the use of the cross because it reminded him of the death of his son.[24]

Shakers found power in bells as well, and there is little question that their use was borrowed from Catholic ritual. At the annual convention at Taholah in October 1984, Bishop Harris Teo said that a decade before John Slocum's "death" it had been foretold that a large bell would come down from heaven. Shakers later interpreted this as forecasting the advent of their religion. A bell with more earthly origins and weighing 427 pounds was hauled over the Cascade Mountains from Seattle in 1910 and installed in the White Swan church house.[25] There are several different kinds of bells used, including the long wooden-handled dinner

bells kept on prayer tables and small bells resembling those rung
to call children to school. Reverend Eells observed that small bells,
rung during Shaker worship services, resembled those used to call
steamboat passengers to board and hotel guests to dinner.[26] In the
Mud Bay mother church,

> The lines form at the outside of the church and enter to the accom-
> paniment of a rhythm set by bell ringers. Many of the men and boys
> will each have two hand bells (bells with wooden handles) which are
> rung with a heavy down-stroke from the wrists. As the Shakers en-
> ter, they often turn around once in a circle. With the men to the left
> and the women to the right, there may soon be two hundred or so
> Shakers circling the room. All are shuffling or dancing in rhythm to
> the bells. As they pass the seated observers, they may touch hands.
> Sometimes the shakers will be seen to make the sign of the cross. All
> the time the rhythm of the bells quickens tempo and is accompanied
> by a most beautiful singing of all participants.[27]

But the sound of Shaker bells has not always been beautiful
to everyone. According to anthropologist George Pettitt, in 1905
the Quileute agent insisted that only one bell be used in services
and that it could be used only for signaling, not for continuous
ringing.[28] Later, government officials on the Quileute limited the
number of bells to two per service, prompting Rev. Robert Lee
and his assistant to explain that they wanted to conduct services
with twelve bells, one for each of Christ's disciples. The two men
reported that tribal police and a judge had stood at their door
to see that the bell edict was enforced. A limitation on the use
of bells, they complained, symbolized the agency's obstruction of
their freedom of worship—it was a hindrance to their efforts to
heal.[29]

At the 1910 dedication of the Mud Bay church, Elder Alex Teio
responded to criticism of bell ringing in Shaker services: "I went
to church at Portland. I saw a great pipe organ extending all along
the side of the church. The people sang. The organ bellowed like
thunder. Is it any more ridiculous to ring bells? We ring bells to
give our people time when they sing. The organ plays to keep the
people in time. It is the same."[30]

There is room for some speculation about the Shakers' attraction
to bells. While they believe that bells are of heavenly origin and
are aware of their prominence in Christian worship, Shakers may

also have embraced them simply because the sounds were pleasant to their ears. It had been a short step from native ceremonies to Shakerism, and a behaviorist could argue that shaking and curing were conditioned by the stimulus of ringing bells. There may also be merit in the idea that bells symbolized for Shakers a break from native traditions and an attempt to achieve legitimacy in the white Christian tradition. Laying aside such speculation, bells are certainly literal bellwethers of Shaker vitality. Those who hear bells pealing from easterly positioned belfries, usually a half hour before Sunday services, are reminded that the Shaker church is alive in their communities.

Handshaking is also important in Shaker worship, although not with the single hand extended. Shakers raise their forearms, with their palms extended outward to touch the palms of those whose forearms and hands are similarly positioned. This practice is reminiscent of the way people extended their palms upward in the *tsiyuk*, an old Quileute curing ceremony.[31] Handshaking occurs at the beginning of Shaker services as people enter the church house.

The precedent for using robes in Shaker services is found in John Slocum's request for one on his return from his first "death." Undoubtedly, Slocum had seen Catholic priests wearing robes, and Shaker robes resemble the white albs worn by priests when they say mass. Interestingly, missionary Sarah Ober defended the Shakers' use of robes as signifying clean living and claimed that the robes did not imitate Catholic robes. Ober also noted, however, that many Shakers had discarded their white gowns.[32] The practice of wearing robes began when Mud Bay Louis wore one in his own services. Louis had dreamed that by wearing a robe he could escape death, and his wife made him one for that purpose. He encouraged the faithful who lived eastward across the Cascade Mountains at White Swan on the Yakama Indian Reservation to wear robes to ensure their own longevity.[33]

Fabricated from imported cotton, Shaker robes covered wearers from their shoulders to their heels. Long sleeves were fastened with one to three buttons along slits at necklines at wearers' backs. Bands were sewn on the fronts of robes, usually of light blue ribbons, simulating chains with hanging crosses. One source reported that both men and women wore similar robes. Over the years, there have been a number of small decorative changes in robes.

Enrobed Shakers at La Push, 1911. The use of robes was a matter of concern in early Shakerism. Bishop Peter Heck's refusal to wear one disturbed some Shaker traditionalists. Some Shakers, as though to shed the image of past lives spent in gambling and Tamahnous practice, burned their shamanist vestments and clothing. At a White Swan Shaker meeting, Wasco Jim claimed to have had a revelation calling for the incorporation of buckskin and feathers as ritual garb for worshippers. The congregation rejected this suggestion. (*Indian Shaker Church Archives*)

During Mud Bay Sam's leadership, Shakers wore white robes with narrow blue bands around the neck. In more recent times, men's robes had no collars and cuffs. Women's gowns had a ribbon sewn at ninety-degree angles, appearing as a bib on the upper part of the chest; on the men's gowns, the ribbon was in a V shape. Both women and men used robes with ribbons sewn in the shape of a cross.[34]

In an undated listing of Shaker church rules, the directives specify that garments (described as "holy raiments") were to be worn only at Sunday services. In earlier times, when robe use was more general, each worshipper entered the church house with his or her gown on the right arm. Once in position, the worshippers put their gowns on over their heads at the same time and later removed them simultaneously. Should evil overtake a worshipper—

as bearing false witness against a neighbor—the broken com-
mandment was believed to "cling on to your garment and be sin."[35]
Robes thus symbolized cloaks of righteousness, much like the purity of robed angels, enhancing the spirituality of their wearers.
Like candle flames and white handkerchiefs, robes symbolized
a divinely sanctioned power used by Shakers to minister to the
sick and potential members and to worship God. Perhaps believing that robes ensured immortality, some Shakers were buried in
them. There has been an inconsistency in the wearing of robes.
Shakers rarely wear robes in the late twentieth century, although
women frequently wear white dresses.

The native practice of painting or tattooing the body was not
carried into Shaker ceremonies. According to Wade Le Roy, a long-
time secretary-organizer and physical and spiritual counselor for
Shakers, in one Shaker church—that of the Siletz—women followed a tribal custom of painting their faces. For them, markings
on the face had religious significance. Le Roy remembered arriving at that church on a motorcycle one day. Riding in the sidecar
was his wife, her face browned by harsh sun and a rough wind. The
white lines radiating from her eyes, caused by wrinkles brought
on by squinting, were believed by the Siletz women to symbolize
the divine nature of the woman's visit.[36]

Many rituals have been introduced in the Shaker Church, some
of which have endured and undergone various refinements. The
church came under severe criticism from Reverend Eells, who
recorded that even though Shakers mentioned Christ as savior,
remarked about his death, and displayed the cross, when they
prayed to confess their sins "they almost totally rejected the
Bible."[37] A Quinault Shaker recorded that confession occurred
when individuals approached the alter and, in scarcely audible
voices, made their statements. In some instances, Shakers made
their confessions by standing with their arms raised until they
began to shake. Shakers believed they were surrendering their
lives to God, whom they approached through the spirit rather than
through earthly intercessors.

Although sporadic attempts were made to institutionalize confession in the Shaker Church, it never became a regularly accepted
practice. John Slocum had formally confessed his sins, and there
were those who supposedly went to him for the same purpose.

But soon after his own "healing," Slocum transferred his confessor role to Mud Bay Louis, who later transferred it to Dick Johnson. After the turn of the century, Joe Riddle, a Yakama Indian and ordained Shaker minister, revived the practice of making and hearing confessions. In about 1903, he traveled to places as distant as Jamestown on the Strait of Juan de Fuca and later to the Klamath Indian Reservation in southern Oregon to hear confessions. Reverend Eells reported Riddle's visit to the Jamestown Shaker church, where its members were induced to hold public confessions. The practice caused a "row" in the church that resulted in the removal of one family and the departure of its minister to Port Gamble.[38]

Riddle also pitched a tent outside the White Swan church and heard parishioners' confessions on Friday nights. He tallied the confessors' sins by laying out a match for each misdeed. In a manner unthinkable in the late twentieth century, Riddle himself openly confessed in a meeting, pointing out and naming women with whom he had had intimate relations. He also confessed to serving time in jail, which had ended, he proudly recalled, when he prophesied it would.[39]

Shaker worship has been modified over time, acquiring uniformity and continuity.[40] Those who convert to Shakerism first have to rid themselves of the *mesache* (or *mesachie*), loosely translated from Chinook jargon as "evil" or "bad" spirit and sometimes "devil." In 1890, Charles Rakestraw, supervisor of the Chehalis school, described the ritual that attended the confession of faith: "[T]he shakers [had] to operate their peculiar enchantments upon him (or her) in order to get the meanness out of the heart of the applicant before he or she can become converted."[41] The process, he explained, began by placing the candidate in the middle of the church house, where he or she stood facing the altar, hands together and arms extended. After the leader or minister put some of "God's medicine" into the candidate's palms, the members encircled the subject, each with one or two handbells ranging in size from four to six inches in diameter. At this, wrote Rakestraw, "the Shake" began. With bells ringing simultaneously, each Shaker jumped violently in unison with the others. Shaking continued until the candidate involuntarily shook in unison with the others. During this process, explained Rakestraw, others approached the candidate, jumping around the person in time with the other members and the bells. They pulled the *mesache* from different parts of the candidate's body and then put burning candles atop one of the crosses to burn up the *mesache*, making certain that none of it remained on their own hands by carefully and frequently singeing them in the candle flames. Sometimes a week or more was required to purge the *mesache* from a person.[42]

Sometimes joiners feel the need of additional strength to resist former evil practices and tendencies. Rakestraw described one such renewal that was achieved in a process similar to that of conversion. The candidate requested a "shake" to gird himself for further battle with the devil. He stood in the half of the room nearest the alter table, with Shaker women assembled around him. These "angels" wore long, flowing white robes, their long hair combed loosely down their backs. The subject held a lighted candle in his right hand as he faced the alter table. Each angel also held a lighted candle. With a stately tread, the angels encircled the subject in a counterclockwise direction to the rhythm of the bells and then reversed direction. The encircling movements were repeated, after which the candidate blew out his candle and stepped into the circle of marching angels. As each woman went by, he took her candle, blew it out, and handed it back. With this, the marching and the bell ringing ceased, and the candidate knelt at the railing in front of a large cross. The angels then arranged themselves behind and on either side of the candidate while other Shakers knelt behind him. Rakestraw noted that "the ceremony seem[ed] to be responsive . . . [with] a marked similarity to the litany of the Episcopal Church." Rakestraw concluded that one young subject had been "fully strengthened 'to resist the devil and all his adversaries.'"[43]

Baptism has always carried some importance to Shakers, but it was some time before the church institutionalized it. John Slocum had been baptized by a Catholic priest before he founded the church in 1882. At the 1883 Big Meeting, Slocum went about baptizing adult Shakers, telling them he had to do so because Reverend Eells's Congregational baptisms were worthless. Some early Shakers took their children to Protestant and Catholic churches to receive the rite. Many elderly Shakers, however, entered their churches on confession of faith, their bodies rubbed, often harshly, by others as a substitute for baptism.[44]

Missionary Sarah Ober reported that Shakers made baptism part of their doctrine shortly after the church was founded. In a 1908 letter from a Yakama correspondent, she learned that some Puget Sound Shakers had introduced baptism on the Yakama Reservation and that nearly all of his people had been baptized. The correspondent testified that his own baptism had enlightened him, bringing him "nearer to Jesus" so he could keep his heart "all clean like Jesus."[45]

In 1930, Joe Connor (Conner), minister of the Siletz, Oregon, church, informed Bishop Heck that four women had baptized themselves in the Klamath River after one of them had dreamed that she should perform the rite. Wade Le Roy told of Jesse Moses, wife of the minister at Concrete, Washington, who shed her old garments and baptized herself in a stream. According to Robert Pope, a Quinault Shaker, a woman who confessed to making home brew shook in her confession amidst candles and then circled the church house three times in freezing weather before baptizing herself in a nearby stream. Joe Daner, a Quinault Shaker, wrote Heck that because Shakers received baptism by other religions in a river they were not true members of their own church. These practices and sentiments are far different from the time when Shakers did not baptize but depended on clergy from other churches to administer that rite.[46]

Although Shakers believe in baptism, they are inconsistent in having their children receive the rite. Church rules now state that bishops, elders, and ministers are authorized to baptize children and new members. When the family requests a baptism it is done in Sunday morning services. During the ritual, the leader calls for the candidate to come forward and for six candle holders to help officiate in cleansing the child. In the Indian Full Gospel Church, a group that split from the original Shaker church, an evangelist performs baptisms in the absence of a minister or a missionary. Some Shakers claim to have undergone considerable change after baptism. Wade Le Roy told of an Indian he knew at Kamilchie (near Shelton), for example, who crawled under the church house in the early 1930s to listen to exhortations above. Finally convinced of what he had heard, he was baptized. He rose from "baptismal waters," Le Roy reported, "a changed man, abandoning his drinking as well as one of his two wives."[47]

It is unclear when marriages were first performed by Shakers.[48] In the 1927 annual convention, delegates decided that because the church was incorporated, marriages were valid when performed by ordained or licensed ministers. In 1931, Enoch Abraham of the White Swan church sought instructions from Bishop Heck for marrying and baptizing. Someone had apparently told Abraham that Fred Shuster, a Satus minister, had said that ". . . we don't carry that [marriage] in our church." Abraham advised Heck that he had "told our minister that we have right to carry everything that other church[es carry]. Cause we are not under no church. Our church is a church like any other church, so please send me the instruction so I can read it to the minister of the two [Satus and White Swan] churches."[49] Records of a 1939 convention read: "Bishop[s] and all ministers . . . [are] to marry and baptize people."[50] Still, Gunther wrote that until the late 1940s she knew of only one Shaker wedding.[51]

In Washington and California, ministers must only hold a church license in order to perform marriages. In Oregon and British Columbia, however, a minister must be registered with the state or province. In the 1970s, Shakers began performing marriages in British Columbia homes and Big Houses. In 1977 three Shaker ministers were registered with the British Columbia Division of Vital Statistics: Gillman Jimmy of Duncan, Theresa Sam of Saanich, and Walker Stogan of Musqueam. In 1983 Bishop Teo directed the Division of Vital Statistics to cancel Stogan's registration to perform marriages because he had made inadequate financial reports to the church. Other ministers were registered in British Columbia in the 1980s and 1990s.

On at least one occasion, provincial officials questioned the legality of a Shaker marriage. On May 25, 1985, Robert J. Nahanee, assistant minister of the Squamish church, performed a marriage for Joseph Michael Siah and Carol Joan O'Brien at Port Douglas. The marriage record was filed in the Division of Vital Statistics. A half year later, a division employee discovered that the marriage had not been performed by a registered minister, and Shaker officials were hastily asked for an explanation. Bishop Teo delayed replying until the provincial government threatened harsh treatment. Following a special meeting at La Push on May 30, 1986,

The reception line at the wedding of Clifford Tulee, later bishop of the Indian Shaker Church, and Oralia Cantu at White Swan church house, September 22, 1990. (*Robert H. Ruby and John A. Brown*)

Washington state and provincial elders decided to relieve Nahanee of his position and pay expenses for a new civil ceremony for the couple. Teo handed over fifty-five dollars for a new license, the civil ceremony fee, and a certified copy of the marriage certificate.[52]

Other procedural ceremonies were also adopted by the church, including the dedication of church houses and the ordination of ministers. On the Colville Reservation at Nespelem in March 1992, one dedication ceremony began in nontraditional fashion with a ribbon-cutting ceremony. The men then filed into the church, followed by the women. Upon entering, some members were given lighted candles. They marched across the rear to the right of the room and up to the front before the alter table. A ten-foot-high cross hung on the wall behind the alter table. At the altar they turned completely around before moving down the left side of the church and across to the back, turning again at the back of the room. They repeated the counterclockwise circling twice. The men then assumed their seats on the left, the women on the right. The dedication concluded with short, spontaneous talks on subjects ranging from how funds were raised for the building to testimonials of the Shaker faith.

The ritual of ordination uses some of the same elements. At Nespelem in 1992, at the ordination of two ministers and a church secretary, each person spoke to the congregation about their new responsibilities. Seven men with bells and seven women holding lighted candles formed a single line behind the candidates. Members of the congregation spoke about how those being ordained needed to follow the laws of the traditional Indian Shaker Church. The three initiates were admonished to use bells and candles only in services and to add no new items, discouraging innovation and nontraditional practices. Another speaker exhorted them to serve only members in the faith. After a song, the seven men and seven women encircled each candidate while the bishop and four head state elders laid hands on the heads of the kneeling candidates. The three received palmed heat from the women's candles and a charge from the bishop. Following the ordination, the entire congregation marched around the church to the front to congratulate the three with handshaking and some embracing.[53]

In no area do Shakers show their independence from mainline Protestant and Catholic churches more than in the absence

Dedication of the new Skokomish church house, September 1, 1962. Leading the procession is Lee Cush. Note the overhead chandeliers and the worshippers ringing bells with both hands. (*Indian Shaker Church Archives*)

of the communion ritual. Lida M. Quimby, a field matron on the Puyallup Reservation, noted that it took "special effort and 'invitations'" for Shakers to participate in this sacrament, a position unchanged to the present. While Shakers avail themselves of services of Protestants and Catholics to baptize their children and perform marriages, they do not accept communion.[54]

Although not a ritual form, prophecies were frequently part of the early Shaker Church. According to Reverend Eells, the Shakers "prophesied very much." The prophecies of a judgment day are reminiscent of those found in Judaic-Christian scriptures, but generally Shaker prophecies were concerned with a more specific time and more local issues. Mary Thompson, Slocum's wife, for example, reportedly said that during her husband's illness a man had prophesied that three stars and the moon would destroy the earth. Another prophecy made reference to the important Shaker Fourth of July gathering time, which was ready-made for Shaker seers to predict catastrophic events. Reverend Eells noted that every prediction of a Fourth of July doomsday had failed. Failed prophecies of worldwide cataclysms may have encouraged Shakers to

Shaker ordination service for Steve Iukes, Jr. (with upraised arms) as secretary of the Nespelem Shaker Church in 1992. (*Robert H. Ruby and John A. Brown*)

concentrate on foretelling local events, although they still occasionally warned of cosmic disasters. Eells reported that he had
also been told that the deaths of several people had been predicted,
but in only one instance were the predictions revealed before the
person died.[55]

Anthropologist Leslie Spier was among those claiming that John
Slocum made no prophecies, but it must be remembered that a
prophet is considered a messenger of God, as Slocum claimed to be,
and not necessarily one who prophesies.[56] One can only speculate
why Slocum was not given to foretelling the future, since so many
native religionists of his time engaged in it. Perhaps memories of
his "death" experience precluded such predictions for him.

Shaker dreams and visions not only foretold of things to come
but also brought wisdom and warnings. Shakers believed that
dreams and visions directed individual and group conduct. One
example of clairvoyance occurred sometime during the first half of
the twentieth century when a man drowned in the Nisqually River.
When locals could not find the body, a Shaker woman from the
Chehalis Reservation who claimed clairvoyant power was brought
in to find it. At the edge of the river, a group of Shakers closed
their eyes in prayer and then began to sing and shake. The woman
prayed: "Oh, Great Spirit, grant us help to accomplish that which
we are trying to do." According to accounts, her prayer was answered, and the body was found in a logjam. On the Colville
Reservation in 1957, shaking that reportedly led to finding the
drowned body of Charlie Moses was believed to be responsible for
the acceptance of the Indian Full Gospel Church east of the Omak
Hills.[57]

There were no formalized rites in the early church for those
whose death was imminent, although Shakers were aware of the
Catholic rite of extreme unction. Any shake for an extremely ill
person is done with the anticipation of recovery. When death does
occur, coffins are used, a practice that dates from the beginning
of the church. Shakers are sometimes buried in their robes. At
midtwentieth century, anthropologist Erna Gunther wrote:

> The coffin is usually not brought into the church, but the Shakers go
> in a body to the home of the deceased, and after the leader has spoken
> a few words there the men carry the coffin to the cemetery. There, by
> the graveside, the leader again speaks, and some hymns are sung.

The hymns chosen are from any standard Protestant hymnal, and
are often more completely used in this case than in other services.
They are sung, standing still, while at other services there is always some movement, even if only the trembling of the hands. Even
though extremely simple, the funeral rites most closely approximate
the ones from the Christian churches from which they are drawn.[58]

After midcentury, however, services changed to the extent that
Shakers began taking caskets to a church house or funeral home.
On the Quinault Reservation, a wake (sometimes lasting three
nights) is traditional when someone dies. At the end of a Quinault
funeral service, after mourners view the body, the casket is rolled
around the room, the congregation following it. It is then turned
completely around three times. Those attending the burial service
at the cemetery remain until the casket is lowered and covered. Occasionally, mourners sprinkle dirt or other objects over the casket
before it is covered. Although Shakers give considerable deference
to Christian burial customs in their own practices, there is at least
one reported instance of implicit resistance to that practice. Elder
Alex Teio complained that on the death of a child, one Shaker minister made his people paint their faces and "March round the dead
body like the wild Indians." The only cemetery owned and operated by Shakers is one at White Swan, which opened in 1911 with
nine burials. Occasionally, non-Shakers are buried there.[59]

Crying has also been an important part of Shaker funerals. According to one Tulalip woman, the Indian way at Shaker funerals
was to make people cry. After weeping at the words of chosen eulo-
gizers, the mourners passed a basin of water among themselves so
they could wash their faces, especially their eyes. After the burial
service, mourners returned to the church, where articles of the
deceased's clothing were passed to each person as a remembrance
and to assuage their grief. In 1914, Dan Hart, a Klamath Shaker
visiting on the Yakama Reservation, informed Bishop Heck that
he had recently conducted a funeral service for some white people
at Selah in the upper Yakima Valley, where he had "made a good
sermon which caused many ones to shed a tear."[60]

Shakers developed other funeral customs as well. In a 1992
funeral service for Muckleshoot Shaker Eva Jerry—a leader,
historian, teacher, and linguist—officials boxed up her personal
belongings and put them away for a year. All of her pictures were

taken down or covered for that period as part of the mourning process.[61]

The Shaker service at the Mud Bay church for Bishop Harris Teo was held on October 12, 1991, corresponding with the annual October convention. Teo's services were typical. A preservice, or "candle service," was held the evening before the burial, with singing and praying and talks of remembrance honoring the dead. Seating was traditional at the funeral the next day, with men on the left and women on the right. Mourners from many Shaker communities were in attendance. Family members, both men and women, sat on the right. The mourners wore plain, simple clothing, some bearing images with Indian themes. Many children attended, and all of them were well behaved, apparently sensing the solemnity of the occasion. White curtains bearing large blue crosses hung over the windows, adding to the plaintive nature of the setting. The coffin was ornamented with typical Shaker funeral objects: flowers, potted plants, wreaths, and even balloons. Mike Davis, a Skokomish who led the service, eulogized the bishop. Conforming to the practice of the Shakers, there was spontaneous singing throughout the service. Several speakers praised the bishop for laying a strong moral foundation for his people. The speakers turned counterclockwise toward the mourners after passing their hands through candle heat. Making the sign of the cross three times, they uttered, "In the name of the Father, the Son, and the Holy Ghost" and rang a prayer-table bell.

A candle service followed. Three women holding candles stood at the right of the casket; three men with bells moved to the left. They repeated three times: "In the name of the Father, the Son, and the Holy Ghost." Several began a song, and others joined in, their tones reverberating throughout the church. One man and his helpers approached the large wood-framed, cross-shaped chandelier, where the man deftly pinched low-flickering candles between thumb and forefinger. The bells rang intermittently. The congregation's singing and praying became scarcely audible with tones rendered in crescendos and diminuendos. First the men and then the women filed by the now-opened casket for a final glimpse of the bishop robed in his gown. The casket was then taken to the nearby Shelton cemetery, where the bishop wished to be buried near John Slocum.

John Slocum's remains were removed from Johns Prairie, a Shelton, Washington, outlying district, and reburied in the Shelton Memorial Cemetery on October 5, 1975, at the time this monument was erected at the new grave site. Harris Teo (*center*) conducts a burial service. It was Teo's wish to be buried in the Shelton Cemetery close to Slocum when he died. His wish was granted. (*Indian Shaker Church Archives*)

Clearly, these ceremonial practices are important to the Shaker church. Yet, even John Slocum had to yield the prospect of dwelling in heavenly mansions to building a church house on earth with a congregation of men and women, not angels. In order for his religion to survive and flourish, Slocum's followers recognized that their faith had to be yoked with funds, their prayers with planning, their reverence and worship of God with a worldly reputation. The need for coming to grips with these earthly necessities marked the passage of John Slocum's religion through the critical transitional stage of its existence.

CHAPTER EIGHT

A Mantle
of Formality

O n October 1, 1882, Edwin Eells was placed in charge of the Puyallup Consolidated Agency, which included ten reservations and four boarding schools. The agency consisted of three subagencies—the Nisqually, the Skokomish, and the Tulalip. Before the year was out, the Quinault Reservation was also placed under Eells's jurisdiction. But on July 16, 1883, the provisions of the Grant peace policy shifted responsibility for the Tulalip agency, with six reservations, to the Catholics, leaving Eells to administer the Nisqually, Puyallup, Squaxin, Skokomish, Chehalis, and Quinault Reservations headquartered at New Tacoma.[1]

Eells's administrative policies were those of Christian-minded reformers of the late nineteenth century who attempted to implement the federal government's forced assimilation of Indians into white American society. This policy was pursued even though assimilation was difficult, if not impossible, among people who lived in reservation enclaves.[2] The government was determined to make agrarians of Pacific Northwest Indians by having them abandon traditional ways of life.

Indian subsistence activities were traditionally collective in nature, but Eells, clinging to a Jeffersonian ideal, sought to have his charges become agrarians under a government landholding

policy that encouraged individual ownership. Even before the 1887
Dawes Indian Severalty Act, which gave Indians the option of own-
ing land, Article 6 of the 1854 Medicine Creek Treaty allowed the
president to divide lands in severalty. In 1874, Eells began allot-
ting land on the Skokomish Reservation and other confines under
his jurisdiction. Based on the land's utilitarian value, allotments
varied from ten acres of bottomland to eighty acres of hilly and
more unproductive land.[3]

After the Dawes Act passed, Eells was exuberant because
now those Indians allotted were citizens of the United States.
They were no longer "wards" of the government, but free-born
sovereigns of their native lands. With this change, he believed, "the
Indian problem has been solved." But Eells celebrated too soon.
As far as the Skokomish and Chehalis Indians were concerned—
particularly the Shakers among them—their problems were far
from over. Many Indians were still forced to seek employment in
and for the white community in order to subsist. Annuity goods
promised under the Indian treaties still came tardily, if at all, and
when they did come, they were ill suited to the physical environment and traditional ways of life of the Indians. Indian children
were forced into day and boarding schools, where they were punished for speaking their native languages. At the same time, their
elders were prohibited from participating in native dances and ceremonies. It was to enforce such edicts that agency courts and police
systems were established to punish violators, especially Shakers,
whose rubbing and shaking were seen as serious infractions. Punishment was also meted out for infractions against general law and
order. In 1884, for example, Eells sentenced some Indian boys to
nine months' hard labor under ball and chain because they were
accused of setting fire to the Puyallup Reservation school.[4]

Many whites continued to look askance at the growing Shaker
religion, and Shakers were persecuted by arrests and imprisonment. These followed a pattern. As photographer and ethnologist
Edward Curtis observed, "In the beginning it [Shakerism] suffered the fate of most new religions. It was vigorously opposed and
its founders and apostles were threatened and actually thrown
into jail by reservation authorities."[5] "Missionary Sarah Ober told
how imprisonment, persecution, and ridicule of Slocum's followers
came from government officials, missionaries, and the white com-

munity, who used every means possible to check, if not to wipe out, Shakerism. She did not overlook the poignant and tragic episode of Big John's incarceration in Olympia, when his followers stood praying about the jail, expecting to see its walls cast down and its prisoners released. John Slocum himself—along with some of his followers—had also apparently been arrested and placed in ball and chains in the Puyallup Agency jail. When the sheriff warned that he would not release the men until they promised to stop their shaking, Slocum reportedly said, "No. It is a gift from God," and refused to surrender his religion.[6]

In 1969 Joyce Simmons Cheeka, a granddaughter of Mud Bay Louis, recounted for Werdna Finley the arrest of her grandfather, Joe Riddle, and another man who were confined with "ball-and-chain" as insane in a military fort that had been converted into an insane asylum at Steilacoom. Even though they had been placed in ball and chains, the men managed to shake. When the guards insisted they stop shaking, they said they could not, for it was the Spirit that made them do it. During their incarceration, they were visited by a priest, who arranged a hearing and told the judge that Shaker teachings were comparable to those of the Catholic faith. Thanks to the priest, the three men, who had never been formally charged, were released without penalty.[7]

In July 1885, Shakers at Mud Bay were so angered by the incarceration of their people for shaking and curing that they hired a lawyer (perhaps Judge James Wickersham) to try to have Eells removed as agent. Opposition to Eells also came from non-Indians, such as R. H. Milroy, former agent of the Puyallup, Nisqually, Squaxin, Muckleshoot, Shoalwater Bay, and Chehalis Reservations. He had a political bone to pick with Eells, since Milroy had lost out to Eells as agent when the Puyallup Consolidated Agency was established. Eells had been appointed during Republican president Chester A. Arthur's administration and had managed to survive Grover Cleveland's two Democratic administrations. Unable to get at Eells at the partisan level, Milroy attacked him on constitutional grounds, claiming that Indians under Eells's control were being denied the First Amendment rights that guaranteed Shakers and others that they could worship as they pleased. It is small wonder that Shakers regarded Milroy their friend and protector.[8]

Edwin Eells, Indian
agent and brother of Rev.
Myron Eells. Under U.S.
government mandate to
prevent "Indian doctoring,"
Eells was initially critical
of Shakerism, believing
there was too much of the
native influence in the
religion. (*Northwest and
Whitman College Archives*)

An important opponent of Eells and supporter of the Shakers
and their religion was the crafty, powerful attorney James Wickersham, sometimes called "Nimble Jim." Wickersham had come from
Springfield, Illinois, to the Pacific Northwest, where he became a
probate judge for Pierce County, Washington, in 1884. It is not
known when sparks first began flying between him and Eells, but
they were fanned into flames over ownership of Puyallup Reservation lands. It was Wickersham's contention that by accepting
provision of the Dawes Act, Indians were entitled to U.S. citizenship and federal protection to do as they wished as long as they
did not harm others. His interest—which brought him into opposition to Agent Eells—was obviously facilitating the opening of the
Puyallup Reservation to whites, his primary clients.[9]

In his annual report for 1888, Eells identified a root cause of the
sticky Puyallup land problem: "The great and increasing value
of the land belonging to the Indians of the Puyallup Reservation
makes it an object of desire to the covetous and avaricious, many of

whom are unprincipled and unscrupulous in the means they take to try to get possession of it."[10] Trouble erupted when Wickersham, serving as attorney for two companies whose efforts Edwin Chalcraft called "land grabbing," attempted to "secure valuable Indian lands illegally on the Puyallup Reservation adjoining the townsite of Tacoma."[11]

Wickersham had marshaled an impressive force, including land speculators, railroad officials, the Tacoma City Council, and others of the political establishment to effect the release of Puyallup Reservation lands. In fact, he was the prime mover in this effort, although he apparently worked behind the scenes for the benefit of these groups. On March 11, 1893, Frank C. Ross, a land developer and local railroad builder in Tacoma, suggested to E. E. Ellis of the Union Pacific Railway that Wickersham was so knowledgeable in Indian matters that he could do the railway much good service in its attempts to obtain a right-of-way through Puyallup lands. But Eells, following government policy, strongly opposed the alienation of Puyallup lands and was a significant foe. Although Wickersham mustered a formidable army from the business community in his fight with Eells, the agent twice won skirmishes of sorts by calling out a company of soldiers from the U.S. Army's Vancouver barracks to prevent Wickersham's forces from physically obtaining the lands.[12]

Unable to extract the Eells thorn from his side, Wickersham settled for having "charges filed in Washington [D.C.] against his reappointment." Eells counterattacked by appearing before a congressional committee to win reappointment as agent, which, according to Chalcraft, occasioned a celebration on the Puyallup Reservation. Yet, where Indians may have celebrated the reappointment of a man whom Chalcraft described as a "sincere Christian man in every way" and guided by "Government instructions only," the Shakers were less concerned about struggles over reservation rights-of-way than about their right to exist as a church.[13]

Nowhere did Wickersham's strategy in his contest with Eells appear more evident than in a letter he wrote in response to an inquiry from the Bureau of American Ethnology. In it, he described the Shaker religion for the benefit of the scholarly community, which knew scarcely more about the church than did the public

Attorney James Wick-
ersham, who played a
dual role as advocate of
Indian Shakers and, at
the same time, advocate of
business interests such as
railroad companies seeking
Indian lands. (*Alaska
State Library, Wickersham
Collection, Photo PCA
20–21*)

at large. Wickersham fulfilled a Shaker request that he advise
the bureau that members of the church not be characterized as
"Ghost dancers," assuring readers that Shakers had "no sympathy
with that ceremony or any other founded on the Dreamer religion
[so-named because of trance experiences of its leaders]."[14]

But at the heart of the animosity between Agent Eells and Judge
Wickersham was the land issue, and Wickersham was not beyond
using Shakerism in a manipulative way. Discarding the finesse
with which he had begun his discourse, Wickersham launched a
bare-fisted attack against Eells, using Shakers as "Exhibit A":

> Imprisonment, banishment, threats, chains, and the general ill will
> of the agent and all his employees were visited on these Shakers who
> continued to practice their forms of worship, and yet they did con-
> tinue it. In spite of the fact that they occupied a place only half-way
> between slave and freemen, and were under the orders of the agent
> and subject to be harassed and annoyed all the time by him, yet they
> continued nobly and fearlessly to practice their religion and to wor-
> ship God and Jesus Christ as they saw fit. To do it, however, they

were forced to stay away from the reservations, where the greater
number of employees were located, and their churches were built on
Mud bay and Oyster bay, far away from reservations.[15]

Wickersham may have been using devious means to achieve a
questionable end, and there is ample evidence that such was his
modus operandi. Most Shakers saw him in a positive light. This
should be no surprise, considering the extent of Wickersham's aid
to his Indian clients. His letters and verbal counsel to the Shakers were full of encouragement. In 1892, for instance, he assured
John (Jack) W. Simmons, a new Shaker convert, that his church
had a right to license preachers and that Simmons and other new
landowners (under the Dawes Act) were as much citizens as was
Pres. Benjamin Harrison. Even John Slocum found a receptive
ear when Wickersham wrote Sheriff D.M. Duckworth at Shelton
inquiring why forty acres that belonged to Slocum had been sold.
Apparently, Slocum had failed to pay his taxes, but the judge assured him that, as the Indians' friend, Wickersham could get the
land "fixed up."[16]

Apparently unconcerned with Wickersham's motives, the Shakers believed that it was through his intercession that their religion
received some measure of acceptance. Was there moral dichotomy
in Wickersham's telling Mud Bay Sam that "I am a friend to
the Indians and help them," while in the same breath asking for
Sam's possessions? In helping the Shakers while taking their arti-
facts, photographs, and lore?[17] The same question could be asked
about Wickersham's request that new Indian allottees vote the
Republican ticket. It is surely paradoxical that the xenophobic
Wickersham, who had tried to trace Indian ancestry to the Chi-
nese, was in the forefront of the fight to remove Oriental people
from Tacoma. Was the information he imparted to Shakers in conducting their affairs a means of preventing them from opposing
private interest in appropriating their land base? Were they aware
that Agent Eells, with whom they associated all the restrictive
policies, might have been a better protector than the self-seeking
judge?

On the basis of just one exhibit in the court of social justice, the
judge might well have stood guilty of being self-serving. His March
20, 1890, letter to Charles Francis Adams, president of the Union

Pacific Railway, revealed at least his ambivalence in offering to help the railroad obtain Indian lands on the Puyallup Reservation, which he claimed were worth a thousand dollars an acre. "We are not trying to rob the poor Indians," he wrote. He assured Adams that the Indians had patents to more than seventeen thousand acres of the best land in Washington, with more than two-thirds of it bonded for sale to Tacoma speculators at from two hundred to five hundred dollars per acre. Wickersham concluded that the Puyallups would be the "richest gang of lazy vagabonds in the United States, for there is not more than 400 of them."[18]

In April 1895, Eells resigned as agent, claiming that the Indians on his agency were more civilized than any others in the United States and there was no further need for his services. The management of the agency was turned over to school superintendents on the reservations. Five years later Wickersham left his Tacoma base for Alaska, where he was appointed a U.S. district judge.[19] Agent Eells had sought to carry out a twofold policy: to protect Indian lands from aggressive acquisitors, in line with his governmental mandate, and to prevent Shakers and other Indians from continuing traditional native religious practices. Wickersham also had two objectives: to advance the desires of his land-seeking clients and, at the same time, to help Shakers legitimize their position in the non-Indian community. Eells's efforts had given the Shakers a more secure base from which to operate, while Wickersham enabled the followers of John Slocum's religion to gain acceptance and stature in the outside world.

During the late 1880s and into the 1890s, the Shaker Church underwent a considerable revival. Reverend Myron Eells, Agent Eells's brother, was apparently displeased with the attention being given the church. On July 16, 1888, Eells recorded in his journal that nearly all Indians on the Skokomish Reservation, except schoolchildren, were reported to be shaking. Rather than attributing any blame to his brother for being unsuccessful in stopping the disturbing activity, he blamed the revival on the impossibility of convicting Shakers in court because no one would testify against them. He also attributed the increased incident of shaking to the Indians' awareness that the Dawes Act had granted them citizenship through allotment and, with it, the freedom to practice their religion.[20] Gunther later offered another explanation:

This sketch by J. R. Blackwood was made from an original drawing done over a century ago. It is of the Indian Shakers' first mother church house at Mud Bay on Eld Inlet near Olympia, Washington. (*J. R. Blackwood, Moses Lake, Wash.*)

In the last two decades of the nineteenth century, many Indians had become aware of the disorganization of their own society. The older beliefs lost their prestige and were externally repressed through the ban on Indian activities by the Indian administration. In such a setting, this Christianized version of Indian religion gained a footing because [as Helen Clark had suggested earlier] it escaped the ban. Where the religion was not adopted, the Indians either still clung to their old faith or to those well-developed missions that served their purposes.[21]

The Shakers' new status was evident in the June 1892 gathering of about forty Shaker leaders at Louis Yowaluch's house on Mud Bay. At the gathering, which Judge Wickersham attended, the group formally organized the church, giving it the name Tschaddam, or Chaddon, church. The name is significant. By adopting the native name that means "to shake," the group announced that they had no intention of minimizing shaking in their religion. Both Wickersham and his Shaker clients believed that the way had been cleared for them to receive respectability in both white and Indian communities.[22]

During the meeting, John Slocum and Mud Bay Louis of the Squaxin, Jack Jones and Bill Jones of the Puyallup, and John Smith, Jim Walker, and Charlie Walker of the Chehalis were declared elders "to serve for good behavior and so long as they keep the rules of the Church and of God." Along with James Tobin of Mud Bay, John Bowers of the Puyallup, and Dick Johnson of Oyster Bay, Slocum and Mud Bay Louis were also appointed ministers. In the election of Louis as "head man," Slocum yielded leadership in a formal and apparently friendly manner. It was agreed that the elders would control all properties, regardless of location. This included the church building at Louis's on the hill, the one at Dick Johnson's at Oyster Bay, and all other church properties belonging to the organization from that day forward.[23] On July 20, 1892, Wickersham made a formal declaration that Shakers had "a right under the United States statutes and laws to belong to this Church and to worship God after the forms of that church." Moreover, he announced that "no one has any right to interfere in the matter as long as they do not violate the laws of our country."[24] The Shakers apparently felt safe and protected. But what Wickersham saw as an open road for Shakers did not prove as smooth as he had hoped. Federal employees and clergy continued to see Shakerism as an extension of old-time doctoring.

Wickersham was not oblivious to white critics. "The spectacle of an Indian church with Indian officers, preachers, and members," he concluded, "and of houses built by the Indians for church purposes, was too much for the average citizen of Puget Sound." He hoped to ward off opponents by warning them to desist. As a measure of his success, he claimed that even "evil-disposed" persons were beginning to respect Shakers and their religion, or at least they were beginning to leave them alone. With an optimism typical of that exhibited by frontier entrepreneurs, Wickersham believed that ending Shaker persecution would open the way to "a day of peace."[25]

Moving toward that same goal, Shakers developed a strong sense of community and an independence from the churches with which many of their members had been associated. This renewed spirit was personalized in Mud Bay Louis's break from the Presbyterian Church, in which he had been an elder. Years later, Joe Simons recalled that Louis had been taken to Presbyterian head-

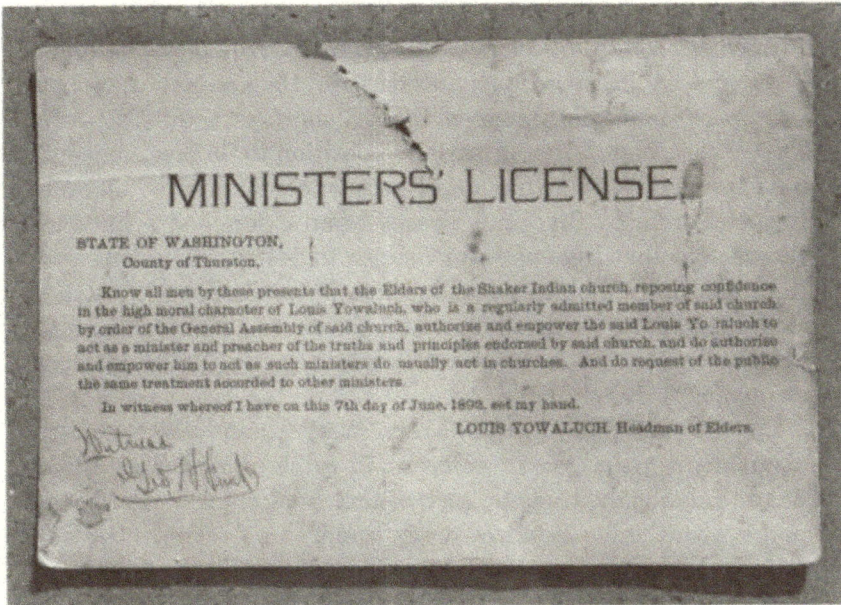

MINISTERS' LICENSE.

STATE OF WASHINGTON,
County of Thurston.

Know all men by these presents that the Elders of the Shaker Indian church, reposing confidence in the high moral character of Louis Yowaluch, who is a regularly admitted member of said church, by order of the General Assembly of said church, authorize and empower the said Louis Yowaluch to act as a minister and preacher of the truths and principles endorsed by said church, and do authorize and empower him to act as such ministers do usually act in churches. And do request of the public the same treatment accorded to other ministers.

In witness whereof I have on this 7th day of June, 1892, set my hand.

LOUIS YOWALUCH, Headman of Elders.

Indian Shaker Church minister's license to preach, issued in 1892, a decade after the founding of the church, by Mud Bay Louis Yowaluch, head state elder. The wording of the license reveals the strong moral cast of Shakerism. This was borne out by the church's indictments against liquor consumption, gambling, profanity, and adultery. (*Robert H. Ruby and John A. Brown*)

quarters at Vancouver, Washington, to see if he had received the "Gift of God." When the Presbyterian officials found his preaching to be such a "Gift," they tempted Louis with a $1,500 annual salary to preach the "Word." The Bible preacher tempted him again, Simons reported, saying, "Your church shall be called the Presbyterian Shaker Church." One of his own people warned Louis that he was refusing too much money, but Louis held fast and refused.[26]

Shakers retained many elements of Presbyterianism, most of which had been brought to them by Louis, since the organizational structure of their church as well as some of its doctrine had much in common with that religion. The most important difference between the two churches was that Shakers did not use the Bible. Shakers believed instead in the "Indian Way," which they claimed to have received from God. Wickersham sought to put to rest criticism of the Shakers' refusal to use the Bible. On June

25, 1893, he explained their position to the Bureau of American Ethnology: "The Bible says there are many roads; the Catholics have one, the Presbyterians another, and the Congregationalists a third but John Slocum gives them a short, straight road—and they choose that."[27] Presbyterian opposition to Shakerism would have been more severe had it not been for a new spirit of tolerance in the church. By this time, Presbyterian elders had abandoned the concept that Indians were doomed to destruction, along with the earth they inhabited as aborigines, in fulfillment of the will of God. Instead, as Wickersham noted, the church occupied "a queer position" among Shakers by exerting "every effort" to claim them as members.[28]

Despite criticism of the Shakers, Wickersham was optimistic about their prospects as members of a viable church. Most Puget Sound Indians, he thought, were either Shakers or were in sympathy with the five hundred or six hundred members of the new religion who lived on the Skokomish, Squaxin, Chehalis, and Nisqually Reservations and on the Cowlitz and Columbia Rivers. In 1893, he also proudly reported a dozen licensed ministers in church houses built at Mud and Oyster Bays, on the Cowlitz River, and on the Chehalis and Puyallup Reservations.[29]

Cooperation among Shaker congregations was an important part of their development. Jack Simmons and Mud Bay Louis sent a written report on June 26, 1893, to the *Mason County Journal* that Chehalis and Oyster Bay Shakers met after mid June to press for the building of a church house for the twenty-six Shakers on the Skokomish Reservation. The meeting on the issue—perhaps the first reported to the press by church leaders—was attended by John Slocum, Louis, Mud Bay Sam, Simmons, John Bowers, John Smith, and George Leshmet, all of whom expressed a willingness to help build a twenty-by forty-foot church house. Everyone at the meeting—including the Skokomish leadership, that stormy petrel Billy Clams, Chehalis Jack, Billy Waterman, and Government Dick [Lewis ?]—swore off drinking, smoking, and chewing, aware that temperance was a strong force in the recognition and continuance of Shakerism.[30] With the Skokomish meeting, Shakerism came home, for it was on that reservation that John Slocum had begun the church.

Not only had Shakers established communication with the lo-

cal newspaper, they also changed their attitudes in their dialogue
with Reverend Eells. On October 20, 1895, Eells recorded in his
journal that a remarkable change for the better had occurred in
Shakerism: Billy Williams had asked him to talk with Skokomish
Shakers in their own church house. Eells obliged by offering a
prayer and pronouncing a benediction. On November 28, Thanksgiving Day, he wrote about his gratitude for what he considered a
changing Shaker attitude. But it was Eells's own attitude that had
made the greater change. He visited the sick with Shakers to hold
services and attended Shaker funerals. In the spring of 1898, he
arranged for the purchase of a stove for the Shakers' new church
house.[31] Other government employees appear to have changed
their views as well. R. E. Newberne, superintendent and acting
agent of the Puyallup Consolidated Agency, reported in 1896 that,
of all church bodies in his agency, Shakerism was the principal
and most helpful religion among the Indians—at least as far as
the drinking problem was concerned. Thanks to the Shakers' influence, Newberne predicted that among Indians of his agency
chances were "16 to 1 that each succeeding generation will be
healthier, happier, wiser, and better."[32]

One Shaker who did not become healthier was its founder, John
Slocum. Although temperate since his second illness, he died in
late November or early December 1897 at his home on Oyster Bay.
As might be expected, a large number attended his funeral. His
body was laid to rest on Johns Prairie outside the Shelton cemetery. Slocum had suffered his share of hardships, not only from the
rigors of logging, but also the deaths of eleven of his reported thirteen children (two daughters survived) and the severe illness of his
wife after a miscarriage in late winter 1887. Adding to his woes
was the 1893 incarceration of his son in McNeil Island Federal
Penitentiary in upper Puget Sound.[33]

As the twentieth century opened, several other actors in the
Shaker story also left the stage. Slocum's antagonist, Agent Edwin Eells, had left the Pacific Northwest in 1895, and Judge
Wickersham left in 1900 for Alaska. From June until December
1901, there is little information available about Shaker activities.
There is some evidence that, during that time, the government
lessened its hostility toward the church. The Skokomish Shaker
church house even served as a temporary schoolhouse until a new

Original grave site of John Slocum. He was laid to rest there in his fifty-ninth year (1897) on Johns Prairie near present-day Shelton, Washington. (*Indian Shaker Church Archives*)

government school was built.[34]

Reverend Eells remained on the Skokomish Reservation, and although he continued to soften his position toward Shakers, he still suspected them of threatening his own efforts. He simply could not erase the thought that the Shaker church was non-Christian. Not only was he anxious about the progress of his own mission on the Skokomish, he was also concerned about its outstation at Jamestown, where the Shaker presence posed a continuing threat. The church might have posed an even greater threat had the Shakers not been experiencing their own troubles with liquor at Jamestown. The nearest thing to an Eells-Shaker rapprochement may have occurred in early 1905 when Dick Lewis invited Eells to the Skokomish Shaker church, telling him that at the close of the service he should not wait to be asked to speak.[35]

Reverend Eells died on January 4, 1907, apparently with a measure of peace after his long struggle with the Shaker Church and resigned to the fact that it had survived and expanded despite his and his brother's efforts to stop it. Eells's successor was Andrew Patterson, an Indian licensed as a missionary of the Congregational Church and assigned to the Skokomish. After white agency employees refused to assist him, Patterson began associating with a group of literate Shakers who read the Bible. He induced them to read the Bible in church services, which prompted some Shakers in the area to discuss whether or not to allow Patterson to join their church. As a result, the Bible-reading Shakers organized a "new denomination" on the Skokomish Reservation and invited Patterson to join and work with them. This began a nidus of literate, sophisticated persons who were less interested in traditional practices than in moving the church in new directions. Among this group were those who would eventually break from the church in the controversy over the use of the Bible.[36]

On March 11, 1914, Agent Eells dictated a report of a return trip with his wife to the Skokomish Reservation. He said "a few years ago" I visited the Shaker church. No longer obliged to execute bans against it, he may have felt more charitable toward the church. At any rate, he believed that by reading the Bible, Shakerism had made a transition to Christianity and assured its adherents that their church had a right to exist.[37] Shakerism had survived, primarily because its members, as Marian Smith, wrote, "meant to grasp the present, not the past."

"In assessing the early development of the Shaker Church," Smith continued,

> it should be remembered that in Indian eyes the Whites were constantly demonstrating power by superior performance. The record shows valiant attempts on the part of the Indians to accept this power and make it their own. The attempts were certainly built upon a whole substratum of native belief but, far from wishing consciously to revive or perpetuate native practices, the explicit aims were in quite the opposite direction.[38]

Notwithstanding Shakerism's zeal in a traditional spiritual direction, the church continued to make the transition in a new one. The next step would be to make its peace with the secular power of the state when its articles of faith were enunciated within another set of articles—that of incorporation.

CHAPTER NINE

A New Era

The Shaker Church entered a new era when it was incorporated as the Indian Shaker Church in 1910. John M. Wilson notarized the incorporation in December, and the church membership elected Mud Bay Sam to a four-year term as bishop. With their church formally recognized by the government, members no longer felt restrictions that accompanied non-Indian skepticism and criticism. During the ten to twenty years after incorporation, Shakers felt free to test the waters, seeking out what they could or could not do in functioning within the corporate structure. Their meetings were no longer held spontaneously but were regularly scheduled. The church also began meeting once a year at annual conventions held to satisfy state-mandated incorporation regulations. These annual meetings and other business meetings were used to solve problems and to conduct the business of the church. Members began keeping minutes and following *Robert's Rules of Order*, their bylaws forming the framework for their operations. Despite this progress, and despite having survived three decades of troubles from outside the church, new troubles loomed as rival Shaker groups began forming the nuclei of doctrinally different churches.

The Indian Shaker Church of Washington state was not the first Shaker congregation to incorporate. Shakers on the Warm

Springs Reservation in north-central Oregon had incorporated in 1907 after their agent had forbidden meetings on the reservation and denied an extension in their shaking time. A lawyer had told them that their incorporation had to be based on grounds other than their belief in John Slocum. There is some evidence that the Oregon Shakers finally incorporated on the basis of their belief in the Bible. The Oregon incorporation paper, issued on February 21, 1907, defined the pursuit of the corporation as promoting and spreading the religious teachings of the Indian Shaker Church of Oregon, especially the doctrine of temperance and the virtues of the Golden Rule.[1]

When Washington Shakers incorporated in 1910, they did so primarily to overcome the criticism and complaints of whites. By using white society's tool, incorporation, they sought to legitimize the church's existence, to define its purpose, and to give it an identity and status. With its new nonprofit status, there were tax advantages to incorporation as well. At the time, the Shakers owned buildings and other properties, although the donations they received did not amount to much. As the church expanded outside the state, Shakers in those areas had to incorporate and register as a foreign body—an out-of-state corporation doing business in Oregon, for instance. The Shakers were helped in their efforts by secretary-organizer Milton Giles, a white man, formerly a "plain everyday butcher," later Olympia justice of the peace, representative for the Mercantile Fire and Marine Underwriters Agency, and fluent speaker of Chinook jargon. It was Mud Bay Sam who brought Giles in to manage the church.[2]

The articles of the incorporation in Washington were couched in noble terms, stating that the Indian Shaker Church would elevate "the Indian race of this state and the North West" and work toward "the encouragement and enforcement of temperance." Especially interesting was the provision for "the elevation of the female Indian," making her "equal in government and of the church." Perhaps coincidentally the document was written in the year that women gained the suffrage in Washington state, a decade earlier than in the nation at large. Wade Le Roy, however, believed that the "elevation" of women was more formality than fact. In 1903 someone told Reverend Eells that Shakers practiced their religion in order to keep their wives in subjection; Eells himself observed

Milton Giles, a white man,
secretary-organizer of the
Indian Shaker Church.
His selection for that office
indicates Shaker dependence
on the counsel of whites. Giles
had to deal with legalities
relating to incorporation of the
Shaker Church under state
law. (*Indian Shaker Church
Archives*)

that women on the Skokomish Reservation had traditionally been treated with considerable propriety. Male dominance, however, did not preclude some women from assuming leadership roles, nor did it preclude their participation in church rituals and ceremonies. Even so, the position of bishop, became the province of males, and to date no woman has held that position.[3]

Incorporation gave Shakers recognition in the white community. The June 22, 1910, *Seattle Post-Intelligencer* reported that the incorporation was "drawn up this morning by Justice of the Peace Milton Giles" and that several of the church's directorship of "Twelve full-blooded Indian apostles" were crossing the state seeking converts.[4] But few other developments put more distance between Shakers and their traditional past than did incorporation. The Shaker document enabled its people to proclaim the right to "the worship of God in our own way" and asserted the church's ownership of its properties. Other provisions involved the non-assessment of dues for church maintenance and ministers' salaries and the acceptance of donations for charitable purposes.

There was no mention of the church's keystone, shaking, although the word "Shaker" appears several times in the document.[5] None of this is to say that the transition was instantaneous, for it was too much to expect Shakers to suddenly grasp the meaning of their newly acquired constitutional rights. Even a most progressive Shaker, Webster H. Hudson, sought help "to secure our liberty to worship God" and not be "ashamed to express ourselves."[6]

At the time of incorporation, Mary Thompson, John Slocum's widow, opposed such church leaders as Mud Bay Sam who had incorporated her husband's church and strongly expressed her opinion that such legalisms destroyed the revelatory, spontaneous, and inspirational aspects of her husband's experience. To her, spiritual matters were to be lived and experienced by each person, not recorded on pieces of paper. Her differences with Mud Bay Sam also involved the correct procedures in ceremonial maneuvers in Shaker services. Where she advocated clockwise movements, Sam, claiming to have had a revelation, maintained that a clockwise movement was worldly and that in heaven everything went the other way. Thompson was also wary of designating certain persons as ministers. For her, the licensing of ministers retarded spontaneity in worship, since she believed such unilateral leadership hampered the free expression of the spirit for one seeking power.[7] Ironically, by the last decade of the twentieth century, many young people, conditioned by organizational structures in both white and Indian society, have dropped out of the Shaker church because of its lack of organization.

The efforts of secretary-organizer Milton Giles were vital to Shakerism, even though he was not a Shaker himself. He kept church records, sent out communications, and often kept peace among the Shakers' sometimes wrangling members. He also served as a watchdog to see that Indian agents did not overstep their authority. In all things, Giles kept a positive image of the church before the public. He was aware of the importance of good relations with political figures. On April 26, 1912, Giles asked Bishop Heck to use his influence with his voting friends to tell them that Washington governor Marion Hay, who was seeking reelection, was a good man and a friend of the Indians and that he thought well of the Shaker Church. But he was aware that as a white person he did not understand the Shaker mentality, and

License to preach of Dick Case of the Chelalis Indian Shaker Church, bearing the date August 20, 1910. Following a schism in the mid-1940s, one branch of Shakerism carried the name "1910 Church" to distinguish it from the Bible-reading Shakers. (*Robert H. Ruby and John A. Brown*)

he made it clear that he wished to serve as secretary-organizer for only six months. He remained much longer, however, to help Shakers achieve incorporation and to guide their officials in administering the church. His picture appeared on the Shaker Church letterhead along with photographs of Bishop Mud Bay Sam and First Elder Alex Teio.[8]

Not everyone appreciated Giles's efforts. Long after Giles had died, one delegate to the 1939 convention said that the "first secretary and organizer of the work" of the church had not been "qualified" because he had lacked membership. Another delegate commented, "White man was always after . . . [the Indians] with the law," adding, "Giles was a white man who straightened out the Indian, then when he finished the members put a qualified man in his place."[9]

Because they thought Bishop Heck, who succeeded Mud Bay Sam, had not been very attentive to their church, Canadian Shakers sought their own incorporation. On November 30, 1917, Peter

Joe of the Koksilah, British Columbia, church on the Cowichan Indian Reserve, wrote Heck asking for the six rules of the church to show Canadian officials: "We find that we have no standing on this side [of the border] because we are not counted as a church at all according to law."[10] Two years later, Heck received a letter from Peter Joe, Samuel Sampson, and Willie Louie enclosing correspondence from their barristers, Moresby O'Reilly & Lowe: "We beg to formally notify you of the obtaining of the Certificate of Incorporation of the Indian Shaker Church of the Province of British Columbia under the 'Benevolent Societies Act' of this Province, the formal Certificate we have obtained in your behalf the official number of same being 590 and dated the 28th day of October, 1919."[11] The branch of the Shaker church in British Columbia was subsequently incorporated as the "Indian Shaker Church of Washington, Inc., 1910."[12]

In Oregon, a group on the Klamath Reservation filed as the "Indian Shaker Church of Washington" in April 1919 after the Bible readers in the congregation split from them. Three months earlier, Warm Springs Shakers had reinstated their lapsed corporate status as the "Warm Springs Branch of the Indian Shaker Church" in order to save their church from threatened closure. A group of Bible-reading Klamaths had filed for incorporation in 1917 as the "Indian Shaker Church of Oregon." Much later, in July 1922, Klamath traditionalist non-Bible readers operated as a Washington state corporation with a new set of bylaws, which stated, "Only an Indian shall be elected to serve during the unexpired term [of bishop]," and included a rule requiring each member to have a prayer table in his or her home. Joiners were given latitude in that they were to continue seeking the "power" if they did not obtain it in one night. John Slocum was mentioned by name in the bylaws only in the Oregon constitution, along with "Christ heals." According to the document, Slocum foretold of a special power of healing that came "when fingers tremble and the body quivers." The words "shake" and "shaking" do not appear in any other Shaker Church constitution or bylaws.[13]

The first articles of incorporation of California Shakers were filed in Sacramento March 18, 1932 by Washington state head elders on behalf of the Smith River group under the name "Indian Shaker Church of Washington." On March 9, 1940, another group

from the Hoopa Reservation filed as the "Indian Shaker Church of
the State of California." Tom Lang, a Klamath Indian, was instrumental in getting the Smith River and other churches established
in northern California.[14]

In many ways, incorporation and its effect on church operations
shocked Shakers into recognizing that they had to conduct affairs
in a new milieu. The secular state, which mandated their incorporation, helped force them into fending for themselves. One result
was a flurry of correspondence to church officials from parishioners asking about procedural matters, such as how to obtain
licenses for elders, as well as congregational matters, such as how
to handle rebellious members who violate Shaker rules. Numerous
queries about bylaws and their enforcement reveal the distance
between the incorporation itself and its implementation.

But the Shakers were not deterred. Reverend Enoch Abraham
of the Yakama Reservation best explained Shakers' confidence in
their ability to rise above dependence on others. Shakers, he said,
did not "have to wait or look at the Government or white people
missionaries to show us how to carry our religion. . . . We can carry
our religion same as whites because we have white's education in
us. We must do all we can in building our church houses all over
the country."[15]

Incorporation gave Shakerism a legal footing, but it would not
have been enough to advance the church had its adherents allowed non-Shakers to further regulate the church. Shakers were
beset with an organization foreign to native traditionalism. Yet
solidification of the offices of bishop and elders under corporate requirements gave the church new status, very unlike that held by
leaders with tribal authority. The new positions of Shaker leadership, according to Marilyn Claire Richen, were by-products of the
incorporation process and not of the need of authority.[16]

It was faith, funds, and feasting at Shaker conventions that
bonded church members and helped the church survive and ex-
pand. Shaker conventions have been likened to traditional Indian
feast gatherings and potlatches, but there are fundamental differences between Shaker and non-Shaker gatherings. Among
Central and Southern Salish speakers, potlatches were a prod-
uct of a structured class society in which the wealthy, served by
persons of lesser status, carried invitations to guests to attend a

Delegates at dinner in a building adjacent to the Shaker church house at the 1953 annual convention on the Skokomish Indian Reservation. Conventions move to various churches from year to year. (*Indian Shaker Church Archives*)

ceremony that centered on one person, the host. Shaker meetings, on the other hand, are the products of an unstructured society of democratic and cooperative groups.

Shaker conventions and native potlatches, however, are alike in that they were both influenced by an imposed Euro-American cultural system. But Shakers adapted more readily to the infusion of an alien culture than did potlatch societies, and Shaker gatherings were attended by people who had acquired a good measure of identification with the dominant white society. The socioeconomic system of that society tended to lessen the rigidity of native societal protocol that found its expression in potlatches.

Annual Shaker conventions have been held in various locations. At the close of each convention, delegates choose sites for the following year. Before modern forms of transportation were introduced in the Pacific Northwest, an important consideration was how participants could reach the next convention site. The locations were usually chosen, then, for their accessibility in addition

Delegates to the October 13, 1953, annual Shaker convention, in front of the old Skokomish church house on the Skokomish Indian Reservation. Delegates attended such conventions from all over Shakerdom, which extended from southern British Columbia to northern California. The logistics of feeding and housing such large numbers of conventioners was a constant concern for Shaker leadership. (*Indian Shaker Church Archives*)

to their importance as Shaker centers.[17] In the early years of the church, delegates reached Mud Bay by canoe and, later, by steam-powered boat. When delegates were able to take the train to meetings, they stopped off near Olympia, less than twenty miles from Mud Bay. By the 1920s, several Shakers owned automobiles, or "engines," but they often broke down and roads were poor. When the Shaker church expanded north to British Columbia, delegates reached convention sites there by boat across the sound and the Strait of Juan de Fuca. Shakers chose October for their annual conventions because the September hop picking was winding down for them and other Indians in the Puyallup and Yakima valleys.[18]

The housing and feeding of delegates and their families, sometimes as many as several hundred persons, posed a logistical problem for planners and delegates. Visitors usually stayed in homes of relatives and friends or in large community houses and slept on church house floors. Convention hosts usually provided food for everyone, but with contributions from their visitors. For years, conventioneers consumed traditional foods such as salmon when meetings were held on the coast. At more recent meetings, food has been largely donated and collections taken to pay for it. Still, the role of host is taken seriously. At the 1930 convention in Koksilah, Vancouver Island, British Columbia, two men offered a canoeload of freshly caught salmon to British Columbia Bishop Peter Joe. He refused to accept it, stating, "I want to give this potlatch for God all by myself." Food was in such short supply at a White Swan meeting one year that Wade Le Roy went with Michael ("Mike") George to kill a deer. When that was gone, George butchered one of his own steers.[19]

Logistics were important not only at annual conventions, but also at interim, or "special," meetings held to discuss matters that surfaced between conventions. Although much discussion at these gatherings concerned mundane church matters, items of a spiritual nature were also considered. Of course, there were also gatherings devoted primarily to shaking and curing. In 1915, for example, U.S. assistant Commissioner of Indian Affairs E. B. Meritt reported a gathering on the Klamath when "numbers" of Indians were "camping" at a house where they treated the sick for several days at considerable expense to its residents.[20]

Agents on the scene at Shaker gatherings were troubled by long meetings, which they described as keeping Shakers from tilling the soil, harvesting crops, and tending livestock. They claimed that the meetings left a legacy of lethargy from shaking, rendering participants unable to perform their chores. The Skokomish Agency farmer reported that about five hundred people attended the annual October 1916 convention on the Skokomish Reservation. They were, he wrote, "about as destitute a bunch as I have ever seen," even after consuming five sacks of sugar, three beeves, two hundred loaves of bread, and a large supply of other foods. Because of the short salmon run that year and the Shakers' inability to secure clams to buttress their larder, conventioneers were forced to adjourn, having not only stretched their food supply but also their credit at nearby stores.[21]

Inspirational words spoken at the annual conventions were calculated not only to secure harmony but also to strengthen members in the fellowship of the Shaker faith. Frank Bennett (who later became a bishop), for example, in his address to the 1930 Koksilah convention, exhorted delegates to

> make use of the power God gives you. Do not look at your brothers and sisters; do what God tells you to. To those who would join, come on the floor and confess your sins and you are done with the past. God will look on you when you confess your sins and you will get the power. Don't come without faith. Don't say you will try the Shaker religion and if they heal you, you will join. Do not try God. Come with your full mind, confess your wrong and you will be healed. You cannot shake without God.[22]

Convention agendas ranged from elections and the licensing of officials to strengthening and extending the Shaker faith. Delegates were aware that such goals could not be reached by faith and revelation alone, for funds were sorely needed to buy the accoutrements of Shakerism, such as candles, and to finance church operations and buy lumber for building and repairing church houses. One source of income came from donations, usually taken after meals and occasionally during services.

On November 17, 1911, soon after the first convention was held on the Chehalis Reservation, the first minister's license was issued to a Chehalis Shaker, John Smith. (The first ministerial license in the church had been issued on June 7, 1892, to Mud Bay Louis Yowaluch.) Cap Carson of the Chehalis church received an elders' license, along with John Cliff of the Humptulips west of the Chehalis and Bob James of the Muckleshoot church just east of Auburn, Washington.

The October 1912 convention was held on the Yakama Reservation in the home of State Head Elder Alex Teio. About a dozen Shakers attended, as did Methodist George Waters from the reservation. Delegates were divided roughly between those who came from both east and west of the Cascade Mountains, with one delegate from Cowichan, British Columbia. The qualification and disqualification and licensing of elders and other officials were discussed. Peter John, elder of the Mud Bay church, was asked to resign because of his gambling, and the group voted to cancel his license. The men agreed that Muckleshoot Bob James, who was both an elder and a tribal judge, had no conflict of interest in holding the two positions. There was also the ever-present mundane matter of money. Although expenditures were perhaps less than those of other churches, the matter of money owed Milton Giles, presumably for some aspect of his organizational work, was discussed. Some trouble surfaced when a delegate from the Warm Springs Reservation reported that someone had sent false reports about Shakers to Washington, D.C.[23]

The records at the Yakama convention were handwritten in English, but statements made in such meetings were also made in Indian dialects and Chinook jargon. In time, annual convention reports would be typewritten to better fulfill the requirement under incorporation that records of Shaker proceedings be well kept and in order. Moreover, Shaker advocates maintained that using typewriters to record their proceedings showed that Shakers were adapting to white ways.[24]

The ability to speak and write English came to be considered an important qualification for holding leadership positions in the church. For instance, at the November 1913 convention at Warm Springs, Oregon, the delegates, standing with right hand uplifted in a vote, elected Harry Miller as head elder. In the words of one who put Miller's name in nomination, "he can talk English language and he can talk good." Replacing Miller as minister, the Rev. Warren McCorkle asked that Tommy Miller be his assistant, since he "can read and write so he can explain and interpret for us."[25]

The June 1914 meeting was back on the Chehalis Reservation, whose Shakers were observing the fourth anniversary of their incorporation. The length of Bishop Peter Heck's tenure came up, a thorny problem that would be discussed in many meetings to come. The disagreement centered on whether Heck had been appointed to fill Mud Bay Sam's term or to a new four-year term beginning at the time of his appointment in 1911. Reverend Peter Kalama chaired the discussion at a July 3, 1915, meeting, and it was decided that Heck should serve a full four-year term from October 18, 1912, the date he took charge of conducting the annual convention. Yet, at the 1911 convention, held in Heck's own Chehalis homeland, the record reflects that he had already been "elected"

(appointed) to succeed Mud Bay Sam "for the term of 3 or 4 yrs."
Further complicating the picture was the fact that minutes of the
1912 convention contain no discussion of Heck's term of office.[26]

Bob James sought to settle the problem by recommending that
Heck remain bishop as long as he was able to "carry all the tools."
The only objections came from Mabel Teo, who wanted the unwilling Heck to wear a gown or robe, and White Salmon, who declared
that he be compelled to wear one. In the midst of the building
pressure over the bishopric at the 1915 annual convention, Heck
tested the waters for his continued tenure: "My dear brothers and
sisters," the bishop said, "as my term is ended, I have served my
4 years now. You must not be afraid to appoint any one that you
choose. I dont know my faults. Maybe you know my mistakes.
Some say I am too slow to answer, because I know I got to consider
what to answer. So it will be right."[27]

With Heck's words, the delegates stood to express satisfaction
with his leadership. The record, however, makes no mention of a
specific vote, only that the speakers expressed confidence in his
ability to strengthen the church. Their words of support would
later be used as evidence of a consensus to have him remain as
bishop. Heck's aim appears to have been to run the church as
harmoniously as possible. But his goal was frustrated by the Bible-
use question. The first documented evidence of this controversy
appears in Heck's October 1915 address at the annual convention:

> I am going to tell you about Tacumseah [Yakatowit]. Yes he was
> appointed as minister [on the Yakama] and the Workers has been
> reporting to me about him. And the reason the people dont like . .
> . [Tacumseah is] because he has a little book, the new Testament
> [which] he said that is his help, because . . . [he] dont receive no help
> [revelation] from God. That is the fault to some of his people.[28]

Those few Shakers who read the Bible were an affront to the majority of traditional Shakers who followed Slocum's precept that
they should live and worship by revelation. The October 27, 1893,
Mason County Journal reported that revelation—not a book of
teachings—played the key role in Shaker belief. Shakers asked,
according to the *Journal*, "What do we need with that [the Bible]?
Our John Slocum was in heaven just twelve years ago, and he can
tell us all about it." At the same time, Shakers made it clear that

their position in no way minimized their belief in God and Christ as savior of the world. The Indians' poor understanding of English and inability to read would have further discouraged them from using the Bible.[29]

This internal argument over whether or not Shakers should use the Bible would eventually escalate into an all-out schism in the church. In the coming years, problems having to do with the requirements of incorporation would be much more easily solved than were those dealing with Bible reading.

CHAPTER TEN

Extending
the Boundaries

Most of the growth of the Shaker church occurred during its first forty years. Like waves spreading from its Squaxin-Skokomish nidus, the church reached from northwestern California north to the midpoint of the east coast of Vancouver Island and the British Columbia mainland. Congregations were also established across the Cascade Mountains to the east, especially on the Yakama Reservation. Despite its success, there were factors that limited the church's acceptance, perhaps most significantly the reluctance of tribes beyond the Pacific Northwest to relate to the shamanic religious elements that had carried over into Shakerism.[1]

It is not too much to say that the spread of Shakerism was both cause and effect of the church's primary activities—shaking and curing. The greatest success for the extension of Shakerism was found in its reputation for healing, and those who converted through healing became ardent extenders of their newly found faith. Some individuals may be credited with helping to extend Shaker influence, but no record could possibly exist of the countless word-of-mouth and face-to-face contacts that testified to the healings that had been effected through the church. Few motivations are more powerful than those pertaining to physical well-being, and therein lay the power of the Shaker Church and the primary explanation for its diffusion.

The Shaker Church also relied on bonds of friendship, blood, and marriage, ties the Euro-American cultural system had sought to disrupt. Shakers depended as well on a new type of relationship to attract new members—that based on fellowship. An early encounter at Mud Bay is instructive. Among those seeking out the religion at Mud Bay was Billy Williams, a Skokomish and a Roman Catholic. When he arrived at the bay, local Shakers, with a zeal bordering on fanaticism, rushed out to meet him, tore the ribbons from his hat and coat, and threw them into the bay. They would not let him enter their church until he prayed. Apparently satisfied that he had met their requirement, they shook over him. Williams hurried back to the Skokomish Reservation to tell his people of the experience. Over the next several days, some Skokomish went to Mud Bay, where two of them were converted to Shakerism. By 1905, most Skokomish Indians, some of them Spirit Dancers, had become Shakers.[2]

Besides the informal personal contacts that helped spread the faith, ardent Shaker leaders put in place a calculated proselytizing effort. First among the missionaries was Mud Bay Louis Yowaluch, who was instrumental in carrying Shakerism to many parts of the Pacific Northwest. In time, Shakers prepared specific persons for missionary work, calling them "traveling missionaries." These traveling missionaries, who are licensed, seek converts, establish churches, and serve as ministers until licensed ones can assume that position. The missionary who most emulated Saint Paul, the early extender of Christianity, was First State Elder Alex Teio. He believed that credentials given him under revelatory light qualified him to extend the faith. After the 1910 incorporation of the church, Teio helped organize congregations from the Klamath Reservation in southern Oregon to other locations in that state, in Washington, and in British Columbia.[3]

In the egalitarian Shaker spirit, not only do appointed missionaries extend the faith, so do various members. One of these was David Hudson, who introduced Shakerism to the Quileute Reservation on the Pacific Coast.[4] For about five years, Hudson was reportedly the only Shaker at La Push. There is some evidence that the wife of Jack Hudson was responsible for spreading

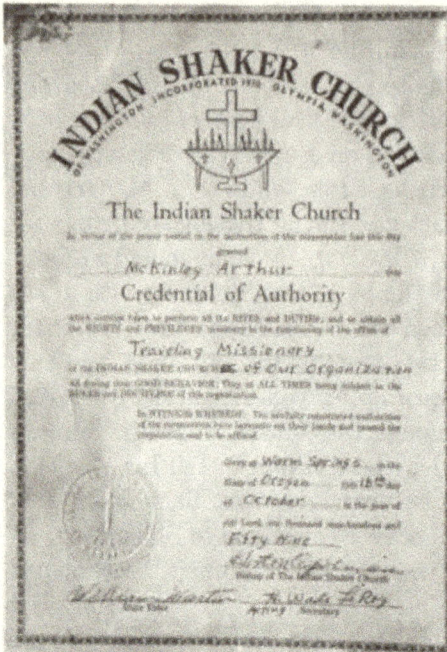

A license issued to a traveling missionary of the Indian Shaker Church. The missionary role was similar to that of a missionary in Christian churches. Whether or not Shakerism should be classified as Christian has been a matter of disagreement among those studying it as an institution. (*Robert H. Ruby and John A. Brown*)

Shakerism from La Push. She was converted in 1906 while she was picking hops at Puyallup, her ill baby "passed away" for an hour. Receiving the "power" she came under the spirit's injunction, and reportedly shook for ten days. The child fully recovered. After that Mrs. Hudson prayed for good weather, and workers returned from the hop fields under rainless skies. These demonstrations of power compelled her to speak to others, and the religion spread.[5] The Quileute church, which had received official recognition in 1904 from the Mud Bay mother church when Rev. Robert E. Lee was licensed as its first minister, experienced a period of growth; the April 6, 1909, *Seattle Post-Intelligencer* reported that a church house had been built by Tommy Brown for the benefit of Shakers and for his sister, Mrs. Jack Hudson. [6]

Tracing the initial appearance of Shakerism on the Quileute Reservation or elsewhere is a tenuous process. For example, Reverend Eells reported that a youth who had been converted on the Chehalis Reservation returned to the Quinault exuberantly claiming that he could "pray like thunder and lightening." But we do not know the date of the young man's return or whether it was before or after Billy Mason and Johnson Wakinas—who were said to have introduced Shakerism on the Quinault Reservation after their conversions—visited Puget Sound around 1885.[7]

The Shaker Church continued to reach out. South of the Quinault, Indians on the Humptulip and lower Chehalis Rivers accepted the new religion. South of Grays Harbor, Shakerism extended to Bay Center on Shoalwater (Willapa) Bay, although it is unclear to what extent its northward spread to the Quinault and the Queets came from the Grays Harbor area. To the north, the church spread to the Makah Indians of Neah Bay, who, like other native groups, had been damaged by disease and drink. In 1902, Makah agent Samuel G. Morse reported that he had been trying to induce some Jamestown Shakers to come among the Makahs to organize a Shaker church there, believing their coming would do the Makahs "a world of good."[8]

A group of nonreservation Clallam Indians lived at the Jamestown settlement near present-day Port Angeles, Washington. Tension developed in the village because whites in the area openly considered the Clallams to be inferior. When Reverend Eells established a mission outpost in their community and built a Congregational church house there in 1878, the Clallams were troubled with the guilt of sin that had much to do with the introduction of Shakerism there by the Skokomish in 1885, the same year Shakerism had spread to another Clallam village at Port Gamble. The Skokomish Shakers had been invited to Jamestown to cure a woman who suffered from some affliction. A Shaker church house was built, and Clallams were converted to Shakerism despite Eells's attempt to combat the new religion. For a short time, the use of alcohol declined, the settlement flourished, and some shamans were converted to the church. Nevertheless, Shakers continued to be threatened by white inroads and the use of liquor. Tribal leadership became weak, and the death of Shaker elders augured trouble for the fledgling Jamestown church. One writer assessing Jamestown Shakerism stated that the Indian settlement was "a conscious, rational attempt on the part of this group of Indians to alleviate tensions and dissatisfactions stemming from the condition into which they had fallen."[9]

Noting Shaker successes at Jamestown, Agent Morse believed

Early twentieth-century Jamestown Clallams in front of their church house. Note the nearly complete conformity to the dress of whites. The suitcase held by the man in the top row was quite unlike bags of native origin. (*Indian Shaker Church Archives*)

its emissaries could lead the way to a healthful environment for the people of the Makah Reservation. His enthusiasm for Shakerism was not shared by Helen Clark, however, whose Presbyterian Church had established a mission among the Makahs in 1904. Where the elderly could withstand Shaker ceremonies, she noted that the young people were withdrawing from Shakerism, thus dimming its prospects on the Makah Reservation. Yet, when traditional medicine men were banned on the reservation and their drums silenced, the Makahs preferred the sound of bell-ringing Shakers to the solemnity of Presbyterian worship. Clark also noted that the government ban on the Tamahnous caused a rise in Makah Shakerism.[10]

At the Makah Neah Bay center, Agent C. L. Woods, exhibiting a common ambivalent view, was quoted as saying, "The Shakers, a peculiar religious sect, are seemingly doing good, as there has been little or no law breaking by their numbers, and no drunk-

House of the 1910 Shaker Church on the Tulalip Indian Reservation, May 2, 1991. This church house is unusual in that, unlike those in traditional Shakerdom, both the belfry and the front door are at the same end of the building. A gambling casino on the reservation, which borders Marysville, Washington, threatens the spirituality of church members. (*Robert H. Ruby and John A. Brown*)

enness whatever." Their professed creed, he added, "is a model of orthodoxy . . . [and] it would be bigotry to oppose their outlandish and queer manner of worship." In 1919, Makah Shakers believed their position tenuous after the new agent wanted them to stop shaking. Woods's replacement may have been influenced by his wife, who said that Shakers did not look good when they shook.[11]

In the general Puget Sound area, Shakerism reached out to the Muckleshoot Reservation, where Shakers had started to build a church house in 1913. It is not surprising that the Shaker faith spread the short distance northeast of Mud Bay to the Puyallup Reservation. At the 1892 organization meeting, John Simmons and Bill James were among those elected church elders on the Puyallup, and Simmons gave a half acre of ground for the church on the confine.[12] To the south, Shakerism was no stranger to Cowlitz peoples. There was a church at Silver Creek, between Mossyrock and Salkum in Washington state, and another east of

Early-day Shakers at Port Gamble at the northern end
of the Kitsap Peninsula in upper western Washington
state. Port Gamble was an important lumber milling
center. Many Shaker males were employed in various
tasks of the logging-milling industry. (*Indian Shaker
Church Archives*)

the Puyallup Valley at Eatonville, in the western shadow of Mount
Rainier.

Inland from Puget Sound, the Snoqualmies, having no reservation, drew Indians from throughout the Snoqualmie Valley to
services in the town of Tolt (later called Carnation). A church house
was also built among Snoqualmies at Falls City. Ed Davis became
minister in 1912 and continued in that capacity for three-quarters
of a century. A church was also established among Stillaguamish
Indians at Darrington, where Johnny Prize was minister. Closely
related to the Stillaguamishes were the Skagits, to whom Shakerism came around 1910. Fourteen years later, the Upper Skagits
to the north built a Shaker church house near Concrete in the
Skagit Valley. A church was also established at Van Horn a few

Shaker church house near Concrete, Washington. Its bell tower, unlike that of many Shaker church houses, is positioned on the west instead of the east. (*Indian Shaker Church Archives*)

miles east of Concrete. The Nooksacks to the North were less affected by Shakerism, although Shaker precepts spread among them.[13]

Because of its schools, gatherings, and celebrations, the Tulalip Reservation near Marysville, Washington, had close ties with Upper and Lower Skagits and other Indians in the Puget Sound area. Shakers had difficulty establishing their religion on the Tulalip Reservation, however, not only because of the influence of the Catholic Church there but also because government officials opposed Shakerism on grounds that its practices were unsanitary and its members were not progressive. A strong Catholic influence was also evident among Lummis to the north, near Bellingham, Washington. But on the Swinomish Reservation, near La Conner, Washington, where Upper and Lower Skagits, Samishes, and Swinomishes lived, Agent O.C. Upchurch noted that by the 1930s the Upper Skagits had a "strong unit" of Shakerism. More isolated than peoples nearer Puget Sound, they made their transition to Shakerism from a strong native milieu.[14]

During Shaker diffusion in the late nineteenth century, there

Left to right: Billy Williams, a minister of the Squamish, British Columbia, Indian Shaker church who died in August 1953; Monica Williams; Mary Louis Williams and children. William's church, north of Vancouver, marked the northernmost location of Shakerism on the British Columbia mainland. (*Indian Shaker Church Archives*)

were widely published accounts of Indian Ghost Dances, especially among the Sioux. Despite the publicity, it is doubtful that most Pacific Northwest whites at the time distinguished between Ghost Dances and Shaker services. The 1890s were also marked by economic hardship and general unrest, which would have tended to retard Shaker diffusion rather than advance it. But before the end of the century, the economy improved and Shakers were seen as less threatening to Christianity and white civilization.[15]

After the turn of the century, Shakerism expanded north to British Columbia and east across the Cascade Mountains. Shaker churches were established on Vancouver Island and on the British Columbia mainland. In 1895, the Shaker Church had reached north from Jamestown to another Clallam village at Beecher Bay on Vancouver Island. Three years later, the settlement was abandoned after its men were drowned off a Japanese sealing schooner. Their widows married men from other villages, and many carried their faith to Esquimalt on southern Vancouver Island. We learn from the pen of Bishop Peter Joe of British Columbia that a church house opened at Esquimalt in 1926. (The church would close in 1961.) Shakerism also appeared among Nanimos, Cowichans, and

Songishes on the island at Nanaimo, South Saanich, Duncan, Chemainus (unofficially Kuleets Bay), Westholm, Port Renfrew, and Shell Beach. Peter Joe's own church house, also on the island at Koksilah, was built in the mid-1920s. Early in the century, there were also congregations off Vancouver Island on the Gulf Islands of Kuper, Galiano, and Valdez.[16]

On the British Columbia mainland, Musqueams built Shaker churches west of Vancouver. Shakerism also spread among Squamishes at Capilano to the north and to Squamish, the church's most northerly appearance. Possibly the first Musqueam to be converted to Shakerism—sometime between 1898 and 1900—was Christine Charles, who visited relatives among Cowichans, some of whom were Shakers. A church was begun on the Musqueams' reservation when another woman was converted. Shakerism also spread east of Vancouver among Semiahmoos at Chiliwack. Another contact for Canadian and American Shakers was the Strait of Juan de Fuca. Sarah Ober reported that on one occasion seventy persons came across the strait from Vancouver Island to Neah Bay to engage in religious services.[17]

Shaker extension east of the Cascade Mountains may have begun when John Slocum went to the Yakama Reservation about 1891 with Mud Bay Louis and three other men to cure Alex Teio's sister-in-law. From White Swan, the faith spread the short distance across the Yakama Reservation to Toppenish, where Alex Teio lived.[18] As Indians traveled between the Yakama Reservation and the Columbia River during salmon fishing seasons, news of Shaker healings spread. In 1900, joiners at Toppenish took their religion to The Dalles, where Seymour, a Wasco Indian, and his wife joined the church. Daily curing services near Hood River, Oregon, and White Salmon, Washington, attracted a number of people. Near the present Dalles bridge, two and a half miles east of The Dalles, Wasco Shakers under Sam Williams built a church on Lone Pine Island. Later, a church was built upriver on Sam Island.[19] There was also a Dalles–Hood River–Cowlitz connection. Williams made several trips down the Columbia to Kelso, at the confluence of the Columbia and Cowlitz Rivers (where Upper Cowlitz Shakers had come); there he met with Mud Bay Louis, who may have been his great uncle.

Southwest of the Umatilla on the Warm Springs Reservation in

Easter Sunday dinner table, Squamish, British Columbia, April 1924. Shakers dedicated Easter more to baptizing children than to observing the resurrection of Christ. Among other holiday gatherings that Shakers attended were those at Thanksgiving time. In some churches trees were put up at Christmas in the manner of other denominations. The Fourth of July was celebrated by Shakers with "camp meetings." In early days Shakers requested permission of government agents to observe George Washington's birthday, but only as an occasion to shake and heal. The New Year's holiday was a most important gathering time; subsistence activities slackened and much shaking took place. This special period resembled the traditional native winter gathering observed with much ceremonial and feasting. (*Indian Shaker Church Archives*)

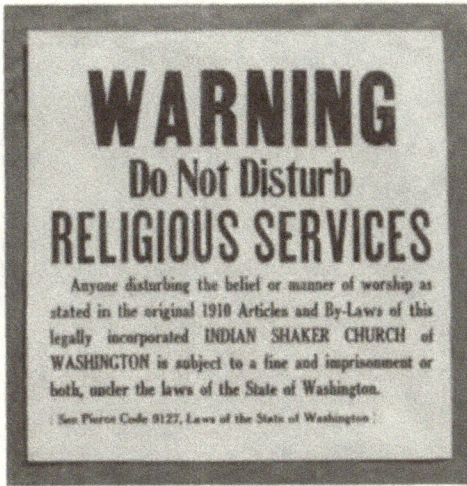

WARNING
Do Not Disturb
RELIGIOUS SERVICES

Anyone disturbing the belief or manner of worship as
stated in the original 1910 Articles and By-Laws of this
legally incorporated INDIAN SHAKER CHURCH of
WASHINGTON is subject to a fine and imprisonment or
both, under the laws of the State of Washington.

See Pierce Code 9127, Laws of the State of Washington

A problem in Shaker churches was the infrequent
disturbance of services by drunken rowdies. This
poster warns against such behavior, citing it as a
violation of Washington state law. Reverend Sam
Williams, of the church at Lone Pine Island on
the Columbia River near The Dalles, posted this
hand-painted warning on his church house at the
beginning of the century:
INDIAN SHAKER CHURCH
You are welcome. Please be orderly
NO ROWDISM ALLOWED
In the services Williams played records on an Edi-
son gramophone, which he obtained, along with
the records, at Portland's Lewis and Clark (1905)
Exposition. (*Robert H. Ruby and John A. Brown*)

north-central Oregon, Shakerism was accepted more readily by
Wascos than by Teninos. There were ties between peoples of the
Yakama and Warm Springs Reservations through gatherings at
fishing places along the Columbia River, so the Shaker Church
could have come to the Warm Springs directly or indirectly. According to one source, when Seymour and his wife moved to Warm
Springs, they did not immediately try to stimulate interest in the
new religion, but "people found out about it" when a woman suffering from tuberculosis was reportedly strengthened by dancing
and shaking.[20]

Farther to the east, on the Nez Percé Reservation of west-central

White Swan church house and adjacent dining hall, Yakima Valley, circa late 1930s. The bell tower, reminiscent of the orientation of early Roman Catholic churches, faces east. The White Swan church was Shakerism's second mother church, second only to the Mud Bay mother church six miles west of Olympia, Washington. It was from the White Swan church that Shakerism spread in the early twentieth century under the influence of Head Elder Alex Teio. (*Indian Shaker Church Archives*)

Idaho, interest in the church was stifled by a strong Presbyterian-Catholic influence that helped prevent the establishment of a Shaker church there until 1979. The Colville Reservation in north-central Washington represented the Shaker Church's most direct northeastern extension across the Cascade Mountains from Puget Sound. The initial seat of Colville Shakerism was geographically isolated at Malott at the southwestern edge of the reservation. Malott became the initial focal point of Colville Shakerism in 1914 when a Yakama convert moved there. First laying aside his Shakerism, the convert resumed it in 1941 when four Bible-reading Shakers from Darrington in Stillaguamish country successfully shook over his daughter. Impressed by their success, the Colvilles took several of their sick west across the Cascade Mountains for healing. From 1940 until 1945, a few more Colvilles joined the church. During the years when the church was divided over the use of the Bible, some Colville Shakers joined the Indian Full Gospel

Church, and two Bible-reading ministers from La Conner began intermittent preaching on the reservation in 1946. The Colvilles petitioned Shaker officials to allow one of the ministers to preach and received permission, as long as he confined his services to ministering at funerals. The church did not extend to Nespelem until 1953.[21]

To the south, word of Shakerism may have sifted into the Siletz in Oregon before 1900 after the Siletz wife of a Yakama man was cured by Shakers. Not until the 1920s did the church begin attracting followers to Otis in Siletz country on the Oregon coast. Missionary Joe Connor, whom Heck appointed to strengthen the church in the south, went to the Siletz in April 1927.[22]

Shaker extension into California via the Siletz involved the conversion of Jimmie Jack, a Yurok Indian living at Requa, California, at the mouth of the Klamath River. After visiting the Siletz and marrying a Siletz woman, he returned to Requa to preach the Shaker religion. Having little success, he asked Siletz Shakers to help him. About thirty of them, including Jackie Johnson and a dozen Klamath Shakers, went to Requa in August 1927, where they met with a small group of joiners and formed the nucleus of the northern California church. On March 20, 1971, Shakers established the Weitchpec–Old Mill Indian Shaker Church, located about ten miles down the Klamath River northwest of the Hoopa Reservation. On their way home to the Siletz, the group stopped at Smith River, California, a few miles below the Oregon state line, where they established a church.[23]

In 1930, Tolowa Indians, assisted by Jimmie Jack and others from Klamath, built a church house at Smith River that became most important in the spread of the Shaker Church in northern California. A pneumonia sufferer at Hoopa–whom a white doctor had failed to cure–was healed by a Shaker woman, and his recovery stregthened people's faith and caused many from the Hoopa Reservation to attend church at Johnson. People from Bald Hill on the reservation had their own small congregation, but most attended the more durable church house at Hoopa until it was destroyed in a flood.[24]

Problems hampered the spread of Shakerism, but no issue was more disruptive than the dispute over revelation, as enunciated by John Slocum and practiced by the Indian Shaker Church, and the

Frank Mitchell of the Hoopa Shaker church in northern California. Some of the churches, like that pictured here, were of plain clapboard; others were painted white. The lumber was usually purchased at local mills. Shakers of one church customarily helped other churches to finance the construction of their buildings. (*Indian Shaker Church Archives*)

use of the Bible. In the early days of the church, Reverend Eells had observed that those who did not use the Bible believed that God, aware of their ignorance, had given them visions that were spiritual instructions straight from heaven. Furthermore, according to Eells, some Shakers regarded themselves as more fortunate than whites who had "an old antiquated book."[25]

In no place was the disagreement more bitter than on the Siletz Reservation. Aggravating the conflict, on Thanksgiving night 1933, traveling missionary Joe Connor sought to thwart a revolt of the Bible users by reading the congregation a letter from Bishop Heck admonishing the congregation not to use Bible teachings. The letter led to the resignation of the Siletz assistant minister, head elder, secretary-treasurer, and local elders, leaving only seven "satisfied" non-Bible readers in the congregation. Siletz minister Sophia Johnson complained to Heck that Connor was the problem in the Siletz church because he had prohibited use of the Bible. According to Johnson, Connor permitted "Bible haters" to function and had told her that she was not to preach

Elwha church house just west of Port Angeles, Washington, on the Strait of Juan de Fuca. Many church houses, like this one, were unpainted, sometimes because of lack of funds. (*Indian Shaker Church Archives*)

the Christian gospel but to preach "John Slocum's gospel."[26]

Connor informed Heck in 1934 that those who had left Shakerism were bringing members of the Four Square Pentecostal Church to the church house to read the Bible. The Pentecostals had told the people that if they did not read the Bible they were "also profits [sic] and worship the evil." Connor's adversary was Wilbur Martin, who not only invited the Four Square people to preach but also got up to preach the Bible himself. Connor told Martin that the Bible users could not elect a minister until they found one who would carry out the "old John Slocum rule." Subsequently, Connor informed Heck that Martin had said that "John Slocums way wasn't any thing but second hand." Because of the conflict, the Siletz church went into decline. It continued to limp along until past midcentury with only a handful of members, and then folded. The church house was torn down in 1969.[27]

In California, the Bible-use conflict continued at Smith River, a community that one student of Shakerism characterized as ex-

periencing "factionalism . . . present in the Shaker community"
indicative of a "deeper factionalism of the community as a whole."[28]
To the north, the Bible-use issue proved to be equally disruptive.
On the non-Bible-use side were Bishop Heck and his successor,
Frank Bennett. A Shaker since 1926, Bennett was minister of the
Elwah Shaker church. Formerly of the Apostolic Faith mission at
Port Angeles, Washington, he witnessed his faith in hospitals and
jails and on street corners. His antagonist was William Kitsap, a
Tulalip on whom "a light" had settled one day after a drinking bout,
after which he had never drunk again. Allied with Kitsap was the
Bible-thumping Pentecostal missionary, Sarah Ober. Apparently
oblivious to how disruptive her crusade might be to traditional
Shakerism, Ober plunged into proselytizing Shakers to join her
church, whose members believed in visions, divine healing, and
speaking in tongues. Ober apparently believed that visions and
healings provided common ground for Shakers and Pentecostals.

Ober wrote a flurry of letters to Bishop Heck, and his wife, trying to convert them. She invited all Shakers to a two-months-long
Pentecostal convention and camp meeting in Seattle in June 1919.
Her correspondence with the Hecks reveals an increasingly imper-
ative tone, bordering on obsession. For some reason, she requested
a Shaker census, claiming that she was preparing "an accurate
record" before Judge Wickersham stopped over for a short visit on
his way from Alaska to Washington, D.C. A census might have
helped her estimate the size of the tent needed for the June camp
meeting, or, believing she was an instrument for saving Shaker
souls, she might have thought an accounting was necessary to
measure her accomplishment.[29]

Ober was not all wrong. Some Shakers felt a strong affinity
to Pentecostalism. One explanation of this appeal, according to
Amoss, is the high value Pentecostals placed on possessing the
spirit as evidence of a genuine contact with God. There was also a
Pentecostal affinity with traditional Shakers, according to Bishop
Harris Teo, because of the Shakers' ability to express their spirituality so exuberantly and because of the Shakers' ability to heal.[30]

Ober was crushed when Heck did not answer her invitiation to
accept camping space and tents for Shakers at the camp meeting; she reminded him that he was rejecting "God's free offers of

Notification of 1919 Pentecostal camp meeting to be held in Seattle. A leading exponent of Pentecostalism was missionary Sarah Ober, who tried desperately, but unsuccessfully, to win Bishop Peter Heck and other Shakers over to her church. Nevertheless, Bible-use Shakers joined Pentecostal congregations, unlike members of the 1910 Church, who adhered to the revelatory principles of John Slocum. (*Robert H. Ruby and John A. Brown*)

precious gifts." She finally resorted to appeal to a higher power "through my unworthy hands," in what she termed God's "last message to the Shakers." She assured Heck that "it is *God* Who is speaking to you—not me—for I have only to give what He sends." What she titled "God's Message to the Indian Shaker Church" was couched in tones of apocalyptic finality:

> My dearly Beloved Children. I, the Almighty God, Ruler of Heaven and Earth, am now again offering you my most precious gifts. . . . I offer you priceless gifts in infinite love and mercy. If you accept them your lives will be blessed above measure—your souls will be filled with the Holy Spirit. . . . If you reject and refuse these free gifts, I shall bring you unto Me through great affliction, sorrow, sickness, trouble, death, such as you have never before known. Already I have withdrawn my Holy Spirit from many of your church—Already I have taken away the powers I gave you from many of your number . . . to heal sick bodies. . . . Have I not saved you from sin, sickness and death? And when I would bestow upon you my greatest and most precious gifts—why do you refuse them? . . . Very soon you will be left

among the lost ones upon earth. . . . Will you not come into the very
fullness of my people? . . . Receive the precious and priceless gifts
that are so freely offered you–Come–Come–Come![31]

Ober's warnings failed to move Heck; in fact, he complained to
Shaker ministers at Jamestown, Taholah, and Skokomish about
her pretentiousness in asking the Taholah minister to come to
her convention in order "that he . . . be taught to preach." Nor
did Heck like Ober's request for a visit with Jamestown minister
William Hall (to whom she had written many times, seeking permission to teach and preach), asking as well for board and room.
Such gratuity was readily offered fellow Shakers, but not Pentecostal ministers. Heck was also disturbed over her letter to the
Skokomish minister advising him that Shakers were lost if they
failed to report to the Seattle meeting. Shaker ministers resented
Ober's condescending lectures that every minister of the church,
regardless of congregation, should be ordained by holy men of God
with the blessing of the church.[32]

Ober responded to Heck in six typed pages, rebutting his charges
against her. She denied, among other things, that she had proposed setting a date for the annual Shaker convention since she
had only offered "our Pentecostal Minister . . . tents for that convention *if* the Shakers *wished to accept them*." She also asked
the Shakers' pardon if she had been "too officious" and again invited them to her Seattle "convention." She attributed William
Hall's refusal to respond to her letters to impoliteness and the
Skokomish minister's lack of response to a misunderstanding. The
olive branch was in her hands, she wrote, not Heck's. Believing she
was God's messenger, she only wanted "to do His Will and help the
Indians." She again alluded to Wickersham's visit to Seattle, possibly hoping she could take advantage of his rapport with Shakers to
influence them to come to her church. She may have been unaware
that he had supported them in their nonuse of the Bible.[33]

It is likely that Bishop Heck was no more receptive many years
later to overtures of the American Bible Society, which sought to
supply him with inexpensive Bibles. Heck would have seen in overtures of the Bible Society the same threat posed by Pentecostals,
namely, the destruction of the revelatory aspects of his religion as
handed down by John Slocum.[34]

CHAPTER ELEVEN

The Klamath Connection

Henry Jackson (Skedaddle), a former slave living at Yainax on the eastern Klamath Reservation, has been credited with introducing Shakerism there. After becoming seriously ill in 1914, he learned of Shaker cures from unorganized converts on the reservation. When they refused to treat him, he called for Yakama church leaders to help him. Responding to Jackson's request, Alex Teio and Peter Heck led a delegation to the Klamath Reservation. They were unable to cure Jackson because he was "too far gone," but shortly before his death, Jackson reportedly implored his brother to retain Shakerism among his people. The promise was kept, and the movement gained members who went from house to house conducting shaking services. Warm Springs missionary Antoine Peppomai eventually organized a church on the Klamath Reservation in 1915.[1]

As on several other Indian agencies, Shaker missionaries to the Klamath had to contend with government officials who looked with suspicion, if not outright disfavor, at the church. In October 1915, Warm Springs Superintendent A. M. Reynolds received an inquiry from Klamath Superintendent William B. Freer concerning Peppomai and other Shakers on the Warm Springs Reservation. Reynolds reiterated his belief that Peppomai was trying to organize a Klamath Shaker church and that he and his coreligionists were a "fake."[2]

Some indication of the Yakama-Warm Springs missionary effort on the Klamath Reservation was word of their September 1915 meetings. The meetings, attended by Shakers from all over the reservation, were held for up to six nights a week at the home of Harry Jackson. Had the Shakers their own way, even prisoners on the reservation would have been released to attend the meetings. Special Agent John W. Lozier could not understand how Jackson could afford to feed the Shakers and their horses during their stay at his place. Nor could he understand how they withstood the "close room and so much noise from the sharp rings of the bells. . . . They seem to be nervous and worn out," Lozier observed, claiming that it had given him a headache and sent him away.[3]

U. S. Assistant Commissioner E. B. Meritt had been apprised of these Shaker activities and found it difficult to ascertain why they continued practicing like old-time medicine men. On October 23, 1915, he wrote Shaker minister Sargent Brown that he did not object to the Shakers visiting the sick and holding services, but he did object to their treating the sick, whose welfare should be left to agency physicians. He advised Superintendent Freer that it was Alex Teio, head elder of the Indian Shaker Church, who had orchestrated the spread of the church on the Klamath Reservation in the summer of 1915. Meritt advised Freer not to allow healings by "incantations" but to permit Shaker worship as long as it did not get out of hand.[4]

For a time, it appeared that Shaker missionary activity might be hampered by Peppomai's marital problems. Peppomai, who officials believed was living in bigamy with Millie Miller, had left a wife on the Warm Springs Reservation. On December 1, 1915, Meritt advised Freer to gather the facts and if necessary to jail the missionary and return him to the Warm Springs Reservation and his "legal wife." When confronted, Peppomai insisted that he had married Miller legally after separating from his wife, a practice that he maintained was according to Indian custom. In communicating with Reynolds, Freer learned that Peppomai had not divorced his wife according to Indian custom, yet Freer wanted nothing to do with him. It would appear that Freer was searching for some kind of moral or legal grounds to keep Peppomai and the

Shaker Church off the Klamath Reservation.[5]

In the meantime, Alex Teio wrote Freer that as head elder he, too, like John Slocum, had tried to overcome destructive habits that whites had introduced among the Indians. He assured Freer that the Indians had distanced themselves from the old medicine spirit quest, adding that Shaker bells were comparable with whites' pianos and organs. In trying to "sell" Shakerism, Teio explained how its people removed sickness from bodies, shrewdly avoiding any mention of shaking. Unimpressed, Freer warned Teio in March 1916 that Shaker curing services had to be conducted in private with no more than three Shakers present in addition to the patient's immediate family. After Teio and the Yakama-Warm Springs Shakers held meetings for a couple of weeks during June and July of 1916, Freer ordered the meetings to cease. Freer also ordered Teio off the reservation by July 15, rationalizing the order on the grounds that frequent meetings were "prejudicial" to the Indians' best interests.[6]

Teio and other Shakers held their large, fourteen-day-long Fourth of July camp meeting that year in temporary wooden structures north of Chiloquin on the Klamath Reservation. Joe Riddle, a self-appointed Yakama confessor, pitched his tent and invited Klamaths to confess their sins and receive instructions. He asked Mrs. David Copperfield to enumerate her sins. Did she "look on" baseball games, horse racing, dancing, moving pictures, or circuses, he asked. She replied that she did. Did she lie or steal things? She did not, she said, but she did get angry. Had she committed adultery? No, she had not since she had but one husband. Had she eaten meat on Friday? Yes, she had, but only before becoming a Shaker. She had joined, she said, following treatment for a partially lame arm that white doctors were unable to cure. Thanks to Peppomai, Copperfield reported, she was now able to swing both arms equally well.[7]

Freer and Fred A. Baker, agency examiner of inheritance, visited the Shaker meeting on July 7, when a number of joiners were received into the church. Arrangements were made to confer the "power" on the joiners, which Baker said signified "the possession of a spiritual potency either over sickness or evil." Joiners and other power seekers stood up, while robed women held burning candles. Ceremonial words, uttered by the congregation, were followed by genuflections and bodily rotations, signs of the cross, and shaking "in full force and vigor." Women with eyes closed stretched their hands above their heads, giving "the appearance of being in a state of hypnosis." They began singing a song "in all its harmonies," resembling "the old Indian dance music." Bell ringers began "a regular and monotonous chime" that resounded progressively louder and faster and harder; members of the congregation and missionaries alike began to shake. With arms raised and trembling and feet stomping rhythmically, the dancers' bent bodies swayed and twisted in a "frenzied orgy of emotional excitement." Baker was concerned about the "hygiene" of the occasion, fearing that some tubercular Shakers could aggravate their illness. He also reported that it would be "unfortunate for Shakerism to obtain a general hold upon the Klamath Indians," for it would reverse their acculturation by throwing them back "into the old forms of Indian dancing."[8]

Wanting to gain more information about Shakers, Freer rounded up several informants to keep him apprised of their activities. But the Klamath Shakers knew little about the founding of their church. Reverend Tom Lang, for example, wanted to return to the Klamath from the Yakama "all the John Slocum preachings and about Mary Slocum's when she got shake and healing of sick." Ten years later, Seeley Griffin of the Requa church wrote Lang seeking information about the Shaker faith, since "There are quite a few members . . . [who] do not know the Rule."[9]

Lacking knowledge of the beginnings of their church, however, did not mean that Shakers lacked zeal or witness for it. Mrs. David Copperfield, for example, told how she had distanced herself from the Methodist Church, having found no solace in it such as she had found in the Shaker Church, whose missionaries brought her people to heal. Copperfield was not alone. One student of Klamath culture wrote that "the Shaker Church had other elements of great emotional appeal which manifested a good deal of aboriginal shamanistic elements—elements absent in the Methodist Church." Members formerly active in that church "were now becoming absorbed in the new [Shaker] movement."[10]

Shaker activity increased on the Klamath Reservation during 1916, primarily because no one tried to stop it. Freer had informed the commissioner of his own mixed feelings about Shakerism and had turned his attention to stressing its negative physical aspects, such as holding protracted meetings in poorly ventilated rooms, which caused mental debility, he said, and spells of "temporary insanity."[11]

Brushing and other physical contacts at Shaker meetings were a continuing concern for Freer. At one meeting at Klamath Marsh, some distance from agency headquarters, stockman E. B. Ashurst reported that Pitt River Dick had been "a little too attentive to the women patients," and others in the curing circle had asked him not to linger too long while passing his hands over women's backs and breasts. Although he told Freer that Shakers did give power, agency policeman Hiram Moore objected when a Yakama in the 1916 Fourth of July camp meeting passed his hands over the legs and breasts of a woman. Basing their action on this and other reports, the Indian Office between 1919 and 1924 sought to eliminate bodily contacts between men and women in rituals that involved brushing.[12]

Ashurst also noted that those being treated appeared to have been stupefied, a condition that did not improve following after-services that continued until three o'clock in the morning. He concluded that the Shakers were sincere in their prayers to give up liquor and gambling and in their resolve to pray before and after meals, yet he believed their services took them unnecessarily from their work and their homes.[13]

After reading Ashurst's report, Freer ordered policeman Moore to Chiloquin to see that the Shakers met no later than ten o'clock at night. (A similar restriction had also been imposed on Quileutes in about 1909.) With no other restriction delineated in the order, the Chiloquin Shakers continued tapping others gently on their mouths, reminding them of a Shaker restriction on chewing tobacco and gum, evidently regarding chewing as the appearance of evil. The chewing practice evoked special censure not only from Klamath Agency officials but also from Mrs. Pedro. In her continuing crusade to stop chewing, she tapped Ed Johnson on the mouth, after which she fainted dead away. Stanley Pedro claimed it was the power of his own hand rather than retaliation that caused him to strike Johnson, bloodying his nose. When called before Freer to explain his action, Stanley confessed, "My hand started leading me . . . and my hand led me down the line down over the men's heads, and was going by Ed Johnson and it turned and hit him in the face like this." Gesturing, he continued, "It must have hit him pretty hard." Freer exhibited his own power by ordering Pedro to deliver ten tiers of wood to the Chiloquin day school.[14]

On November 16, 1916, Freer ordered police chief Edward Cookman to restrain persons from going to Daisy Paddy's place to perform incantations over her sick body. Cookman reported that four Shakers disobeyed his order. Freer was so concerned about other health problems for Shakers that he ordered policeman Moore to enforce the rule that windows be opened for ventilation when they met. He also offered them the alternative of attending another church.[15]

The Klamath Shakers began 1917 by disobeying a number of Indian Service regulations. On January 2, 1917, Freer wrote Moore, James Jackson, and Stonewall Jackson that they must agree to close their meetings by ten o'clock at night and must desist from using incantations, bells, and brushing. He also reiterated that Shakers could participate in no practice that hindered Indians' thrift and industry. But the Klamath Shakers refused to cooperate.

Freer then issued an order for the closing of the Klamath Shakers' Chiloquin church building on January 6. In response, Moore and the two Jacksons agreed to close down the meetings by ten o'clock. Freer also apprised them that there would be no more curings, which he still believed to be "old medicine men" practice. Nor had his concern about Shaker brushing, bell ringing, and candle burning to help effect cures lessened. In the face of these restrictions, the Klamaths maintained their connection with the Yakama by inviting missionary John Johnson to come down to lead their usual New Year's activities.

Ignoring the curfew for closing, the Shakers met until three o'clock in the morning on New Year's Day. Freer instructed Private Harry Jackson to report whether the Shakers had complied with his order. But Jackson's wife was a Shaker and Jackson himself was affiliated with the Shaker group, so he disobeyed Freer's order. Consequently, for a brief time Freer was unaware that the Shakers had not shortened their meetings. When he finally learned of the infraction, Freer immediately closed the hall to Shakers, leaving them in a quandary. Ironically, the rowdies who were drinking and gambling in the building next door had been released shortly after being arrested.[16] On January 6, Freer explained his edict and assured the Shakers that he would reopen the hall when their leaders had signed an agreement to abide by his order.

Instead, the Shakers began meeting in other places. Freer continued to dog them about disobeying his orders to stop incantations and to have no more than three or four persons gathered to pray for the ill. He still objected to their dancing, their bells, and their candles, but the Shakers remained as determined as he and refused to stop. Freer hoped to meliorate the situation by ordering the visiting Yakama–Warm Springs missionaries—Johnny (Johnnie) Johnson, Fred Shuster, and Waller Dick—to leave the reservation by January 8 and Antoine Peppomai to leave by January 15. In reply, Johnson told Freer that Shakers were responsible for the Indians' progress in lifestyle and added that he could not leave the Klamath for lack of funds.[17]

When Freer learned that Peppomai, who had signed an agreement to obey Indian Office regulations and the superintendent's "reasonable" orders, was not at the New Year's meeting, he permitted him to remain on the reservation. Peppomai's wife, who had business on the reservation requiring her presence there at all times, was also allowed to stay.

On January 23, Shakespeare Hicks went to Freer's house seeking permission to treat the elderly Long Wilson and his wife. As Hicks explained to Freer, it was a church tenet that it was "absolutely necessary" for Shakers to respond to the request. Freer sent police chief Cookman to check on the situation, only to find healers shaking over the couple, rubbing them gently to the accompaniment of ringing bells. Advising them that they had disobeyed agency rules, Cookman arrested Sargent Brown and his wife, Mabel, Charlie Brown and his wife, and Colly (Coley) Bill. Cookman asked Hicks and Wilson's son, Robert, to appear the next morning at the agency. There, Hicks admitted witnessing the scene where the Wilsons were prayed over and rubbed to the accompaniment of bells. Charlie Brown pleaded guilty but explained the need of ringing bells and burning candles, since the whites' medicine had failed to cure.[18]

Freer was in a quandary. If he punished the Shakers they might be seen as martyrs. Wishing to make no "tactical mistake," he frankly admitted that handling the Shaker "problem" of healing the sick had "very much puzzled" him. Seeking to solve the situation, on February 3 he met with twenty-five or thirty Shakers in a schoolhouse. Freer "explained to them painstakingly" that his main concern was the Shakers' disregard of his orders, particularly those orders regarding working over the sick, and their refusal to sign an agreement that they would obey the orders. The discussion kept returning to the prohibition of incantations, and the Shakers continued to express their unwillingness to give up treating the sick. About a half-dozen people testified that they had been cured by incantations. Freer tried to persuade the group that any benefit they received in their ceremonies was from prayers, not from dancing, which had nothing to do with healing.[19]

During this time of confrontation, the Klamath Shakers received support not only from missionaries in their midst but also from the ISC, especially its leaders on the Yakama Reservation. Stanley Pedro wrote Commissioner Cato Sells on January 23 asking why Freer had the right to "close their Christian Shaker Church." Pedro informed Sells that Shakers did not discriminate as to racial and economic status and insisted that the church should be reopened. In short, Sells should instruct Freer and the lawbreakers next to the Chiloquin hall, Pedro said, not to bother the Shakers and others who wished to be Christian men and women. Because of restrictions against them, Pedro went on, there were about seventy-one Shakers on the Klamath Reservation who were "shedding tears when they are praying to the almighty."[20]

Acting Commissioner E. B. Meritt wrote the Wilsons' daughter-in-law that no attempt had been made to interfere with Shaker churches as long as their congregations complied with agency regulations. Meritt said he supported Freer because he was only trying to follow guidelines laid down by the Office of Indian Affairs, which considered the passing of hands between genders in healing services incompatible with its regulations. Meritt reiterated that men should "heal" men and women should "heal" women, except for members of their immediate families. But to some, at least, this principle had never made sense. On January 24, the day following the Wilsons' "healing," Mabel Brown wrote Freer: "According to my belief I do not believe that I was doing wrong to doctor [a] man as we know in our own Agency we have a man Doctor who doctors women as well as men." On February 2, Freer wrote Head Elder Teio, defending the requirement that all leading Shakers sign agreements to obey the established rules. If they did so, he wrote, he would reopen the hall. Meanwhile, the Shakers continued shaking in their homes.[21]

In addition to support from Shakers in other churches, the Klamaths also received aid from non-Shakers. Stwire G. Waters, a Methodist minister on the Yakama Reservation and member of his church's Columbia River Annual Conference, was besieged by Shakers to ask Freer to open the Chiloquin hall. Waters complied, writing that as temperate Christian people Shakers were opposed to saloons and did not practice in the manner of the old Indian doctors. He stressed the earnestness of Shaker prayers. Waters told Freer that when his wife had almost died after a white physician had failed to restore her, she had been healed in the Shaker church. It was with satisfaction that Waters could report that she was alive ten years later, having survived the white doctor's prognosis that she had less than two years to live. Freer was unbending, explaining to Waters that Klamath Shakers, under instructions from Washington, D.C., would be restricted from congregating in a church house unless they gave up their incantations and other actions in healing services.[22]

As help for Klamath Shakers came from outside, so did opposition. Reading about developments on the Klamath farmer William Miller of the Skokomish Reservation extended his "heartiest sympathies" to Freer. On arriving on the Skokomish Reservation, Miller wrote, he had found "about 500 or more Indians congregated around and about my quarters, yelping, howling, sweating and otherwise expending their physical entergies [sic]." Among these Indians, he wrote, the Shakers were "the most ignorant, shiftless and lazy." In conclusion, "Shakerism being wholly Indian tends to make it contageous" while containing "more the worship of John Slocum than anything else, unless it be to make a tyee [chief] of ones self."[23]

Freer responded to Miller, explaining that he had ordered the visiting Shaker "propagandists" off the Klamath Reservation. These men, wrote Freer, had been ordered to leave and the Shaker meeting hall closed because the Shakers had not followed his regulations, authority, and instructions. Less harsh than Miller, Freer explained that the government permitted Shakers and all others to worship as they saw fit as long as "ordinary customs and proprieties are complied with." Moreover, responded Freer, "Some of our best Indians have recently joined the Shakers."[24]

Believing that Freer had acted harshly, Milton Giles, secretary-organizer, asked Washington state Congressman Albert Johnson, a Republican, to take up the matter with Indian Office personnel, seeking to get the banishment edict either modified or repealed. Defending the Shakers, Giles wrote that they liked "ceremony and form . . . [and] pictures, robes and music to lend reality to their worship." They were not savages, he wrote. They wrote letters on a typewriter and rode in automobiles. They merely liked to feast and to practice their religion, and their "barbaric spirit" called for "vividness." Interestingly, Giles's letter to Johnson was the subject of a cover story in the March 11, 1917, *Mason County Journal* under the headline "Shaker Evangelists Put off Reservation." Giles may have been trying to mobilize public opinion on behalf of the Shakers as well as seeking congressional intervention.

Amidst the troubles, Special Agent C. H. Asbury inherited Freer's problem. When he sought Yakama Superintendent Don M. Carr's opinion of Shakers and their religion, he was informed that Shakers should be allowed to worship as permitted within the bounds of morality and progressive leadership but should be restricted in ministering to the sick since Carr believed such treatment sometimes did more harm than good.[25]

In late summer 1917, Superintendent John M. Johnson took charge of the reservation. By that time, Dan M. Hart, a minister and leader of a growing Shaker Bible-use group, was attempting to meet with the new superintendent. He wrote Johnson, expressing the wish that their relationship be compatible so that the superintendent could help his Shakers in a way "that will better them while they live and also be prepared when their Last Day Ends in this world." Johnson responded with a conciliatory letter expressing regret that he had not yet met Hart.[26]

Hart also appealed to Bishop Heck for help in building a Shaker church house on the Klamath Reservation. He asked Heck to appeal to all ministers, as was Shaker practice, for funds to complete the project. He informed the bishop that he was working on a temporary church house that would be used as a dining hall when the larger church house was built. Hart's project must have been un-

Shaker leaders: Alex Teio, Yakama (*seated left*); Dan Hart, Klamath (*seated right*); and Joe Dan, Skokomish (*standing*). Teio was the foremost extender of Shakerism. Hart prided himself on his ability to preach with much emotion. (*Yakama Cultural Center Museum, photo neg. 137*)

der construction the following year, for on May 13, 1918, Johnson authorized church officials to purchase nearly a hundred dollars of dressed lumber, since the agency mill had burned. The retired agency school bell would have been an important addition to a Shaker church house, but in 1918 Meritt refused a Shaker request for it.[27]

There was still tension between the Shakers and the government, but the authorization to purchase lumber indicates that the contest had been temporized. There were other signs as well. Seeking assurances that Shakers could continue practicing their religion on the Klamath, Sargent Brown and Judge Wickersham visited the commissioner in Washington, D.C., in 1920. Brown discussed the agency's lingering interference with Shaker services.

He received the commissioner's word that the Shakers "could go and practice the religion" and that he would notify the Klamath superintendent that he was to ease his interference in such matters.[28]

While church and state relations were improving, relations in the church itself were growing more difficult. A Bible-reading majority had managed to work its way into the church, and its members refused to function under Washington state ISC rules. By the end of the 1920s, Bible-use Shakers had become an important force on the Klamath Reservation. Marilyn Claire Richen recorded that Chiloquin Bible readers had broken from the original ISC group in 1917, filing for incorporation as the "Shaker Church of Oregon." This breach more likely occurred in 1918, the year when Joseph Jackson, the secretary of the newly organized Bible-reading group, informed the Klamath superintendent that the group refused to operate under the ISC corporate rules. Meeting at Jackson's home on March 11, the Bible readers had elected Garfield Jack as their bishop. In his letter of March 12, Jackson asked the superintendent to recognize the church.[29]

The Bible users on the Klamath Reservation toyed with writing their articles and bylaws by combining their own ideas with those of the traditional ISC. The ardent, fastidious non-Bible-using Sargent Brown, however, refused to give the group a copy of the ISC articles of incorporation. (In time, the Bible users obtained a copy from Alex Teio and Peter McGuff.) ISC officials became alarmed when Klamath Bible users filed for corporate status in Oregon, concerned not only about having two Oregon bishops but also questioning the right of the traditional, direct-revelation Shakers to gain corporate status.

Because the traditionalists lacked such status in Oregon, ISC leaders went to the office of the Oregon secretary of state to ascertain the legality of the Bible-use group. As to their own right to exist in that state, they were informed that the Bible users were functioning legally as a Shaker Church and that the traditionalists could file with the state as a foreign corporation doing business there.

The Oregon schism, still centered at Chiloquin, did not go unnoticed or undebated outside the Klamath Reservation. Other churches were also experiencing uncertainty, although not necessarily over the use of the Bible. For example, the corporate status of the "Warm Springs Branch of the Indian Shaker Church" had lapsed, and that church had forfeited its rights as a legal entity. Its people looked forward to filing for a new corporate status, since the agency had threatened to close down their church if they did not do so. One of its members, Arthur Simintire, who likened his church to "a warm coat in stormy weather," said he wanted to be free from agency restrictions.[30]

Fearful of his own status as well as the future of the ISC, Bishop Heck called for a "special convention" of the Oregon churches to be held at White Swan on July 5, 1918. When the Warm Springs and non-Bible-use Klamaths did not arrive, the meeting was postponed for a day. A Klamath in attendance, Ralph John, called for solidarity, likening Shakerism to a stream flowing from Washington into Oregon and, with time, into California. Directing his remarks to the absent Warm Springs Shakers, he scolded: "I wish every Warm Springs to live up close. You can not do this business by sitting in tents distant away as this is an important business." The Warm Springs contingent did not arrive until July 8.[31]

The ISC now faced a crisis, with many questions yet unanswered. The splintering and establishment of corporations with different rules and philosophies left the identity of John Slocum's church in doubt. Who had the right to administer church functions and ordain ministers? By what right did groups who ignored ISC rules exist and should they be recognized as Shakers? Perhaps apologizing for the Klamaths for causing these vexing questions to be brought before the church, Sargent Brown said, "[M]y people are weak minded weak in the head. . . . I think we had better not shake if this matter will [go] on this way. My brothers and sisters are losing their power in their shake meetings. . . . I have asked many to join . . . but no they say you people [Klamath non-Bible people] split too much." Theodore Stern cited the controversy among Klamath groups as involving tribal politics energized by the clash of personalities by which "the church was riven."[32]

Concerned with his own ministerial license, which Bishop Heck had issued in Washington, Sam Williams of The Dalles told a gathering at a special convention held in White Swan on July 8, 1918, "Now [in] Hood River the light of Shaker religion is nearly out. Here of late the laws of our country is chasing us like a band of dogs. I have been in Klamath and found good Shaker people . . . I see the Klamath people very good in their work in this religion. This is what we want to grow."[33] Eventually, Williams joined the Oregon corporation of Bible readers and became bishop.

The Warm Springs dispute was eventually resolved. On January 8, 1919, the "Warm Springs Branch of the Indian Shaker Church of Oregon" filed its articles of incorporation, carrying that document until its revocation on December 31, 1945, for failing to file annual reports. The preamble to the incorporation articles stated that it was the desire of the Warm Springs Shakers "to form a corporation under and by virtue of the Laws of the state of Oregon providing for the formation of religious, benevolent, literary, educational, scientific, fine art, musical, sculptural, engraving, architectural and charitable societies and trade organizations."[34]

The dispute on the Klamath Reservation was less easily resolved. In the early 1920s, two corporate structures functioned as both Oregon and Washington churches. Bishop Heck was disturbed that the Bible-reading group was allowed to operate as a Shaker Church outside his control, completely separate from the ISC of Washington. He wrote the Incorporation Department of Oregon on January 19, 1921, pointing out that the Bible users were not a legitimate Shaker group. To him, that group should not have been allowed to operate as a Shaker Church.[35] He found it hard to understand how another group could incorporate using "Shaker" in its name.

In 1922, the ISC of Washington on the Klamath Reservation saved itself from extinction with a brief revival of interest. According to Richen, sixty-five members at a meeting at Chiloquin agreed to unite under the Washington ISC, which resulted in the 1923 dissolution of the Oregon ISC. This is not supported by records extant in the office of the Oregon secretary of state. It would be strange for the group to join the small non-Bible-reading faction and act under the latter's incorporation, which they had opposed all along.[36]

The precise relationship between the two Chiloquin groups in 1923 is not clear. It may be that the ISC of Oregon wanted to obtain materials, such as official records, from the original church. The Bible readers were having trouble obtaining the official stamp, or seal, of the church from Bishop Hart, who refused to give it up.[37]

In addition to Colly Bill, who made his thumbmark, on December 18, 1925, nine Klamaths signed their names to the articles of incorporation for the ISC of Oregon. In addition to Hart as bishop, the officers were William Moore, head minister; Abraham Charlie, traveling missionary; Harry Jackson, secretary; and Robert David, head elder. Their annual meetings (which were not called conventions) were held at Chiloquin on the first Friday in July to coincide with the annual Fourth of July camp meetings. The group adopted the name "Annie Lee Shakers."[38] The name was taken from Ann Lee, commonly referred to as Mother Ann, founder of a sect of Shakers from England who settled at Watervliet, New York.

Anthropologist Hiroto Zakoji, who studied Klamaths during the twentieth century, recorded that Bibles were not used in the two meetings he attended at the Annie Lee Church. He did not indicate if these meetings were for worship or strictly for business, however, or whether Bibles were even in evidence. He did mention finances as a possible cause for the schism, but did not explain in what way they might have been. Zakoji cited friction among unnamed power-conscious personalities as a cause of the rift. Because most Klamaths were literate, he found it difficult to explain the conflict as one of revelation versus literacy, but he did explain that those espousing revelation wished to retain their Indian heritage.[39]

In 1922, there were no more than thirty-five Klamath Shakers, although others, including Methodists, attended their meetings. Klamath Shakers appeared to have little tolerance for non-Indians of other faiths in their church. Bible-reading Klamath Shakers sometimes attended services of non-Bible readers, although the two factions only tenuously accepted each other. According to Klamath non-Bible-user Tom Lang, missionaries of the Four Square Gospel Church widened the rift, especially since both Bible and non-Bible users left Shakerism to join the Pentecostal group.[40] For their meetings, Four Square missionaries in 1926 used the Chiloquin church house built by Bible users. When the church burned down, the Annie Lee group rebuilt it but continued gravitating to the Four Square church. Eventually, the Pentecostals obtained a deed to the Shakers' church land. In 1991, Wade Le Roy sought to have the transactions reversed and the lands put back in trust for the ISC. There were only occasional ISC meetings at Chiloquin, but Le Roy persuaded Cecil Tulee, the Warm Springs minister and one of three Oregon state elders, to hold monthly meetings at Chiloquin in order to keep that church viable.[41]

The schism on the Klamath Reservation, involving a troublesome triangle of Bible and non-Bible users and Pentecostals, was an extension of forces that had appeared in Christian churches for years. Spun from another triangle of Catholicism, Protestantism, and nativism, the Shaker Church was caught in a process quickened by twentieth-century travel and communication that scattered religious offspring from one end of Shakerism to the other. These events may not have been in the minds of Yakama–Warm Springs Shaker missionaries who spread their faith to the Klamath. Nor perhaps could they have known that the same divisive process was even then at work in Shakerism's northern quarters, the homelands from which these missionaries had come.

CHAPTER TWELVE

Schism within
the Indian Shaker Church

A half century after its founding, the Indian Shaker Church experienced a schism—the so-called Bishops' Fight over Bible use—which threatened the unity and future of the church. The seeds of the schism were sown early in Shakerism when John Slocum declared that because Indians could not read the Bible they would not be held responsible for wrongful living. The early members of what was then known as the John Slocum Church rejected Bible use but still held the book in high esteem. Still, they found it difficult to reconcile the behavior of whites with the Bible decalogue, believing it a blanket that whites wore only on Sundays to cover their sins.[1] Above all, these non-Bible readers believed that because God knew they were illiterate the heaven-sent visions and spiritual instructions of Slocum's followers were as efficacious as the words of the Bible.[2]

But over the years, some Shakers began to see the Bible in a different light. In 1936, William Kitsap, a Tulalip, declared that Shakers needed the Bible: "For 24 years the word of God has been out of these Shaker churches, and now we must get the word of God established in all churches," he proclaimed. A Kitsap follower confirmed the belief that it was impossible to be guided in the right direction without the Bible. "You can shake without it," he

William Kitsap, first bishop of the Indian Full Gospel Church, under whose leadership in the mid-1940s it broke from the traditionalist 1910 Church of John Slocum. (*Leotah Bustillo, Tulalip Indian Reservation*)

said, "but you need it to know whether you are right or not." Some Shaker churches and homes began to change as Bible users hung Christian images on their walls and sang hymns.[3]

In 1910 traditional Shakers had faced competition from Bible-reading Pentecostals who were proselytizing Clallam Shakers. Even Jamestown Shaker minister William Hall had been attracted to the "new kind of religion," whose adherents did not "jump around" or engage in "hard work like the Shake." The new religion, he thought was "so easy in every way." They had a "Power to Preach," he wrote Bishop Heck, and cured any kind of disease and even raised the dead by prayer and faith without using crosses, candles, bells, and garments. Lest he appear too heretical, Hall had advised Heck that despite the advantages of the Pentecostals he was not abandoning his Shaker faith.[4]

Bishop Heck continued to receive pleas from Shakers to adopt Bible worship. A. P. Peterson—who had ties with Skokomish, Dun-

Reverend and Mrs. William Hall of the Jamestown church. The prevalence of seaborne liquor (his church house was close by the Strait of Juan de Fuca) was a constant irritation to Hall, whose Shaker religion rejected the consumption of liquor. (*Indian Shaker Church Archives*)

geness, and Port Gamble peoples, among whom Pentecostals were making inroads—wrote an unyielding Heck: "I believe no religion can live without the Bible. Our Shaker Religion I am sure will never live beyond the present generation unless we accept the Bible as our guide and authority in our religions work. . . . I do not say that we have to stop shaking. Our church would still be the Indian Shaker Church, and we would shake same as before, but we would use the Bible more in our worship."[5] Shakers who agreed with Peterson's position had already distanced themselves from their native culture, adopting from whites the need to keep records in English in order to legitimize their position on Bible use. This did not mean, however, that they had broken completely from tradition. In their meetings, off-the-record prayers were still offered in native languages and Chinook jargon.

Shaker records detail the main skirmishes in the Bishops' Fight. Partisans attempted to keep their disagreements within

Bishop Peter Heck, Chehalis Indian, prominent in the establishment of the Indian Shaker Church. In administering the church, he used a great deal of diplomacy, but he was also overly given to compromise, a trait that helped bring on a schism within the church. (*Indian Shaker Church Archives*)

the bounds of Christian charity to avoid being contentious. Consequently, it is often difficult to ascertain which of the champions of the two groups, Heck or Kitsap, was supported by which delegates. As in all human polarity, however, personalities in the Bishops' Fight moved in tandem with matters of policy.

Heck's opponents saw his retention as bishop ever since his appointment in 1911 as an unwillingness on the part of the church to change policies, especially on the issue of Bible use. Confusion over the elections of bishops had persisted since the premature death of Mud Bay Sam and that first "election" of Heck in 1911. First Elder Alex Teio had appointed Heck, who had then been approved by the convention, but it was unclear whether Heck was completing Sam's four-year term, which would end in 1914, or was beginning his own.[6] Now with advancing age, Heck had become increasingly passive, which made it unlikely that he could ever heal the widening rift in the church or prevent his opponents from advancing Kitsap as their leader. The first major attempt to seat Kitsap in the bishop's chair occurred at the annual convention on October 13, 1927. Heck called the meeting to order and led the group in electing Harry Teo as secretary. Then, perhaps fearing he might not win reelection—or maybe even thinking he had—Heck left the meeting without calling for an election of bishop and without proper adjournment.[7] Anthropologist Erna Gunther gave a different version of the meeting. The delegates, she wrote, believed that Heck would not seek reelection. His supporters had supposedly said he was determined to resign, but a dream had warned him of imminent death if he did so. Thus, Gunther wrote, the elders ruled that Heck had to serve during his lifetime.[8]

Unhappy with this decision, about thirty self-appointed delegates met at Mud Bay on November 12, 1927, to take up the problem of the bishopric. Johnnie James was elected chairman, representing the Tulalip church and the churches at La Conner, Neah Bay, and Stillaguamish. Also attending were Charles Boome of Concrete, Andrew Wilson of Lummi, Johnnie Johnson of La Push, and Lee Cush of Skokomish. Their goal was to elect a bishop for a four-year term, and their choice was William Kitsap. Those present were apparently aware that they had overstepped the bounds of proper procedure, and they retained as their counsel attorney Ivan L. Hyland of Seattle.[9]

Heck's informant at the meeting, Jerry Keenum (Kenam) of Carnation, returned with a predictably negative impression of what had transpired there. He warned Heck that something had to be done with Johnnie James, whom he called a "Boot-legger and . . . a leading man at the gamble." He also warned that George Adams of Skokomish and James "take your [Heck's] name and rub it into the dirt." James and Adams had served as chairmen of the meeting. One nominee for the bishopric, Robert E. Lee of Skokomish, had turned his votes over to Kitsap despite opposition from Heck supporters Keenum and Mary Starr. Lee's votes had clinched the election for Kitsap, who had been immediately ordained as bishop. Keenum later warned Heck, "If you let these men get away with what [they are] doing maybe some other day another big headed man will start the same trouble." He was "glad that none of our head Elders were present at the meeting," since it showed "that what they done is not legal."[10] Nevertheless, from

Back view of the present White Swan Shaker church house. In 1910 a 427-pound bell was hauled over the Cascade Mountains and installed in the White Swan church house tower. (*Robert H. Ruby and John A. Brown*)

1927 both Heck and Kitsap acted as bishop, and the Bishops' Fight was fully engaged.

Four years later, in 1931, few Washington Shakers attended the convention on the Siletz Reservation, mostly because of the distance and lack of funds. The Kitsap people stayed away, having been deliberately misled by Kitsap supporter Carl Jones, who told them that the convention would be held at Tulalip. Such confusion caused a growing frustration and disappointment in the church. Those attending the convention were mostly Heck partisans who supported him as lifetime bishop.

Back in Washington State, after the Siletz convention, Carl Jones wrote Heck, asking about what had transpired there concerning elections: "I can not sleep good until I hear from you," Jones said. Kitsap had spread the word that no business had transpired at the Siletz convention and that Heck had resigned. Because of these reports, Jones, who hoped to legitimize Kitsap

Carl Jones, bishop of the Indian Full Gospel Church, who succeeded William Kitsap in that position. The Full Gospel mother church was on the Tulalip Indian Reservation. (*Leotah Bustillo, Tulalip Indian Reservation*)

as bishop, called for a substitute convention to meet on December 22 at Tulalip to settle the bishopric question "once and for all time." Delegates to the second convention were requested to come with letters authorizing them as delegates. Only those bearing such credentials were considered eligible to attend. At the convention on Kitsap's home turf, his followers reelected him as bishop.[11] Presumably, Heck did not attend.

The annual convention for 1932 was held at White Swan on October 14 and 15. Bishop Heck presided at the meeting, at which all Washington state churches were represented and "regular and official business of the church organization" was acted upon. During the July 4 camp meeting held the year before at Mud Bay, Kitsap forces had determined that an election would be held at the annual convention. Heck departed White Swan, while the other conventioneers remained until Monday to hold an extended convention for the purpose of electing a new bishop and secretary.

Nominees for bishop were William Kitsap, Charles Howeattle, and Peter Heck. The unusually large number of delegates at the

Charles Howeattle, minister of the Shaker Church at La Push on the Quileute Indian Reservation, circa 1930. The cross on his vestment is similar to the symbol used in Catholicism. Howeattle held two certificates ordaining him as minister, one from Bishop Kitsap and the other from Bishop Heck. (*Indian Shaker Church Archives*)

meeting gave 239 votes to Kitsap, 177 to Howeattle, and 9 to Heck. Charles Boome of Concrete was elected secretary. Writing up minutes, Boome noted that the meeting had been "for the purpose of electing a Bishop of said Church and a Secretary of the Bishop, for the term of four years."[12]

There was no open confrontation between the Heck and Kitsap forces at the 1932 meeting, but the conflict smoldered into the new year. The dispute surfaced in a lawsuit filed in the Thurston County (Washington), Superior Court. Heck, as plaintiff, had decided to seek recognition of his position as ISC bishop against the defending Kitsap. It was charged that Kitsap, acting as ISC bishop, had fraudulently collected and used monies for his own activities, that, in un-Shakerlike fashion, he had accepted funds from talks at various Christian churches. On September 27, 1933, Judge John Wilson ruled that Heck was the lawful bishop and incumbent of the office. Kitsap was enjoined from usurping duties and functions of the bishop's office and from performing acts authorized for the bishop. Wilson further offered the "simple" suggestions that the first state head elder "preside at all conventions" if the bishop was absent. The judge further defined Shaker factions as of the "old school, [which was] used to following the Indian customs rather than conforming to the regular procedure," and the younger generation, which wanted to follow more formal procedures. Wilson ruled that no legal election could take place before the next quadrennial convention in 1935 if Heck were to choose to remain in office. Apparently seeking a face-saving solution for Heck, Wilson declared that "Bishop Heck is an old man" who had served long and faithfully, but he questioned if it would not be a "fitting close to his honorable service if he could see his way clear to tender his resignation at the coming annual convention this year and thus create a vacancy which would be filled by appointment by the elders." The one appointed, Wilson wrote, would serve until the 1935 convention. But Wilson underestimated Heck's staying power.[13]

Strengthened by his victory in court and perhaps by his desire to avoid death as presaged in his revelation, Heck remained in office. In February 1936, he again refused to turn over church records and the seal after Kitsap again laid claim to the bishopric in the 1935 election held at Taholah.[14]

Kitsap called a July 4, 1937, meeting at Mud Bay, but Heck chose not to attend. Kitsap's reply was that any good Shaker, regardless of his leader, should have been in attendance. But Heck was attending another meeting at Smith River, California, seeking to solidify his position as bishop in that state, where reverberations of the schism were being felt. Heck's belief that Shakers should not use the Bible was solid. In the mid-1930s, he had sent missionary Joe Connor to the Siletz Reservation to expel Wilbur Martin, the Bible-reading missionary, from the church there. Heck had instructed Connor to order any Bible readers to leave the Shaker Church and join the Pentecostal mission or the Four Square Gospel Church.

Kitsap presided at the 1937 annual meeting, held on October 9 at Neah Bay. He sought to assure his position by establishing a treasury by asking "our Lord and members for a donation of fifty cents per year from all members." This was done by passing a resolution prefaced by the clause "Whereas that this shaker religion is to go on for the best interest for all the shakers in our country and whereas we are looking forward for more members and more conventions for the future."[15]

Kitsap traveled around Puget Sound trying to gain support for the bishop's office. His stronghold was his own Tulalip Reservation, while Heck's was the Chehalis and the Yakama. Shakers who lived far from the sound, such as the Quileutes on the coast, did not recognize Kitsap, and neither did Shakers who lived farther away on the Siletz Reservation.[16]

Heck and his supporters considered 1938 to be an election year, and their annual convention opened on October 15 on the Chehalis Reservation with Heck in charge. The dates for elections were once again a matter for dispute. The Heck people, unwilling to cooperate with Kitsap, refused to follow Judge Wilson's recommendation that election years be quadrennial from 1911, which the Kitsap group had adopted.[17] Kitsap's people had gained support for adopting the judge's recommendation among the congregations. Nevertheless, the delegates to the Chehalis meeting unanimously voted to retain Heck as bishop for another four years. On the same day, Kitsap's followers attended a convention of their own at Neah Bay.

During the nine years from 1933 to 1942, when Heck would be retired, Shakers often held two annual conventions and other factional meetings. Heck sidestepped and walked out on elections in 1935 and 1939, giving Kitsap room to act as controlling bishop to call meetings on his own. At one meeting Kitsap held in Concrete in the upper Skagit Valley on June 17, 1939, Gaspar Dan of La Conner told the delegates, "We are in the same boat as the white man, we must adopt a ruling for our church, which is badly needed; So we must amend our by-laws." Gaspar Dan explained that the church had to function just as white Christian churches did. Kitsap explained that in order to exist as a corporation, the Shaker Church could not base its beliefs on John Slocum's teachings but must base them on the Bible. Mike George of White Swan moved that an amended constitution and bylaws be put to the people for their approval at the coming annual convention. Isador Tom of Lummi seconded the motion to amend. The amendment passed with ten in favor and two opposed. Jackson Harvey then closed the meeting with a prayer and a song, which lent sanctity to the transaction.[18]

Delegates from seventeen churches attended the 1939 convention, held on October 6 at White Swan. Kitsap presided, but it was Carl Jones and Gaspar Dan who asked the delegates to pay strict attention to business in order to prevent discussion. Their primary concern was to adopt a new constitution and articles of incorporation. Kitsap urged quick adoption of the constitution, stating that the amendments that caused quarreling among delegates could be amended by vote at any time. On the second day of the convention, delegates adopted a constitution and bylaws. The meeting adjourned after the quadrennial election was held. Kitsap was placed in office for four more years. Johnnie James's nomination to retain five elders was passed, but Enoch Abraham, a Heck supporter, declined the nomination. Mike George of White Swan was chosen to fill that position.[19]

Kitsap thought he had put Heck out of the way by having future elections figured from 1939. The new constitution and bylaws called for the bishop to be elected for four years and his own election to begin with the year 1939. The Bible-use position of the Kitsap group was evident in Article IV of the bylaws:

> The Indian Shaker Church, because its work is based upon the word of God, has adopted the Bible which is the basis for all true Christian Faith, as its guide, and encourages its members to read and pray, and take healing as it is taught in the Bible, especially according to Jas. Chapt 5 vs. 13 thru 16.

The constitution and bylaws were signed by Kitsap and three state elders—Mary Krise, Carl Jones, and Henry Jackson. The documents were filed with the State of Washington under the title "Indian Shaker Church of Washington and the Northwest." A huge wedge had now been driven into the Shaker Church.[20]

In the Bishops' Fight, possession of the corporate seal of the ISC prevented the Kitsap faction from gaining control of the church as completely as it had envisioned at White Swan. On his own Tulalip turf, Kitsap called for a series of whirlwind meetings. At his suggestion, the 1940 annual convention was held in Tulalip on October 26. At the gathering, Jerry Keenum said that the matter of "who is legal Bishop is not yet settled in the minds of the People." Despite the conflict, delegates discussed the disrepair of the Muckleshoot church house and the necessity for building some church houses and fixing others.[21]

It is unclear what meetings Heck's people might have held during that time. Heck's forces, other than holding their own annual conventions, appear to have been immobilized as Kitsap sat in the bishop's chair in meetings with state elders. ISC records contain several letters from Heck's partisans begging him to explain developments in the church rift, and asking him to try to fix it.[22]

In the face of the aged Heck's faltering leadership, Frank Bennett, minister of the Elwah Shaker church, sought to salvage the traditional church. Bennett was aided in this effort when Kitsap's people asked church secretary Mary Amundson to resign her position. Amundson had carried reports of the 1939 convention to Heck and had made it clear that she considered the Kitsap meeting to be illegal. She attached her personal notes to a copy of the minutes. She maintained that nominees for bishop were required to state their platforms, and since Kitsap had made no such statement, she considered the constitution and bylaws he presented to be his platform. As such, she believed them to be ineffectual until he was elected. Amundson's notes concluded: "Therefore:— According to PP. 47, page 20, Roberts rules of Order, *all votes cast were contrary to Bishop William Kitsap's own Constitution* which was adopted before the election of officers began, therefore, *null and void*." Thus, according to Amundson, the new constitution was in conflict with the previous constitution of California and Oregon and with the 1910 Articles of Incorporation.[23]

The Bishops' Fight moved from church to church. At a March 16, 1941, meeting at Neah Bay, Clarence Cheer stated that whites closed down the church at Concrete when they discovered it was not founded on the Bible. When Kitsap visited Concrete, he ordained Harry Moses, who used the Bible, and the church reopened.[24] Tensions at Concrete increased when the non-Bible users complained that those using the Bible played their musical instruments until eleven o'clock at night, leaving the non-Bible users too tired and with little time to hold services and minister to the sick. Such complaints supported fears that Bible use could destroy the church by tampering with its principles and symbols. Eight years earlier, some Tulalip traditionalists had written Heck:

> We do not want these white people [Bible readers] running over us
> as they are. We do not understand what its all about when they sing

The official seal of the 1910 Indian Shaker Church symbolized not only the legal status of the church but also its authority. The seal was a bone of contention between the Shaker groups involved in the schism, since the defecting Indian Full Gospels sought unsuccessfully to obtain it. (*Robert H. Ruby and John A. Brown*)

and play instruments in front of the altar table. We want to worship Our God in our own original way. The way it was put before us. We do not want to lose our rights to our church. Therefore we ask you—do not fail to not give up your rights as head of our church.[25]

They had also asked Heck to keep their names secret from their fellow Tulalip, Kitsap, who had the backing of the Tulalip police chief, among others. Eight years later, the sentiments of the non-Bible users had not changed.

Kitsap's hold on the bishop's post focused attention on the church seal. Following the October 1939 White Swan meeting, Kitsap's people tried to obtain the original seal from Heck. Failing in this effort, Kitsap had another seal made for himself with similar wording.[26] Seeking the authority to restrain Heck and his followers, Kitsap called a meeting of his own forces to be held at La Conner on May 17, 1941. Delegates at the meeting, however, decided not to go to court against their opponents. As Secretary Foster Jones put it, "The word of God forbids his children to go to law, and a restraining order means trouble."[27]

Annual meetings focused on one question: Who is bishop of the Shaker Church? As a result, no decisions were made on questions of assessments, memberships, and building and repairing church structures. At the center of the controversy was the continuing problem of determining election years. The Kitsap people hoped that the question had been settled with their adoption of a constitution and bylaws that specified elections every four years beginning with 1939. The Heck-Bennett people, however, called for a special Shaker Church meeting at White Swan on October 4, 1941, the time of year when annual conventions were usually held. Their plan was to make 1942 an election year.

Neither bishop attended the October meeting. Ed Hudson, temporary chairman, told delegates he had "no grudge against bro. Kitsap [except for] just one thing where he does not carry out the Shaker Faith." Gaspar Dan made a motion that 1942 be an election year. With sixty-eight members attending, twenty-six delegates voted favorably, none opposed, and forty-two abstained—a clear repudiation of Kitsap's bylaws. Bennett exhibited his new leadership by holding up the original 1910 incorporation papers and a copy of Kitsap's 1939 constitution and bylaws. "We want to get back to the original [1910 Articles of Incorporation]," he said, adding, "I want to be on [the] right side and how are we going to make Kitsap and Heck love one another."[28]

Bible and non-Bible users alike seemed to exhibit a cooperative spirit and a weariness, if not disgust, with the Bishops' Fight. Both bishops were censored at the meeting and found to be "guilty" of improper conduct. Heck was faulted for retaining church properties—the seal and official records—for refusing to step down from the bishop's office after being defeated at Taholah in 1935, and for carrying on as bishop and making "disturbance to the shaker organization." Kitsap was found guilty of issuing licenses without the church seal, for violating unspecified church bylaws, for instructing churches not to attend this special meeting, for drawing money from the treasury without approval, for drawing up a constitution and bylaws to replace articles of incorporation, for causing division in Shaker membership, and for refusing to yield control of church properties.

Frank Bennett played an important role in the proceedings. Now the key figure in a non-Bible-use resurgence, Bennett benefited from close ties with Heck supporters, including those on the Quileute and Quinault Reservations. Like Bishop Heck, Bennett sought to maintain John Slocum's opposition to Bible use, but he had not always held that position. Bennett's former Pentecostalism was very different from John Slocum's faith, which put more emphasis on inspiration and revelation than on Bible use.[29]

Early in the meeting, Bennett said, "I want to explain and understand that Kitsap and his board have been recalled and also Peter Heck and his board are recalled." The delegates then voted for the immediate removal of both bishops. Lee Cush, a Skokomish and non-Bible user, was made acting bishop for a year. In the aftermath of the meeting, Heck sought counsel of an Olympia attorney, who advised him that he could not be removed from office without just cause.[30]

Although Cush served as acting bishop, Bennett took over the church program, and it was he who called the 1942 annual convention for October 17 on the Chehalis Reservation. Having been left out of deliberations, Heck came to the meeting only because someone stopped by to pick him up. Acting as chairman, Bennett called the meeting to order and explained the differences between the two church groups. Traditionally, when a person became a church member, he explained, he or she had to be "a full-fledged Shaker," adding that the Bible was not used in early Shakerism because Indians could not read. He confessed to having read the Bible himself but asserted that the proper course was to preach what John Slocum taught by spontaneously letting God direct members in what to do and say. "The Shaker must not plan out what he is going to do," explained Bennett, but "must follow the power of God only."[31]

In order to elect a new bishop, Bennett said, another person of that office was needed to ordain him. Therefore, the Cush appointment had been ineffective and lacked proper ordination. Heck was "retired," Bennett asserted, and he would not recognize Kitsap as having been a legally elected bishop by asking him to ordain the person elected to that post. He called on Heck to speak. The bishop began, "Brothers and sisters, I still call you brothers and sisters even though you are trying to put me out. You say that I am too old, well thats alright, but I did not know that I am retired Bishop." Admitting to having had little voice in the deliberations, he said,

"I do not want to say very much to you people while I am retired Bishop, but I have stumbled now." With that, he sat down, yielding the floor to others, but not yielding his belief that he had been elected for life.

When Bennett asked for nominations for a permanent chairman, both he and Heck were nominated, along with John Wapat, who declined. Forty-nine members were present, but only nineteen voted—only one of them for Heck. Heck again rose to his feet, scolding,

> I thought that you people understood this meeting. The first time I was elected for Bishop I did not know anything about this church and its laws, but I thought that the Bishop is to be chairman at all meetings of the church. Well today I am fooled again. I have the license to give to my Head Elders. I thought that was the right way for you people to put in your new man for Bishop. But now I have no Head Elders and I cannot go ahead so I guess I'll just walk out and let you people run this the best way you know how.[32]

But Heck didn't walk out. Instead, Bennett turned the meeting over to him to act as chairman, believing that would legalize any action taken. John Logan, newly elected head elder and minister of the dwindling, almost defunct Siletz church, reminded the delegates that Heck had to be recalled in line with the previous year's vote and that the church had to be reorganized. Logan expressed his desire to reorganize and reunify the church and to stay its falling membership and lack of leaders. At that, Heck again threatened to walk out of the meeting. Sam Elmore and others asked him to remain to finish his work, with Elmore reminding delegates that "without Peter Heck you cannot ordain anyone." The meeting was adjourned for lunch in the midst of an argument over whether any election was legal if it lacked a majority of the membership to vote.

Reconvening at three o'clock, Bennett turned the meeting over to Heck with the comment that only Heck could appoint head elders and officiate at their meetings. With that, Heck appointed and licensed Bennett as first elder, Gilbert Sotomish of Taholah as second elder, and George Sanders of the Chehalis Reservation as third elder.

Once again Heck raised the troubling bishop question. Determined to get in the last word, he stated that because Lee Cush had been elected at a special meeting to fill the bishopric for a year with Kitsap's head elders, his election was illegal. Finally, the board of elders recommended Bennett as bishop. Thirty delegates stood to vote for him, with nine delegates opposed. Asking California bishop Archie Roberts to stand with Bennett, Heck began the ordination by asking Bennett about his past conduct and other things. "Frank Bennett takes the chair for Bishop after I get through with questioning him," said Heck, "then he starts work for the Convention. Maybe he will get mad and not want to be Bishop when I ask him the Questions I am supposed to ask him but I will not ask all the Questions because I do not want to take up [your] time and will make it short." After the questioning, Heck and Roberts prayed for Bennett, and Heck invited delegates to shake hands with the new bishop.[33] Minutes of the meeting do not reveal how well the questioning went.

On Monday, October 19, the elders traveled the short distance from Chehalis north to Olympia to seek assurances from the state attorney general that their meeting had been legal. The attorney general advised them that the "present set was on the level" and properly done within the law of incorporation. He also advised them to "get after the Other Party [the Bible-use group] who are disturbing the Corporation." On Wednesday, October 21, the bishop and elders filed papers with the secretary of state for the corporation, listing Bennett as the new bishop and Gilbert Sotomish, George Sanders, and Joseph Mitchell as state elders.[34] Bennett and his people decided to go after the Kitsap faction with a restraining order, which the attorney general filed in the Snohomish County Washington, Superior Court.

Throughout all of this, Kitsap was not idle. He called for a meeting of his followers on the Tulalip Reservation for October 8, 1943, almost a year after Bennett had been elected bishop at Chehalis. At the meeting, Kitsap presented the matter of Bennett's restraining order against him for acting as bishop. Alex Young urged the delegates to keep the matter out of the courts, warning that they would only be restraining themselves if they continued in the fight. Young's remark could have been a threat meant to encourage Kitsap to stop acting as bishop, although Young also stated, "I think

Harris Teo, late bishop of
the Indian Shaker Church
at home in White Swan,
Washington. His paternal
roots were Hawaiian;
his maternal roots were
Native American, primarily
Skokomish and Wishram.
(*Robert H. Ruby and John
A. Brown*)

the people ought to put up a petition to disqualify both men." The
assembled members did not accept the suggestion.[35]

The Kitsap people had wanted Bennett to attend the Tulalip
meeting, since it was being held in the Bible users' election year.
With Bennett present, they hoped, he and Kitsap could be advanced for election to settle the matter once and for all. Although
one Kitsap elder asked Bennett not to attend the meeting, he
stayed away primarily because he was not about to subject himself to another election in an ISC off-year, especially one held in
the presence of those who did not support him. Charles Strom
suggested that they meet Bennett at a special gathering at a
convention that Bennett had planned on holding in mid-October.
Instead, they decided to bring Bennett to the Tulalip while their
meeting was still in session. A delegation left the Tulalip Reservation by auto for Bennett's Queets home at five o'clock on the
afternoon of the ninth and returned at eight o'clock the next
evening with Bennett in tow.

Harris Teo opened the meeting that day by calling for the election of a temporary chairman. Charles Boome won the honor and officially asked Bennett to explain his position. Before doing so, Bennett sang a song and offered a prayer. He then told how he had been chosen at a general election on the Chehalis Reservation the previous year and how he had traveled to Olympia to report the new slate of church officers and confirm the authenticity of the ISC seal. "I do not want to be God," he said. "I only represent the Indian Shaker Church." His position as bishop, he was careful to add, had been recognized by state officials. A motion was passed asking Bennett to officially withdraw his restraining order. He countered: "If you accept me as your Bishop, I will withdraw the restraining order." Breaking his silence during the deliberations that followed, Kitsap clearly felt confident in his home territory. Trying to force a vote for bishop, he said, "You know the floor has been opened on the motion. . . . Are you afraid of [Bennett]?" With that, the Muckleshoot delegate nominated Bennett and the Darrington delegate nominated Kitsap.

At no time before, during, or after the meeting did Bennett concede to being a candidate for bishop. He stood firmly on the ground that he already held that position, and he walked out of the meeting when he received no consensus for acceptance as ISC bishop. The delegates were troubled, and the issue of Bible use continued to influence their thinking. One Lummi delegate said, "I dont care who the Bishop is. No man can come and take over our church. . . . If this isnt settled right now, we will have two heads. If I was Bennett, I wouldnt condemn the Bible." The delegate also revealed an important gap within the church—that between generations: "I belong to the younger generation. . . . Days are changing . . . we read the Bible." In the end, the delegates gave Bennett fifty-seven votes to Kitsap's sixty-six.[36]

The Tulalip convention widened as never before the gap between the two factions. Kitsap became so agitated by demands of the non-Bible users that he turned over church properties to them and called for yet another meeting on the Tulalip Reservation on November 6, 1943. At this meeting, Carl Jones spoke in favor of Kitsap's suggestion that they retain an attorney to combat the Bennett group, but Alex Young objected to the vote since the matter involved spending money and the finance committee was not present at the meeting. Tempers flared. When Kitsap accused

Indian Full Gospel church house on the Tulalip Indian Reservation, May 2, 1991. The church house was a former army barracks moved to the Tulalip. (*Robert H. Ruby and John A. Brown*)

Young of making trouble, Young replied, "How can you talk to me like that and I have backed you for seven years?" To that, Kitsap snapped, "Like the devil you have." At that juncture, Jim Price reminded the delegates that Bennett still claimed the bishop's position and suggested that the best solution was to borrow the money to put out the "fire burning." On motion, his suggestion was carried, with ten in favor and two opposed. The group pledged seventy dollars to retain an attorney, with Price and Kitsap pledging twenty dollars each.[37]

Three months later, on February 26, 1944, Kitsap and some of his supporters met in Tulalip to consider a resolution to recall Bennett. Kitsap reaffirmed his wish to seek a peaceful solution to the schism so that Shakers could "continue our worship of God, as we are based on His Word"—an allusion to the Bible. His people were blaming him for pushing the church into court, but Kitsap claimed to have worked hard to prevent that from happening. He also explained, that he had depended on attorney Ivan L. Hyland to save Shaker churches. Obviously annoyed by the bickering, Hattie Johns said that Bennett's and Kitsap's followers were acting "just like a bunch of little kids." Johnny James said that lawyers, who were "only after the money," were not helpful in settling the problem. The thing should be stopped, he said, "even if we have to hog-tie Frank Bennett to avoid court proceedings." Lee Cush pointed out that the Bible-use matter was not as big as that of a two-headed Shaker church.[38]

The Kitsap faction met again at Tulalip in July 1944. Mary Krise announced that church membership cards had been credentialed by Kitsap's hand-picked secretary, Foster Jones, and that only those signed by Jones and Kitsap would be accepted. Those signed by Bennett, she said, had been voided by his election and his performance as bishop, which she termed "unlawful infringement." Krise and Jones were authorized to consult Hyland concerning such "infringement" by Bennett on "our Incorporation in his ordaining ministers and thereby obtaining supplemental mileage and other rations."[39]

The next move was Bennett's. He filed charges against Kitsap in the Snohomish County Superior Court for usurping and intruding into the office of bishop and for causing him humiliation. Bennett asked that Kitsap be excluded from exercising the privileges and franchises of the Indian Shaker Church. Bennett was represented in this action by attorney W. H. Cameron of Centralia. During pretrial hearings, the two factions agreed to an out-of-court settlement that divided the church into separate entities, as suggested by Judge Ralph C. Bell, and the case was dismissed on November 29, 1945. Under the arrangement, the Kitsap people assumed the name "Indian Full Gospel Church." Bennett's people held rights to the original name, forcing Kitsap to accept a name without "Shaker" in it.[40]

Still, all matters of the settlement had not been finalized. Both parties had agreed that each congregation in the church would nominate a delegate to attend a meeting at the Thurston County Court House on July 15, 1945. The purpose of the meeting was to vote whether or not to formally divide Shakerism into two organizations and to determine to which organization each congregation wished to belong. Delegates were given full authority to vote for the church of their choice. Those who chose to go with Kitsap's Indian Full Gospel Church were Port Gamble, Tulalip, Neah Bay,

La Conner, Colville, and Lummi. Remaining with Bennett's ISC were churches at Taholah, Chehalis, Muckleshoot, Yakama, and Skagit. Quileutes at La Push were considered too inactive to be listed. It was also agreed that each church that opted to go with the IFGC would have its properties conveyed to that church.[41]

The transfer of property was not always a simple matter. The IFGC expected to obtain a deed to two acres of land at Priest Point Park on the Tulalip Reservation. The church there, however, discovered that on August 28, 1932, Mabel J. Stiels had donated the property to the ISC and that three of its members had been named trustees for the land. Of the three, one, Alexander Johnnie, was deceased. The second, Carl Jones, signed a transfer of land to the Full Gospel Church on February 25, 1946. The third trustee caused the problem. Henry Shelton, who favored the ISC, refused to sign a transfer. On March 11, ISC trustees Alex Young and Levalla Johnny signed a deed awarding the property to the ISC. Bennett then took Kitsap and Jones to court over the disputed piece of land. Judge Bell awarded the property to the ISC.[42]

The Indian Full Gospel Church was formally incorporated on June 13, 1945. Kitsap sought to keep one foot in Pentecostalism and the other in Shakerism, apparently finding enough spiritual bonding in both to tie them together. By using the Full Gospel standard, he sought to salvage what he could in his struggle with the non-Bible-use traditionalists.

The Bishops' Fight seems to have centered less on personalities than on the use of the Bible. In the spirit of Christian charity, rancor was suppressed beneath matters of policy. Yet the struggle had dragged on, with each group believing it could win. Consequently, each had fallen exhausted and there were no clear winners. The result, however, was the emergence of definite, identifiable church congregations. Two elements prevented the breach from being total: reverence for John Slocum and the practice of shaking. Furthermore, non-Bible users continued to have high regard for the moral principles enunciated in the Bible, and it was not unusual for non-Bible users to associate with those who used it.

Although negative in many respects, the schism served to bond the Shaker Church more deeply to United States constitutional practices and to American society at large. Placing the Bishops' Fight in a positive light, Marilyn Claire Richen stated that the

The Indian Shaker Church in Washington state usually holds annual conventions in October and interim meetings throughout the year. Attending this annual convention, October 13, 1958, on the Muckleshoot Indian Reservation were (*left to right*) Johnson Mowich; Herman Goudy, of the Muckleshoot church; William Martin (later a bishop), of the church at Concrete; Horton Capoeman (also later a bishop), of the Taholah church; Clifford Tulee (also later a bishop), of the White Swan church; Clarence McKinley, of the Warm Springs church; and Ted Pulsifer, of the Skokomish church. Although some members live on the Muckleshoot Indian Reservation, others come from the greater Seattle area to attend services. (*Indian Shaker Church Archives*)

"decision to go to court was an admission that no one could win without widening the political field. It was," she stated, "an appeal to outside authority to determine legitimacy, but more important it was an effort to mobilize a new kind of support." Moreover, she concluded, the schism "was the best of the available mechanisms to bring about a restoration of the peace. Schism settled the conflict by creating a separate organization and a separate political status for each candidate. The legitimacy of each contestant was already accepted by his own faction. With schism, the court validated this

Shakers at the 1958 convention in the new Muckleshoot church house. Since 1910 annual conventions have been held in October. Those attending come from throughout the Pacific Northwest to tackle the issues of church business, to worship and heal, for friendship and feasting. Since now many have permanent employment and obligations at home, they hurry home following the convention. The early days of the Indian Shaker Church roughly coincided with the founding of the hop industry in Washington's Puyallup, Snoqualmie, and Yakima Valleys. Shakers would linger for meetings and visitations in the hop fields where they worked and extended their faith to others. (*Indian Shaker Church Archives*)

legitimacy and the legitimacy of the consensus group."[43]

But Shakerism did not come through the Bishops' Fight unscathed. The fallout for the church and its members would have long-reaching consequences.

CHAPTER THIRTEEN

Schismatic Fallout

The resolution of the Shaker schism did not end doctrinal and political contention in what had once been a unified church. The Indian Full Gospel Church (IFGC), commonly referred to as "Full Gospel"—the Bible users—had made its break from the ISC, commonly referred to as "the 1910 Church." The fracturing of the Shaker Church continued. On January 12, 1953, at White Swan, the ISC stronghold, a group of Shakers who had been restricted from reading the Bible in the 1910 Church formed the Independent Indian Shaker Church of White Swan (ISCWS), commonly called "the Independents." While the Independents remained on good terms with the 1910 Church, ill feelings remained between the 1910 group and the Full Gospels. At the same time, following the common pattern of crossover church attendance among Shakers, the Full Gospels attended the Independents' services without abandoning affiliation with their own church.

The corporate papers of the ISCWS stated that the church's purposes were the elevation of the Indian race, including its women; encouragement of temperance; maintenance of virtues such as worship of God; and adoption of the Bible as the basis of the church's teachings. In writing, joiners vowed to abide by the ISCWS's principles, which specified more numerous strictures than

Independent Shaker church house at White Swan, with dining hall on the left, August 20, 1991. Independents were one of the groups that broke away from the main body of Shakers. As is to be seen here, Independent Shaker buildings emulate those of traditional Shakers. (*Robert H. Ruby and John A. Brown*)

those of either the 1910 or the Full Gospel Churches. The Independent Church was governed by a president, vice president, treasurer, and secretary, all elected annually by a board of five directors empowered to make bylaws that could be amended or repealed by the membership. Only Indians of half-blood quantum or greater could qualify as directors.

The only unit of the Independent Church outside Washington state was on the Hoopa Reservation in northern California. In the 1970s the ISCWS bishop deserted his wife on the Yakama Reservation went to live with a Hoopa woman and became a member of that branch church. But this incident was just one of the problems facing the fledgling church. The church house on the Hoopa Reservation was burned and never rebuilt. Then a bishop fell off the Shaker temperance wagon. In 1991 the minister defected to the Seven Drum religion and the church could not find a replacement.[1] The church membership had little interest in expanding, though there were members among the Colville and the Makah.[2] A church was finally established on the reservation for the latter, but it has since been disbanded.

During the 1970s, Gerald Enick from the Skagit area visited the

Umatilla Reservation in northeastern Oregon, seeking to organize
a Shaker group there. He led a group to White Swan to counsel
with Head Elder Harris Teo. Perceiving that the group was unin-
terested in establishing a traditional 1910 Church, Teo informed
them that the Full Gospel constitution and bylaws were unlawful
in Oregon because the church was unincorporated there. He also
told them that the California church had drawn up papers as a
California corporation with articles that were in conflict with the
corporate document of the 1910 Church. Teo implied that Enick's
group should avoid that path.[3]

Returning to Umatilla, Enick realized that the needs and wishes
of his followers were incompatible with those of both the Full
Gospel and the 1910 Churches. Thus they formed a separate
group, the All Nations Shaker Church (ANSC). They wrote articles of incorporation stating that their "object, business and
purpose" was to promote the spirit of brotherhood and a closer
association of their members and to uphold the Constitution of
the United States. The ANSC's intent was to maintain law and
order, to transmit to posterity the purity and righteousness of
individual freedom, and to assist in charitable work. The ANSC operated under a three-person directorate, but otherwise it bore little
resemblance to other Shaker corporations. The articles of incorporation made clear that the church would issue no capital stock,
although no other Shaker organization mentioned such stock in its
articles of incorporation. The ANSC was more like a fraternal order or service club than a church, although its members did shake,
read the Bible, and pray for the sick. Its board members, all from
the Umatilla Reservation, included Daniel and Amelia Broncheau
and Gerald Enick, its incorporator and prime mover.[4] The ANSC
did not endure. Enick dropped out of the Shaker Church to join
a Pentecostal group, and other ANSC members joined the Full
Gospels.[5]

Drawing historical parallels is fraught with risk, but it could
be maintained that the rise of various Shaker branches after the
schism was somewhat similar to what happened following the
Protestant Reformation when its bodies challenged the catholic-
ity of the Roman church. As in the universality claimed by that
church, there was in Shakerism an attempt to bring under its blanket of faith both young and old. The Independents were the first

Shaker group to consider membership for children, the only restriction being that they have their parents' consent. Soon other Shaker groups followed the Independents' practice of accepting children as members. In the 1930s Bishop Heck had been careful to see that Shaker youth did nothing to weaken the faith. On the Warm Springs Reservation, for example, he had opposed young people singing in English. When some California youth sought to establish an organization within their own Shaker church in Crescent City, California, assistant minister Mattie Charles was so concerned that she wrote Heck about their proposed organization, explaining, "They're adding to many new ways here lately. Now some of the younger people want to have young people's meeting. I want to know if thats right. They don't want any elder people in the meeting. They say if we don't put up with it they say they're not going to be good."[6]

Despite the ISC wish to keep things as they were, its youth faced a period of greater cultural change than that experienced by their elders. This, coupled with a generational gap from which the Shaker Church was no more immune than any other religious group, posed a problem for church leaders during the twentieth century, for it was their youth to whom they looked to perpetuate their faith.

Another shift in ISC ministries was a widening of its outreach in diverse types of healings. Shakers have a long record of treating alcohol abusers, and beginning in the 1970s they shook to cure Indians living both on and off reservation who were addicted to illegal drugs. Also warning Indians of the dangers of tobacco, they shook over smokers to cure them of their habit. In 1978 R. Putman of the McNeil Island Federal Penitentiary in Washington state, at the request of the inmates, asked 1910 Church members to minister at that institution. But because the Shaker program was incompatible with penitentiary rules that banned all-night shaking activities, the visit had to be canceled. The Shaker plan of ministering in the government Indian school at Chemawa near Salem, Oregon, was abandoned for lack of space. In 1991, however, ISC members began ministering to Native Americans in the Oregon State Penitentiary at Salem.[7]

ISC administrators were deeply involved in the fallout that resulted from the years of schism. Bishop Horton Capoeman, a

Shakers cooking oysters at the Mud Bay church house, 1950, the year Bishop Frank Bennett died. Bennett had carried on the traditionalism of the 1910 Church following the term of Bishop Peter Heck. (*Indian Shaker Church Archives*)

Shaker minister and restauranteur at Taholah, succeeded Bishop Bennett, who died prior to the 1950 annual convention.[8] Capoeman undertook his official duties just as the church was beginning to recover from the schism. He had joined the church when he was sixteen and was schooled in the old ways, having known elderly Quinault tribal leaders. During his tenure as bishop, he took credit for planning, building, and rebuilding twelve churches.[9]

Capoeman called for a meeting in a cabin near the church house at White Swan on November 26, 1950, only a month after being elected. At the meeting, he sought to bring together not only the Bible-reading White Swan group, but also to bring the Full Gospels back by holding out an olive branch to their bishop, Carl Jones. The White Swan Bible readers met first with Capoeman and clarified their position of wishing to adhere to precepts of the Bible. Otis Shilow, a Warm Springs dissident, attended the meeting in order to convey Capoeman's remarks to Enoch Abraham of the ISC. Willie Waput accused Shilow of purposely misinterpreting Capoeman, claiming that Capoeman would "drop all the

Shakers celebrate the birthday of Bishop Horton Capoeman, who is shown holding the cake with candles. (*Indian Shaker Church Archives*)

Amendments to the Original articles and follow only the 1910 articles of Incorporation" if Jones would unite the ISC. Eventually, Jones was called from the church house to the meeting so Capoeman could ask him to dissolve his corporation and return Full Gospels to the original ISC. Capoeman assured him that he could still preach the Bible, yet he was careful to state that there would be no compromising with the beliefs of the original Shaker church. Jones asked for a copy of the original ISC articles of incorporation before making a decision. The result was the Full Gospels' refusal to join the ISC, and the dissidents subsequently broke from the ISC to become the Independent Indian Shaker Church of White Swan.[10]

Wade Le Roy had better relations with Capoeman. He became the secretary-organizer under the new bishop, and the two became friends. With his various positions in the church, Le Roy exerted great influence, first aiding Capoeman in administrative matters and then giving aid to Capoeman's successor, the semiliterate but deeply spiritual William Martin.[11] Le Roy had an interesting background. After returning from a tour of duty in France in World War I, he had been diagnosed as having a brain disorder and given only a short time to live. He went to a Pentecostal church in Walla Walla, Washington, where they prayed over him and reportedly cured him. After preaching for a year and a half in a Pentecostal church at Kamilchie near Shelton, Le Roy said he was directed into Shakerism by spirit power. His official conversion occurred at La Conner, despite the disapproval of a woman who spoke against him because he was white. As a visible token of his conversion, he was given a Shaker gown by members of the White Swan church.

Le Roy's responsibilities as secretary-organizer often took him from home and away from his Puyallup, Washington, surveying business. An airplane pilot, he frequently flew from place to place, where he was warmly greeted by the faithful who regarded him as a Shaker mind and spirit and revered him as a catalyst sent by God to enhance their own spirituality. Matching Le Roy's reported ability to heal was his skill in managing church publicity and policy. In fact, he often stood in for Bishop Capoeman, who it soon became clear was an alcoholic.[12]

In the early 1960s, Bishop Capoeman was taken to the Lummi Reservation, where Shakers unsuccessfully shook over him to help cure him of his drinking. He then went before the people to confess his weakness but promised to remain in office if the elders accepted him. Aware that he had violated a most important Shaker injunction against using liquor, Capoeman submitted his resignation at an annual meeting, only to have it rejected by a vote of the delegates. In 1965, he wrote First Elder William Martin asking that he be allowed to resign. Later that year, at the annual convention in October, he again asked to be relieved of his duties, but the elders and delegates again decided he should remain.[13]

When Capoeman resumed drinking the month following the convention, Le Roy called Elder Martin and then wrote State Head Elder Harris Teo that he would come to White Swan at Thanksgiving time to discuss the matter with him. On November 18, Le Roy wrote Capoeman at Taholah informing him of the meeting and assuring him that the reason for this meeting was that his followers were "all . . . behind you 100% to get [you] back on your feet again."[14]

A congregational meeting was called for December 4, 1965, at the Skokomish Indian Shaker church because of "the continued misbehavior of the elected bishop of our organization and of his neglect to take proper action to keep our organization alive and that proper action may be taken by our people to protect the rules and bylaws of our organization."[15]

Capoeman eventually succeeded in removing himself from the bishop's position because of his inability to resist alcohol. Still, it was only after he presented his resignation at the 1968 annual convention on the Chehalis Reservation that delegates finally accepted his resignation. Capoeman's experience reveals the agonizing conflict between Shakers' tolerance of wayward members, seeking every means possible to keep them in the fold, and their strong opposition to liquor. The board of elders promoted Elder William Martin to fill out the remaining two years of Capoeman's term.[16]

In 1970, Martin was elected bishop in his own right. After his death in 1974, another Yakama, State Head Elder Harris Teo, was appointed to fill the few months left in the bishop's term. Later that year, Teo was elected bishop at the annual convention. With Martin out of the picture and Teo as bishop, Le Roy lost his former clout and influence. A strong leader, Teo completely assumed church headship, and the two harbored a soft resentment toward each other.

An important era of Shaker history ended with the death of Bishop Teo in 1991. Teo's family name had been embedded in Shakerism from its beginnings, and he had resolved to hold the bishop's office for life and to control elections. Customarily, most bishops had either yielded their office or had died in it. Those who had died in office had been replaced by the first state head elder, appointed by the state board of elders to complete the unexpired term. The appointed bishop was then customarily elected bishop during an election year.[17] Teo attempted to break the precedent by arranging to have his nephew, Third State Elder Floyd Teo of Tacoma, appointed to succeed him.[18] At a meeting held on November 16, 1991, at Mud Bay, precedent won out with First State Elder Clifford Tulee's appointment as bishop, an act that polarized

Shakers arrive at Mud Bay to prepare food in the dining hall. The occasion was the October 12, 1991, funeral of Bishop Harris Teo, which was preceded by feasting. (*Robert H. Ruby and John A. Brown*)

some Shakers.

The number of bishops in the Shaker Church has been declining. Currently, there is no 1910 Church bishop in British Columbia, the last being Bert Underwood, who was near the century mark when he completed his term. Because their corporate status has lapsed, California Shakers have no bishop, and efforts to establish a bishopric in that state have failed. There is also no bishop in Oregon. The Full Gospel Church bishop administers the few churches on the Colville, Makah, Umatilla, and Nez Perce Reservations. Confined to the White Swan area, the Independents have neither bishop nor minister.

Other areas of the church have also gone through changes. The Full Gospel arm of the church experienced change in organizational matters resulting from the May 24, 1982, lapse in its corporate status for failing to file an annual report with the Washington secretary of state. The church had managed to survive under Kitsap's successors: his fellow Tulalip Carl Jones; Robert James, a Clallam; and David Nanamkin, a Colville. In the Independents' Church, Willey Miller succeeded Bishop Russell Billy, and Miller was followed by Jasper Andy who died in 1994.

Clifford Tulee (*left*) and Bishop Harris Teo (*right*). Amid political contention, Tulee succeeded Teo as bishop at the latter's death in 1991, the year this picture was taken. (*Robert H. Ruby and John A. Brown*)

Under David Nanamkin, the Indian Full Gospel Church was infused with new life with members on the Umatilla and Nez Perce Reservations and with its constitution and bylaws amended on June 3, 1989. The reconstituted church was to operate in accordance with "New Testament standards" and with a "Teen Ministry." The document was exclusive in that Indian believers were primary members, and bylaws were amended so that officers were elected in February rather than October. Elders, secretaries, treasurers, and directors were to be elected annually. If a bishop died in office, the first elder would serve in that capacity until the next quadrennial year. Annual meetings were to be held in June, and a quorum had to be present to conduct business.[19] The revised 1989 constitution adopted a new name, "Indian Full Gospel Shaker Church," finally being permitted to insert the word "Shaker" into the name of their church.

Shakerism remained within bounds of its early spread from

Bishop David Nanamkin of the Full Gospel Church standing by a prayer table in his Wapato, Washington, home. Prayer tables are central, both physically and spiritually, in Shaker worship. The Bible on the table indicates services of a Bible-use group rather than of 1910 Church non-Bible users. (*Robert H. Ruby and John A. Brown*)

Washington to British Columbia and to Oregon and northern California. To the east, the Indian Full Gospels established a spiritual beachhead on the Nez Perce Reservation. On April 23, 1969, Fay Compo, an Idaho Nez Perce, joined the Indian Full Gospel Church and was ordained a minister in 1984. Membership ranged from five to seven persons. At first, her followers received criticism from other reservation Nez Perces, but later, Compo said, many came to her for healing.

In the Tulalip Indian Full Gospel mother church, with which the Nez Perces had close ties, Ed Davis, a Snoqualmie, held services until 1987. After his death, evangelist Leotah Bustillo held services with small, but lively congregations, meeting mostly in homes at different reservation locations to which members traveled for weekend services. The Full Gospels have no churches in British Columbia or in California. They no longer wear gowns, but they do observe communion.[20]

Faye Compo, Nez Perce minister of
the first Indian Full Gospel Church
in Idaho at Lapwai on the Nez Perce
Indian Reservation, August 31, 1991.
Her group remained small compared
with the larger bodies of Roman
Catholics and Presbyterians long
established on the reservation. (*Robert
H. Ruby and John A. Brown*)

On the Colville Reservation, the Full Gospels and the 1910
Church congregations maintain a polite if distant relationship.
In 1945, the year of the schism, the church at Malott on the west
end of the Colville joined the Full Gospels. They then spread to
the Nespelem area in 1955, with members coming from Malott,
Omak, and Monse for services. The group was small but openly
expressed its IFGC affiliation.[21]

It was not until February 20, 1970, that a group was sufficiently
interested and strong enough to organize a 1910 Church on the
Colville Reservation. In 1987, that group began building a church
house on donated land in Nespelem. The 1989 convention was
held there, even though the building was not completely finished.
Earlier, the 1910 and Full Gospel congregations had shared meetings in homes and joined together for services, with leaders of
each group alternating for Sunday services. During Bible-reading
periods on Sundays, the 1910 group would leave for dinner. The
two groups had an extra measure of unity, not only because they
had joined together until the 1910 Church was established at Ne-

Nancy Nanamkin at a Shaker prayer table in her Nespelem home,
February 16, 1966. Benches such as that on the lower left were
placed along the sides and the back of the room in the same manner
as they are arranged in Shaker church houses. Unlike the furniture for which eastern Shakers are noted, that of Indian Shakers
was crude. (*Robert H. Ruby and John A. Brown*)

spelem in 1970, but also because members of each church had in
common their withdrawal from Catholicism, long an important
force on the Colville. Factionalism is not as much as factor on the
Colville as it is on other reservations.[22]

Less rooted in traditionalism, the Full Gospels placed greater
emphasis on youth programs. On the Tulalip Reservation, they
established a teen ministry and even ordained their youth to that
service.[23] Bishop Teo received numerous queries about youth activities in his 1910 Church. His policy ran counter to that of most
Christian churches that had youth activities, especially when it
came to sports programs. Believing there was a connection between competitive sports and gambling, Teo was troubled by the
resurgence of Indian gaming enterprises on reservations. On the
Tulalip Reservation, even the Full Gospels left church duties to
participate in managing the evening games. For that matter, they
were even joined by a small 1910 group, which quit meeting

altogether when the Tulalip bingo parlor was built. After that, the only occupant of the church was a caretaker.[24]

The schism, which had pitted traditionalist followers of John Slocum against those espousing Bible use, was in essence one of "use" more than "truth." Yet both factions believed they had a corner on the truth. While some hoped that the official split in the church would put personal rivalries to rest, both the Full Gospels and the 1910 church continued to face vexing problems. Fragmentation continued, and some Shakers drifted further from their traditional faith. One of the threats to that tradition was the Spirit Dance of the Smokehouse, which lured some Shakers.

The relationship between Shakerism and Smokehouse Spirit Dancing is complex. The word "smokehouse" comes from a large dwelling or meeting house in which Central and Southern Coastal Salish Spirit Dancing is held. In British Columbia, the building is also called a long house; in the States, two terms, long house and big house, are used. Attendance at both Shaker and Smokehouse ceremonies is often a quest for healing. In northwestern Washington and extending into British Columbia, it is not unusual for Shakers and Smokehouse people to attend the Smokehouse in winter and Shaker churches in summer. In Washington, smokehouses are found on the Tulalip, Swinomish, and Lummi Reservations. Ironically, the areas of Smokehouse strength correspond with a strong Catholic and Pentecostal tradition.

Some Shakers are drawn to the Smokehouse in their quest for the same thing that draws them to Shakerism: physical and spiritual healing. As anthropologist John Kew pointed out, there are close conceptual and behavioral parallels in Shaker and Spirit Dance rituals, where dancers seek supernatural power to locate sources of trouble so it can be isolated and dispersed. Pamela Amoss agreed with Kew: "[T]he two systems are not so much competitive alternatives as complementary," she said. But there are some significant differences in belief. Participants in the Smokehouse claim to see both good and evil, while some Shakers maintain that only good is found in their ceremonies. The Smokehouse group charges fees for curings, while Shakers do not. Some Shakers claim that when money for seeking Smokehouse healings runs out, the ill turn to Shakers for help. IFGC minister Leotah Bustillo told of a woman who exhausted funds for Smokehouse

Old Lummi Smokehouse. Note the roof apertures to allow smoke from fires within the structure to escape. One element of the Shaker-Smokehouse connection was the claim of Smokehouse adherents that they, like Shakers, affected cures in their traditional rites. (*Robert H. Ruby and John A. Brown*)

doctoring only to remain ill, but when she sought money to pay for a Full Gospel healing she was told there was no fee.[25]

Perhaps nothing tests the Shaker spirit of tolerance more than its members' attendance at Smokehouse ceremonies. This kind of tolerance has a long tradition in the Shaker Church, as evidenced by the church's willingness to restore backsliders to fellowship. But this tolerance only facilitates a Shaker retention of the symbiotic relationship with the Smokehouse.[26] Shaker records do not conceal its members' involvement in Smokehouse ceremonies.

A Smokehouse building was constructed on the Tulalip Reservation in 1913, for example, replacing an earlier one that had been destroyed under government bans against Indian doctoring.[27] At Neah Bay, an agent ordered Shaker minister Joe Sly to tear down his smokehouse in 1914. In 1916, Joseph Jefferson, a Lummi, told Bishop Heck that Lummis were attending Smokehouse ceremonies on Fridays and Sundays because Heck had not advised them to stay away. Jefferson later informed Heck that Lummi Shakers were "getting hotter" for the Smokehouse. He had heard, he wrote, that Shaker dancing powers were greater in the Smokehouse than were their powers to shake. Only three Shakers would not go to the Smokehouse, unlike the nine and sometimes more who went there because their husbands or wives were dancers.[28] At the White Swan convention in October 1941, Gaspar Dan confessed his wish "to work to be chairman for the Smoke house and a Shaker at the same time" and requested delegates to help him through his ambivalence with their prayers.[29]

In the 1970s, the public was made aware of Smokehouse ceremonies through the press. In December 1976, it was reported that a nineteen-year-old had died on the Swinomish Reservation during an initiation.[30] Reports of a similar death of a woman brought the FBI to the Lummi Reservation to investigate her drowning by Smokehouse people for reportedly refusing to participate in their initiation rites.[31] Also on the Lummi Reservation, a teenage girl suffered injuries in a 1982 ritual. In March 1983, another girl required hospitalization after having been bitten until her sides "felt like jelly." Six men were charged with involvement in ceremonies in which subjects were said to have sought the help of protective spirits of past warriors. It was also reported that initiates were pounded by deer-hoof rattles and forced to fast and meditate for ten days.[32]

Young people are often targeted for Smokehouse initiation, especially, it seems, on the Lummi Reservation. When Arthur and Ann Humphrey and Paul and Clara Harvey tried to protect children from the Smokehouse, they ran into a literal roadblock on the Lummi's Scott Road when the Smokehouse people served them with a temporary restraining order. The order kept them from "interfering with the physical well being . . . harassing or molesting . . . the people around the . . . smokehouse."[33]

Confronted with such accounts and with no sign of diminishing Smokehouse activity, Shakers' reaction to the Smokehouse ceremonies appeared to stiffen in the late twentieth century. At an ISC convention at White Swan on October 10 and 11, 1986, an ISC missionary was boldly cited as being affiliated with the Smokehouse. Also cited was a missionary among the Nooksacks who six years earlier had held Smokehouse ceremonies in his home, where he performed marriages and conducted funerals with his Shaker missionary license. Elder Ted Morris said that he had talked with young people on the Swinomish Reservation who had been taken for Smokehouse initiation. Especially alarming to him

Smokehouse on the Tulalip Indian Reservation, built in 1967. A Smokehouse building had been constructed on the Tulalip in 1913, but was torn down in the mid-1950s to be replaced by this structure. The 1913 Smokehouse had replaced an even earlier one destroyed under a government ban against Indian doctoring. (*Robert H. Ruby and John A. Brown*)

were statements of Swinomish elders to their youth that Shakers and Smokehouse people were one and the same. Morris took credit for having young people report to authorities that they had been "kicked, bitten and clubbed," some of them so badly that hospital physicians had also reported the abuse.[34]

It was also reported that Smokehouse people had attended Shaker meetings where they had been "very dominant and [in] control, they go up to the altar and take over . . . meetings." Bishop Teo exhorted ministers to exercise more authority in keeping order in their churches, citing La Conner as a place where anyone could walk in and the minister allowed his people to move easily between church house and smokehouse. "A person that goes to Smokehouse and Shaker church," he warned, "and mix the two together . . . won't mix, one or the other will dominate, all the time never have peace of mind." He told of "a man that went to a smokehouse in Canada and he saw what was in there, it was so evil and so bad he blacked out [and] ran out of that smokehouse [and] never went back." Because of such behavior, Teo concluded, Shakers were "forbidden to go run back and forth."[35]

Strong as Teo's anti-Smokehouse words were, they appeared to make no serious dent in Shaker-Smokehouse intermingling. On the Swinomish Reservation, Gary and Ada Wilbur were threatened with being turned over to the Smokehouse for treatment of

An interior view of the Lummi Smokehouse. Note the two fire pits and the benches along each wall. A two-bed recovery room for initiates is off to one corner. (*Robert H. Ruby and John A. Brown*)

alcohol and drug addiction. At the suggestion of Ada's mother and Paul Harvey, her initiation would "straighten up their lives." Fearful, Ada phoned Shaker Ted Morris (who would later be state elder) for help, but he postponed taking action for a day. By then, Ada had been taken to what she believed were Shakers for help. Seeing black-painted faces, she immediately knew she was in a smokehouse. Kept "incommunicado," she reported that she was beaten. When she complained of feeling ill, she was slapped. At the end of her ten-day confinement, she was so ill that she had to be hospitalized with bruised knees and welts on her legs from whippings. She also suffered from diarrhea and leukopenia, a condition in which the sufferer has insufficient white blood corpuscles. In the hospital, she told nurses and others to keep the Smokehouse people away. Nevertheless, a confrontation ensued when the Smokehouse people told the Shakers to leave Ada alone since she wanted to be with them.[36]

The conflict between some Shakers and Smokehouse Spirit Dancers in British Columbia is even stronger than that in Washington. In British Columbia, Spirit Dancing was banned from the Fraser River Canyon to southern Vancouver Island between 1884 and 1951. Canadian Spirit Dancing practitioners claimed they were simply conducting an ancient religious custom and told their mostly Christian adversaries to cease their opposition. Their Canadian and Washington state opponents cite examples of vandalism and of persons held against their will. The Spirit Dancers, however, are not without sympathy, even among the Christian clergy.[37]

The sharing of ritual participation between Shakers and Spirit Dancers continues in the 1990s.[38] But the attraction of Smokehouse practices is not the only thing troubling Shakers as the church approaches the close of the twentieth century. Equally troubling to John Slocum's spiritual successors are problems with Shaker places of worship, the interference of intruders, and prospects for the future of the Shaker Church itself.

CHAPTER FOURTEEN

Ashes, Activists,
and Attrition

Shakers faced continuing trouble as the twentieth century came to a close. To the south, for instance, a problem stemmed from termination of the Tolowa Indians' Smith River Rancheria, where the Shaker church house was located. Two lots had been assigned in parcel to the church when it was organized. When the federal government terminated the rancheria by Public Law 85-671 on August 18, 1958, the land was conveyed from the Howonquet Community to the Howonquet Community Association, with the stipulation that entities with use agreements be given title to particular lands and that allotted Indians receive deeds. The two Shaker lots were to be for religious purposes; otherwise, they would revert to the association for the Howonquet people. But the Howonquet Community Association did not recèive title to the rancheria until February 18, 1966. The association paid taxes to the state of California on the two lots after they were freed from trust status. Shakers wanted the deed to the land, but the association was not about to give it to them since the church was incorporated as a Washington state entity. The church sent Wade Le Roy, then retired in California, to resolve the matter.[1]

Under Bishop Teo, the Washington church had approved a resolution on October 16, 1976, to force the measure by bringing suit

Members of the Smith River Indian Shaker Church: *left to right*, Woodruf Hostler, Willie Norton, Frank Moorehead, Ellen Lakewater's father, Ellen Lakewater, Mr. Norton, and Frank Mitchell, and *in front*, Ben White. This church was most important in Shakerism's spread into northern California. (*Indian Shaker Church Archives*)

against the Howonquet Community Association. The 2.44 acres involved were conveyed by title to the church by court order, provided that the church reimburse the association for taxes it had paid on the lots. Not until May 1981 was the matter settled.[2]

One problem at Smith River was the attrition of members who had begun attending the Pentecostal church. Diminishing membership created another problem. In the summer of 1987, Elders Nadine Gutierrez, Shelly Morrison, and Brenda Gensow asked Bishop Teo for help in defining the roles and responsibilities of church officials as ministers, secretaries, and head elders, especially since fewer members necessitated having persons double in these positions. Teo responded that members could hold two offices, but that ministers should deal with spiritual matters, not with those pertaining to business.[3]

Paying taxes was another Shaker problem. On becoming bishop, Teo found that the church was paying thirty-five dollars a year to Washington state for each parcel of land it owned, regardless of size. This amounted to a substantial sum, which burdened the small church treasury. The taxation was relaxed when, by arrangement with a Washington state tax official, the church was

New Skokomish Indian Shaker church house dedicated in 1962. John Slocum, the founder of Shakerism, spent time on the Skokomish Reservation, receiving many of his religious precepts there as well as learning such occupational skills as logging. This church house is still in use, though many Shaker church houses have suffered from fires, floods, and general deterioration. (*Indian Shaker Church Archives*)

assessed thirty-five dollars a parcel only every three years.[4]

Another source of trouble was the condition of Shaker church houses. Those at Mud Bay and Koksilah burned down from leaking gas. The Jamestown Shaker church house burned down just before 1940, and no attempt was made to rebuild it. One of two Shaker churches on the Lummi Reservation, the Old Time Indian Church (OTIC), burned down some years ago. The other Lummi church, a hybrid Smokehouse structure run by Frank Jefferson, was not tolerated by strict Shakers and was not being used when it burned.

Other church houses were destroyed or suffered damage from vandalism, floods, and desertion of members. Loss of church properties was heavy on the eastern shores of Vancouver Island and on the western side of the lower British Columbia mainland. What formerly might have been termed the British Columbia mother

Second Mud Bay church house, circa 1950. Note the automobiles by which Shakers traveled to the bay. In earlier times they traveled to Mud Bay afoot, by boat, or by train. Boat and train travel continued into more recent years. (*Indian Shaker Church Archives*)

church at Koksilah suffered the loss of its house by fire on two occasions. When the church house up the Cowichan River burned down because of a gas leak, it was rebuilt in the mid-1980s near Duncan. The Duncan church was the only Canadian church house in use in 1992.[5] In late 1989, the Saanich church house near Sidney burned. At Chemainus, an old church house was condemned when its foundation became unsafe. Minister Nelson Alex photographed the rotting floor beams, and the building was eventually demolished.[6]

The northernmost Shaker group, at Nanaimo, met in members' homes because they were without a church house. On the British Columbia mainland, the home used by Musqueams for a church house fell into disrepair in the 1960s and was dismantled. Eventually, the Musqueams were assigned another home to use. The Squamishes built a church house with monies that Capilano Shakers received from sale of land on the northern periphery of Vancouver to make way for Park Royal, a shopping center. Until the 1990s, when dry rot forced its abandonment, the church house was used by Squamishes and sometimes by Musqueams.[7]

An indication of the Mud Bay mother church's staying power

was its recovery not only from one fire, but two, which destroyed successive replacements of the old church after it had been repaired and refurbished at midcentury. After a 1948 convening of a special meeting to repair the church house, it had been reopened and rededicated on May 21–22, 1949. But as time passed, the church had again suffered much disrepair; roof shingles and sheathing rotted away, windows were broken, some parts of the ceiling were torn down, and the prayer table and bell tower disappeared. The mess hall kitchen caved in during the 1969 annual convention. Shortly thereafter the church house was dismantled, each piece of lumber respectfully removed, and the remainder burned. Its $100,000 replacement, erected in 1971 by church members with a design and lumber donated by the Simpson Timber Company, was dedicated in 1974. But the new building was never in harmony with traditional church houses. Its destruction by fire on January 4, 1979, was believed to be caused by an overheated stove. It was rebuilt in a more traditional manner with donated labor, money, and materials. A subsequent roof replacement was paid for by Lutherans. The Tulalip 1910 church group were not so lucky finding a benefactor. When they replaced the roof on their church house in 1972, they looked to the proceeds from an October salmon bake to pay for it.[8]

California church houses fared only slightly better than did those in other places. One that burned down had been used by Independents on the Hoopa Reservation. Destruction and abandonment of other California church houses no doubt contributed to the ongoing presence of the Smith River church, its congregation held together by spiritual bonding under persons such as Charlie Bighead. Becoming its third minister shortly after 1960, he battled California tax and land problems, believing he was fighting for the survival of the church.

There was a sizable building program in northern California in 1971 under the leadership of Wade Le Roy who used his surveying skills to ensure that county legislative requirements were followed; he also arranged for several money-making projects. That same year, the old Johnson-Pecwan church house, which had stood for over a century (although originally not a Shaker building), was torn down. Some of its redwood lumber was sold to help pay for the new building. The new Johnson-Pecwan church house was

The Johnson-Pecwan church house being built in June 1972 as a memorial to Cindy Simpson, daughter of a former state elder. Cindy drowned in the Klamath River. (*Indian Shaker Church Archives*)

built in June 1972 as a memorial to Cindy Simpson, daughter of a former state elder, who had been drowned in the Klamath River. Involved in the rebuilding were churches of Sacramento and Oakland, which donated funds and labor for the project. The rapidly completed work was accomplished by eighty-four college students who brought $7,000 in donations from Sen. Jack Schrade of San Diego and his senatorial colleagues.

The Requa church house on the coast was lost in the 1945 Klamath River flood, and the Hoopa 1910 Church house was destroyed in a flood in 1955. The first attempt to rebuild the Hoopa church house came in 1971, when a special meeting was held to dedicate the land. In July, a building committee was formed and $783.64 was collected for the project. When no further action was taken, those funds were turned over to the California state church in 1977 for a new dining hall at Smith River. By the last half of the twentieth century, only two California church houses remained: the one at Smith River and the one rebuilt at Johnson. Many small groups deserted to Pentecostal churches, and the few numbers remaining in 1910 Church groups reflect this attrition.[9]

Oregon Shakers also suffered losses in membership and church houses. The Siletz church house was torn down after being severely damaged in a windstorm. The Chiloquin church house, built among Klamaths by a 1910 Church group, eventually passed to the Annie Lee Shakers. When it burned down, it was rebuilt. By the 1960s, Chiloquin Shakerism gave way to Pentecostalism. An old-time Annie Lee Shaker, Nora Hawk, attended the October 17, 1964, White Swan convention of the 1910 Church and explained that she was licensed "in the Kitsap Incorporation" as a minister. She said she was struggling to hold healing and other services to keep the church intact. Bishop Capoeman explained that she should "strike out the charter [of the Bible-reading Indian Shaker Church of Oregon] and then reorganize under the 1910 Incorporation." Wade Le Roy noted that there remained only two die-hard 1910 Chiloquin Shakers—Lula Lang and Clara Jackson. They turned church property over to an outside group, prompting Le Roy as early as 1971 to seek to retrieve the land and have it deeded to the 1910 Church. By the mid-1970s, the 1910 Church group proclaimed, rededicated, and reactivated their Smith River church, but it later passed into Pentecostal hands.[10]

A "cleansing" ritual of church houses was a matter of discussion at the annual convention in 1987 at Elwah. It was noted that a few members were using Clorox and salt, making them into a solution to symbolically cleanse church houses two or three times weekly by scrubbing the floors and walls. This practice met with the general disapproval of the assembly. In 1988, a couple from Taholah on the Quinault Reservation used Purex and spread ashes outside around the Duncan, British Columbia church house. Because the couple would not discuss their intentions with Canadian Shakers, a meeting was called with British Columbia elders, the church secretary, and the minister, Wilfred Aleck. Believing the couple was following an old spirit, the group sent a letter to Bishop Teo, reporting the activity. The elders believed that because there was danger in Purex cleansing and that it was carried on under cover of night without explanation, the practice should cease. When the couple did not desist, Shaker officials considered contacting immigration authorities. Responding to the complaints from Duncan church members, Bishop Teo counseled the use of reason and peer pressure to solve the problem. Quinault church members also voiced opposition to the practice by the same couple of using Purex and spring water to purify their church house and home altars.

The use of bleach and salt to purify church houses supposedly originated in a vision experienced by the wife of Johnson (Johnnie) Bastian on the Quinault Reservation. The use of bleach and spring water came from a trance that her husband experienced. He purified home altars by washing them down with spring water, prized for its purity. Going from house to house, he also cleansed prayer tables with the water. The man said he had learned of the use of ashes from Horton Capoeman one evening as they camped up the Quinault River. After finishing their evening cup of coffee, Capoeman had ringed their camp with the ashes, explaining that they represented the devil and protected persons within that area from evil. According to Anthropologist Pamela Amoss, the question of spiritual purification by using Purex, spring water, ashes, and salt illustrates tension between Shaker community tradition and novel practices by persons who believe they are acting under directions from an ancient spirit.[11]

In addition to the problem of maintaining its properties, the church was plagued by another problem in 1971. "We have our own deputized officers to maintain 'Law and order,'" proclaimed the report from a special meeting on June 16,

> but we need the cooperation of the parents to control the children. Last year many windshields were broken by children throwing rocks at cars on the freeway. At dedication time children damaged the new buildings and indoor toilets and other facilities. We also had complaints from neighbors of damage done by our children to their property. . . . Our children should be orderly in church services and at all times during the meetings. Children causing disturbances or damage will be detained by the officers until the parents can arrange for their release.

The report included what amounted to an apology for having to take this action, pointing out that it was necessary "to abide by our 'By-Laws' and the 'State Laws' for the protection of our meetings."[12]

Shakers continue to wrestle with old power spirits that are un-
acceptable in the Shaker faith. At White Swan, for example, a
Nooksack Shaker addressed the congregation in the dining hall
about problems with the dead, citing the need to take food outside
for them. Because the Nooksack was a strong leader, the congregation felt constrained to follow his instructions. But there was
ambivalence on the part of the congregation about whether to compromise their behavior by adopting such practices, since ancient
spirits could easily be put aside. It is important to note that this
incident did not result in the removal of the practitioner from the
congregation.[13]

Another problem came from outside the church and involved
people whose work towards socioeconomic reform set poorly with
older traditionalists on reservations. Their projects, although al-
truistically conceived, often did little to minimize the generational
gap between the elderly and the young people in a tribe. When
the Grant Peace Policy was in effect during the 1870s, Roman
Catholic, Methodist, Presbyterian, and Congregational Churches
were placed in charge of Indian agencies in the Pacific Northwest.
Caught up in sectarianism and government-imposed secularism, the policy failed. A century later, in the 1970s, the same
churches—minus the Congregationalists but with the addition of
the Lutherans—sought to end the plight of both reservation and
urban Indians. At the same time, Indian and white activists, some
of them sponsored by churches, appeared on various Pacific Northwest reservations. More extreme reformers among them would, if
necessary, abandon the policy of peace attempted a century earlier for one of war. As part of the Indian community, Shakers
were affected by the reformers' actions. Because of their religious
traditionalism, Shakers generally became the bedfellows of reservation conservatives who did not welcome reform. By the same
token, non-Shaker liberal forces allied with activists seeking to
solve continuing socioeconomic problems on the reservations.

Among activists were urban Indians who returned to reservations to join in the crusade for reform. These urbanites and their
tribal cohorts opposed Indian traditionalists and conservatives
in seeking to throw off the yoke of the Bureau of Indian Affairs
and to extend Indian sovereignty. While they did make inroads
into tribal governance on some reservations, the liberals met re-

sistance on others. When successful in their efforts, these urban Indians became consultants, and some were elected to tribal councils. Quarreling between activist and traditionalist tribal factions on the Makah and Quinault Reservations extended into organizations other than tribal councils. On the Quinault Reservation, for instance, when progressives aligned against the traditionalists, Shaker minister Robert William James sided with the traditionalists. Although sought after as a religious leader, James seemed to be so confused in his perception of things that he functioned poorly as a political leader.

Throughout this period, politically active urban Indians and whites, some of them non-Christian, composed the National Indian Lutheran Board (NILB), which was administered by a Sisseton Sioux, Eugene Crawford. The board dispensed an unsupervised, no-strings-attached, half-million dollars annually to politically active Indians working in conjunction with Indian officeholders and committee appointees. Opponents of these activists regarded them much as post–Civil War Southerners had viewed carpetbaggers from the North.

Lest one think such divisions a novelty, it should be remembered that factionalism and personality conflicts had always been found among tribal groups. Now, much like blacks in the 1950s and Hispanics in the 1960s, the Indian activists who arose to protest their own menial status and station, seeking self-determination and respect, found that their efforts resulted in polarization and brought out the worst in people. This was especially so among urban Indians and their counterparts on reservations who sought to rattle their conservative opponents even while they sought to eliminate the heavy influence of the U.S. government in Indian affairs.

Several Shakers on the Quinault Reservation, a small number of them on the Makah, and an even smaller group on the Puyallup were among those siding with the activists in the 1970s. Against an undercurrent of repression, Quinault and Makah Shakers accused tribal officers of fraud and deceit, according to Lutheran maverick Marvin Fisher. Besides hurling accusations of theft and forgery, they accused those officials of tapping telephones and opening mail. The conservatives countercharged that the progressives lacked sufficient blood quantum to be considered Indian.

Suspicions were also aroused when it was discovered that buildings had been erected on the Makah Reservation using inferior materials. A Shaker minister, Dorothy Chamblin, was given the job of inspecting buildings for the Department of Housing and Urban Development (HUD). In making her rounds, she found faulty construction in which flooring was only partially nailed down. But Chamblin was summarily fired when she said that "when we have a shake there, the people are jumping on the floor and moving, and our Indian people are heavy people, and they are going to go right through that floor. . . . "[14]

Besides criticizing the NILB and the "new Indians," the traditionalists and conservatives also criticized the Presbyterian and Catholic churches of Seattle and Seattle's Church Council, which columnist Robert Wallace of the Bellevue (Washington) *Journal American* termed "a purely political body masquerading as a religious organization."[15] Marvin Fisher, the dissident Lutheran, agreed and opposed large sums of money being transferred from his church to Indians for political purposes. Understandably, his opponents judged him to be anti-Indian and racist. In what amounted to a crusade, he found sympathizers on several reservations, many of whom had axes to grind with local tribal governments. Shakers on several reservations also jumped on his bandwagon. He accused his opponents of attempting to stop his campaign by offering him a financial interest in a motel.[16]

Undaunted by Fisher's efforts, many Lutheran and Catholic clergymen and other church officials, along with members of the Church Council of Greater Seattle, appeared before congressional committees to testify on issues of a political nature, not, as their critics claimed they should, on social issues. These critics, among them Lutherans who thought their contributions had been supporting Indian social welfare programs, reacted strongly to what they perceived as a change of policy under which the church was organizing Indian study groups to deal with political issues.[17]

On the Quinault Reservation, this came down to influencing tribal chairman Joe DeLaCruz to undertake plans, which included Shakers, having the express purpose of getting Lutheran Church funds to implement programs Shaker minister Robert James did not want. James became increasingly displeased with DeLaCruz, blaming him for trying to unseat him as minister. James also blamed Bishop Teo for siding with the Quinault tribe on various issues and latched onto Fisher's coattails.[18] Shakers, however, saw James as having disturbing attitudes and actions, and they were uncomfortable with his unusual spiritual visions. Although visions were an important element of Shakerism, James's were considered out of line. Nevertheless, in traditional Shaker manner, his people did not excommunicate him. Some Shakers believed that his problem was a mental one.

In the late '70s, three Pacific Northwest Lutheran judicatories supported tribal officers among the Quinaults and other tribes. They gave the Quinaults $89,000 to build a greenhouse. Those who supported the traditionalists feared that tribal officials were skimming funds and attempting to control projects that were funded from outside the reservation. They also feared that urban Indians who returned to the reservations wanted to revamp tribal governments and line their own pockets.

In this setting, Quinault church members had tried to collect $24,000 for a church house but had fallen about $13,000 short. Some tribal members approached Justine James (no relation to Robert), who was vice-chairman of the Quinault Business Committee. James, who was not a Shaker, became involved because the tribe was ready to condemn the dilapidated church house. He offered to seek tribal assistance for financing a new church, but Robert James opposed the help, fearing that the building would be taken over by the tribe.[19] A special meeting was held in the church dining hall on January 27, 1979, to discuss finances for building a new church. In attendance was tribal vice-chairman Justine James, who said the tribal council had designated him to go to the bank "and work with shaker people." Because church members shook and stomped, it was emphasized that a solid floor underpinned by subflooring was needed. Justine James warned that the church organization could be at the mercy of a contractor, exposing its people to legal problems. He also offered the services of tribal attorneys and the tribal inspector.

At that point, Robert James interpreted the offer as a concerted effort by tribal representatives to take over the church. Nevertheless, members present voted to use tribal funds to complete the project. The only negative vote was Robert James's.[20] Two weeks later, on February 12, the Tribal Business Committee passed Resolution 79-19, signed by tribal chairman Joe DeLaCruz, stating that it would negotiate "on behalf of the tribe" a time certificate in the amount of $13,000, using the tribal mill as collateral. The new church would be built. Bishop Teo approved the committee's decision, which disappointed Robert James. In December 1979, with James finally too ill to carry on, State Head Elder Ted Strom arrived to take over as Quinault Shaker minister.

Certain that DeLaCruz had sought his removal, Robert James wrote Marvin Fisher on November 30, 1979:

> I need a call for a May Day here in our village of Taholah.
>
> There has been changes made, here, since our Chairman, Joe DeLaCruz has taken office; things, my people do not understand.
>
> There has been a government formed here, without my people's knowledge; a State tribe is what I mean. This government and Bureau of Indian Affairs have been working together and have . . . [many] people in a very bad way. (Broke and Hungry, I mean). They have closed our river when the fish run good and opened the river when no fish were moving. People have been trying to please the tribe by selling land to said tribe for a fair market price set by Bureau of Indian Affairs people; land that is in trust to the U.S. Government.
>
> Most of the State tribes have gone to many courts in several States and have claimed the *Treaty Rights* of many Reservations and they have won. I believe they have won all said cases in all said state courts and whatever all business of these said state tribes somehow fail. Yet, all people who work for said tribes seem to have a lot of money. The Chairwoman of Puyallup, Romona Bennette [Ramona Bennett], has retired and has such funds.
>
> My Shaker members of Neah Bay have the same problems with their leaders, all projects seem to fail. Note: Bureau of Indian Affairs has pushed our church members of Neah Bay around and when they objected, one . . . [of] our ministers of the Shaker Faith in Neah Bay was put in jail, Dorothy Chaimberlin [sic], was her name. I feel that the Neah Bay people have a state tribe, also.
>
> Note: When Joe DeLaCruz came into office we did have a council and reservation, now we have a tribal government that I know we do not need.[21]

Following the emotionally charged process of ousting James, the few members who held records dealing with the incident burned them.

Although James was no longer a factor in church governance, he remained in the politically turbulent atmosphere, joining Fisher in a concerted effort to undo efforts of Lutheran Church assistance to reservation Indians. Fisher made his intentions known by filing a suit for $1 million against Bishop Clarence Solberg of the American Lutheran Church.

The suit was based on accusations that the American Lutheran Church was negligent in working with Indian leaders who lacked credibility and integrity, that separation of church and state had been breached, and that Lutheran Church funds had been used for tribal political purposes rather than being given to spiritual needs and missionary work. Numerous individual complaints were also listed.[22] Drawn into this troublesome situation, Shakers were divided; some accused DeLaCruz and others of his staff of seeking monies and other resources under the name of the Quinault Reservation. They also charged that the tribal chairman and his staff had then reallocated these acquisitions for their own purposes. On April 14, 1980, Fisher filed copies of depositions from Shaker members, alleging such offenses, in the Superior Court of King County, Washington.

Urban Indians, who many suspected had come on reservations to stir up sentiment for their cause, were ordered off the reservations, but residents, especially on the Quinault, continued their activism in the emotionally charged atmosphere. To meet what he considered to be a threat to both Indians and his church, Fisher filed complaint on September 30, 1980, amending his suit and raising the amount asked to $5 million. He added as plaintiffs Robert James, Frances Hobucket, and Robert Comenout, Snoqualmie tribal chairman. He also added as additional defendants Marilyn Bode, the inter-Lutheran coordinator for Native American concerns in the Lutheran Church, and Bishop A. G. Fjellman, president of the Pacific Northwest Synod of the Lutheran Church in America.[23]

Now DeLaCruz was accused of carrying the feud to the Snoqualmies, with tribal leaders warning that should they not abandon their support of Comenout the Quinaults would not support them in seeking federal acknowledgement. The threat was probably meaningless, when, in fact, the Quinaults and other federally recognized tribes were little interested in helping other tribes achieve that same status since their own fish allotments might be diminished under the terms of the (Judge George) Boldt decision. Comenout was ousted from Snoqualmie leadership in favor of a pro-DeLaCruz person.[24]

DeLaCruz, now called the "Ayatollah of Taholah" by his opponents, told both the *Seattle Times* and the *Post-Intelligencer* that he was resigning on October 13, 1980, because his tribal leadership had been attacked by "a small group of people." His opposition was led by Frances Hobucket, head of the Concerned Citizens of the Quinault Reservation. This group was composed not only of Shakers but also of fundamentalists on the reservation who threatened to ask for DeLaCruz's resignation. They claimed that he had chosen "to listen to technical advisers instead of the Quinault people." Three days after the news stories appeared, DeLaCruz called Marilyn Bode, Indian affairs coordinator for the Lutheran Church, advising her that Fisher should be taken seriously. But DeLaCruz did not resign his tribal chairman post.[25]

When Bode notified Dr. Solberg of the amended suit, Solberg was with NILB leader Eugene Crawford. When Fisher arranged for a KIRO-TV news conference on October 3 with a representative of the Interstate Congress for Equal Rights and Responsibilities, church personnel judged the conflict to be not intra-Lutheran but, as Bode believed, a nationwide backlash organized by non-Indians. For Bode, advocacy of Native American efforts involved political activity differing from ministrations to other minorities. But Fisher disdained the "unfair influence over tribal governments" used by urban and other Indians as well as the misuse of funds to promote their own programs.[26]

News of the Lutheran Church suit over tribal funding reached across the country. To help counteract such news, Bode wrote friends of the church, citing "Lutheran credibility" and hoping that urban activists such as Mary Jo Butterfield on the Makah Reservation and DeLaCruz on the Quinault would not abandon their efforts. Supported by the Concerned Citizens of the Quinault Reservation, Fisher continued to dog Lutheran Church meetings, even though church leaders refused to yield the floor to him.[27]

To defend himself, especially against Shaker officials, DeLaCruz wrote Bishop Teo, describing Fisher as one whose intent was to "destroy our Indian Nation" and aligning himself with persons seeking "our remaining lands and rights in the name of equality." It was "unfortunate," DeLaCruz wrote, "that our misguided members bring the Indian Shaker church into an area they don't understand." "Traditional Indian people," he went on, "understand the fine line separation between religion & political leaders in the old days." He then went on to tell how the "spiritual leader gave guidance, support and prayers to leaders who had to walk another path on this great circle [and], maybe when our people come to understand this again there will be harmony" among them. Then, on an almost benedictory note, he concluded: "My heart is out to you and the church. I hope your prayer is with us as ours be with you. May you continue your walk with the lord."[28]

DeLaCruz explained the problem as a Shaker Church argument carried over from the Bishops' Fight, with Quinaults as a tribe having no involvement in it. Shaker Church fighting, he maintained, was "an internal political dispute amongst Shakers themselves" in which their elders ousted their minister, Robert James. The entire matter rested in changing church leadership (as that which found minister Robert James and Bishop Harris Teo on opposing sides). He perceived the conflict as being between traditionalist Shakers and Shaker Bible users. "I stay out of it," he claimed, explaining that "church politics amongst the Shakers gets pretty thick."[29]

There was a widening of what DeLaCruz called the "fine line separation between religion & political leaders." Under white cultural influences, the separation of the Shaker Church from the state—beyond the necessity of filing articles of incorporation, paying marriage license fees, and so on—had altered for Shakers the close political-religious bonding found in native society. Moreover, progressives who advocated sociopolitical reform in the Indian community jeopardized the Shakers' goal of "elevat[ing] the Indian race of this State and of the North West."[30]

The period of activism on the reservations lasted from the '70s through the mid-1980s. As far as Shakers were concerned, they had virtually no part in its promotion; its impetus had come from outside the membership of the church and the reservations. Nonetheless, Shakers were affected by it. The activism caused them to align with conservatives in order to protect their traditional practices. What Shakers could not prevent, however, was the government's new leniency toward native religious practices, which attracted some Shakers and lessened membership in the church during what might be termed a neo-shaministic period.

In September 1991, Jasper Andy, new bishop of the White Swan Independent Shaker Church, said that its young minister had left the 1910 Church to join the Seven Drum religion. Shaker Independents were falling apart, he said, with fewer and fewer dedicated workers. "They are all joining the native church," he lamented. Some Shakers had also defected to the Smokehouse and to non-Shaker Christian churches, especially the Pentecostals.[31]

Rapid change in both Indian and non-Indian society has threatened to unravel the threads of the robe woven and worn by John Slocum. Wade Le Roy, in seeking to explain the decline in church ranks, pinpointed education. Education, he said, had negated and threatened the revelatory aspects of Shakerism, citing the Biblical passage, "The letter killeth," to prove his point.[32]

Le Roy's assessment notwithstanding, other factors have contributed to Shaker attrition, leaving Shakers hard put to retain and practice the principles advanced by John Slocum. Many of these factors may be attributed to the non-Shaker community, of which Shakers themselves have become a part. In Slocum's day, opponents of the Shaker Church were easily identified as a skeptical public and a restrictive government. In the late twentieth century, however, opposition became more subtle, coming in the form of materialism, secularism, tribal and family dysfunction, and, not least, an increasing temptation on the part of Shakers to turn to modern medicine instead of trusting traditional healing practices.

Will the tides of time, like those washing upon the beaches of John Slocum's homeland, erode the impact, vitality, and memory, of his religion? Or will Shaker roads, like those Slocum cleared in the forest, be swept of the tangle of underbrush by his spiritual descendants who stand now at a major crossroads?

Afterword

Indian Shakerism has existed for over a century of time and a thousand miles of space. It remains to be seen if John Slocum's legacy will endure. Among the various "particles" falling out of Shakerism is the debate over whether the church is Christian or not. Many non-Shakers believe it does not qualify as Christian, believing that it retains too much of the aboriginal. According to Shaker Harold Patterson,

> the cosmology of the Indian people is animistic . . . [meaning] that they believe in the elemental spirits of the universe which dwell in the rocks, trees, rivers and the animals etc. When the people became Shakers the world view did not change [since] they still live in the same world. I think that is what John Slocum meant when he said an Indian can be a Christian because he did not have to renounce those things which he knew to be true about the world.[1]

While some may judge the Shaker church and its principles harshly, no one should minimize the role its founders played in leaving their imprint on an important Indian religious movement.

John Slocum and Mary Thompson have been lionized as cofounders of Shakerism. Certainly their role in its founding should not be minimized. Yet their religion did not emerge in a vacuum,

for they built on aboriginal precedents, however weak they might
have been. Their good fortune was that their religion arose at the
right time in history and at a place where it could be introduced
to the larger non-Indian community surrounding them. Although
many Shakers believed their religion should stand on its Indian
bases, they were forced to recognize the significant efforts of a few
early non-Indian advocates.

Shakerism's staying power may be attributed to the twin practices of shaking and healing, which developed not only physical
stamina in the church's adherents but also spiritual stamina.
Shakerism's survival can also be attributed to its ability to adapt
to the demands of an alien culture. Although its shaking practices
have changed little over time and place, Shakerism has managed
to remain viable in the midst of great societal change. Near the
beginning of the twentieth century, Indian Agent O. C. Upchurch
noted that such tradition was based on

> the surrender of the individual to his individual spirit and his idea of
> it in the old ceremonial to a surrender of the group of individuals to
> the approved community conception of how the "Power of The Spirit"
> may be manifested in physical acts. There is a two-fold transition;
> from the individual to the community (although there are distinc-
> tions of type in individual reactions) and from the multi-spiritual
> concept to that of one Supreme Spirit.[2]

Only those with prophetic insight can predict the future of
Shakerism as it stands on the threshold of a new century. We
would suggest that the increasing racial heterogeneity of its membership, their improved self-image, and their tolerance by the
non-Shaker community pose lesser threats to Shakerism than
does a diminished spirituality. The question posed to the faithful
is this: Can we, who healed the sick by the power of "one Supreme
Spirit," immunize our faith from social ills pressing in upon it?
More simply put: Can we retain the life and vitality of John Slocum
at the time of his near-death experience?

If anything, there is as much rationale today for the existence
of Shakerism as there ever was. Many problems facing Indians
during the early days of the church continue to plague the tribes.
The Shakers' emphasis on temperance still finds relevance on the
reservations, and it is encouraging to see Shaker young people

turning their backs on liquor and other drug use. In a larger
sense, for Indians the spiritualism found in Shaker healing ceremonies can be an antidote to the materialism pervading the larger
American society.

With their candles to light the way, it is hoped that Slocum's
followers will travel roads leading to the fulfillment of their faith—
not to its destruction. Continued and renewed spirituality does
not lessen responsibility resting on Shakers themselves as well
as on others who must regard them tolerantly. Like all others on
spiritual quests, Shakers

> Must light to men
> The fires no other can
> And find in . . . [their] own eye
> Where the strange crossroads lie.
> —*Communion*

Notes

N.B. Folder numbers specified in Indian Shaker Church Archives (ISCA) citations refer only to those copies in possession of the authors. The original papers are being held in the Washington State Historical Society, Tacoma, WA. They are subject to reorganization.

Abbreviations

ISC   Indian Shaker Church
ISCA   Indian Shaker Church Archives
ISCR   Indian Shaker Church Records
KIA   Klamath Indian Agency
NBIAR   Neah Bay Indian Agency Records
TIA   Tulalip Indian Agency
WSIA   Washington Superintendency of Indian Affairs
YIA   Yakama Indian Agency

Chapter One John Slocum and the
Beginnings of the Indian Shaker Church

1. James Mooney, "The Shakers of Puget Sound," 752. Mooney placed the year of Slocum's "death" at 1881 (ibid., 746). Anthropologist Homer G. Barnett did likewise in *Indian Shakers*, 23. We accept the year 1882, as given in Myron Eells's notation in his journal (Journal 8, December 7, 1882). Eells wrote of considerable excitement at about the time

when Slocum of Skookum Bay died "two or three weeks ago," prior to his journal entry, making it November; Myron Eells Papers, Box 2). Indian Shaker Church (ISC) records confirm the date as October 20, 1882. See Indian Shaker Church, Mud Bay, Washington, Records, Folders 4–7, Indian Shaker Church Records, Ms. 118, Washington Room, Washington State Library, Olympia.

2. Charles D. Rakestraw, "The Shaker Indians of Puget Sound," 704.

3. *Mason County Journal* (Shelton, WA), October 27, 1893.

4. Rakestraw, "Shaker Indians of Puget Sound," 705.

5. Ibid.; Mooney, "Shakers of Puget Sound," 752.

6. Daniel L. Dawley, "Some Ante-Mortem Good Indians," 22.

7. Nancy George gave her eyewitness account of Slocum's death to Jean Todd Fredson in "The Religion of the Shakers," Folder 1, ISCR. Slocum died at ten o'clock one evening and awoke at six o'clock the next morning. See Indian Shaker Church Archives, Folder 48, "Historic Events," Washington State Historical Society, Tacoma. Most accounts give a death period of six to eight hours, but some extend it to as many as three days. Myron Eells recorded that Slocum was "dead six to seven hours" (Journal 8, December 7, 1882). Dick Lewis, an ardent early convert from shamanism to Shakerism, said Slocum was dead for six hours (Records of the Memorial Meeting of the Shaker Church, Skokomish Indian Reservation, August 21, 1913, Folder 27, ISCA). Edwin L. Chalcraft, head schoolmaster on the Chehalis Reservation, gathered testimony of several Indians at Mud Bay and concluded that Slocum had died at four o'clock in the morning and had awakened "at mid-afternoon" (Edwin Chalcraft, "Memory's Storehouse," 24). Yet Chalcraft also reported two days, as related to him by Pike Ben, a Chehalis (Chalcraft, Diary, February 19, 1888). After interviewing Shakers, Jean Todd Fredson stated that Slocum was dead for one whole day, from noon to noon (Fredson, "Religion of the Shakers," 7). Mooney reported that the "death" lasted about twelve hours, from four in the morning to late the following afternoon (Mooney, "Shakers of Puget Sound," 752). Slocum's sister-in-law, Annie James, claimed that Slocum was dead for a day or two (Frank Bennett, "Beginning of Shaker Faith among the American Indians," ISCR). Accounts of most Pacific Northwestern native prophets who "died" give a three-day "death" period. Only Werdna Finley, who befriended Shakers and wrote their history, records a three-day death for Slocum (Finley, "As My Sun Now Sets," 229).

8. Records of the Memorial Meeting, Folder 27, ISCA.

9. Finley, "As My Sun Now Sets," 230.

10. Bennett, "Beginning of Shaker Faith," ISCR.

11. Mooney, "Shakers of Puget Sound," 753.

12. When Slocum was "resurrected," a messenger was sent to Olympia, Washington Territory, to intercept the two men who had been sent there to purchase a coffin. (Barnett, *Indian Shakers*, 21)

13. Sarah Endicott Ober, "A New Religion among the West Coast Indians," 594.

14. Myron Eells, "Indians of Puget Sound, Notebook 6, 90–92; Mooney, "Shakers of Puget Sound," 753.

15. Marilyn Claire Richen, "Legitimacy and the Resolution of Conflict in an Indian Church," p. 1; Barnett, *Indian Shakers*, 18, 21; Erna Gunther, "The Shaker Religion of the Northwest," 40; Chalcraft, "Memory's Storehouse," 25; "Birth of the Indian Shaker Church," *Seattle Times*, May 2, 1971, 24; Rakestraw, "Shaker Indians," 703.

16. Physician Raymond A. Moody, Jr., explained the syndrome in 1975 in *Life after Life* and later conducted more extensive interviews with subjects who had experienced it. Psychologist Kenneth Ring conducted a similar investigation, confirming and reinforcing Moody's studies. In 1990, Seattle physician Melvin Morse published a study of children who had experienced "deaths" similar to Slocum's (Raymond A. Moody, Jr., *Life after Life*, *The Light Beyond*, and *Reflections on Life after Life*; Kenneth Ring, *Heading toward Omega* and *Life at Death*; Melvin Morse, *Closer to the Light*).

17. Mooney, "Shakers of Puget Sound," 752.

18. Ring, *Life at Death*, 56–60, 71; Morse, *Closer to the Light*, 27; Moody, *Reflections on Life*, 6. Prior to his "death," Slocum was reportedly a "confirmed gambler," a man of "sporty proclivities, with a powerful and consuming thirst for fire water" who lived a life of "wicked ways." See "Indian Shaker Sect," *Mason County Journal*, October 27, 1933. See also Rakestraw, "Shaker Indians of Puget Sound," 705.

19. Rakestraw, "Shaker Indians," 706; Ring, *Heading toward Omega*, 50–55; Ring, *Life at Death*, 59.

20. Moody, *Light Beyond*, 27; Ring, *Heading toward Omega*, 8.

21. Ring, *Heading toward Omega*, 90.

Chapter Two Pacific Northwest Native
Religion and Early Christian Missionaries

1. Ella Clark, *Indian Legends of the Pacific Northwest*, 46.

2. Myron Eells, "Do-Ki-Batt: Or, The God of the Puget Sound Indians," 392. A modern interpretation of the Changer is given by anthropologist Pamela Amoss, who cited an equivalence between Christ and the Changer and even John Slocum. She wrote that among early accounts of the founding of Slocum's church is the claim that the faithful expected the world

to end soon, the dead to rise, and unbelievers to be changed into animals, "but the specific punishment of unbelievers by turning them into animals is rare enough to suggest a more than coincidental comparison of Slocum with the Changer, who, as part of establishing the order of the cosmos, changed myth-age people into animals" (Pamela Amoss, "Resurrection, Healing, and 'the Shake': The Story of John and Mary Slocum," 101).

3. Myron Eells, "Indians of Puget Sound," Notebook 6, 94. Many native rituals associated with health and curing are fairly well documented and described, many of them by Reverend Eells.

4. It was believed that persons suffering loss of the soul would die if their souls were not recovered. See Edwin Eells, "Skokomish and Clallam Tribe Attitudes towards U.S. Government and Religion." Among Skokomishes, guardian spirits that granted powers to shamans were different from and less elaborate than guardian spirits that granted powers to laypeople. Shaman spirit power enabled its practitioner to cure or induce illness and even to bring on death. In fewer instances, the power to cause illness might not be accompanied by the power to cure. See W. W. Elmendorf, "The Structure of Twana Culture," 500–501.

5. Elmendorf, "Structure of Twana Culture," 516, 517; E. A. Starling to Isaac I. Stevens, December 10, 1853, Letters from Agents, Washington Superintendency of Indian Affairs (hereafter cited as WSIA), No. 5, Roll 9; Myron Eells, "The Religion of the Clallam and Twana Indians," 13.

6. Myron Eells, "Indians of Puget Sound," Notebook 6, 105. Even before Eells arrived on the scene, a period of disenchantment had followed the natives' introduction to Christianity, for they believed it had failed to bring them a hoped-for powerful "medicine." This disenchantment was not shared by John Slocum's followers, but Slocum's religion contained significant references to elements of native spirituality and tradition. For an account of Skokomish soul beliefs, see Elmendorf, "Structure of Twana Culture," 514–21. On the Black Tamahnous ceremony, see Mooney, "Shakers of Puget Sound," 748; Johnson Williams, "Black Tamanous, the Secret of the Clallam Indians," 296–300.

7. T. T. Waterman, "The Paraphernalia of the Duwamish 'Spirit-Canoe' Ceremony," 135, 146.

8. Marian W. Smith, "Shamanism in the Shaker Religion of Northwest America," 121.

9. Wilfred P. Schoenberg, S.J., *A History of the Catholic Church in the Pacific Northwest, 1743–1983*, 9.

10. Clarence B. Bagley, ed., "Documents-Journal of Occurrences at Nisqually House," *Washington Historical Quarterly* 6: 272, 274–75; 7: 70. The journal noted that the Indians used the devotional dance as the mode to show "they were pleased that they knew who their Creator was." See

Bagley, 7: 158.

11. Harry Holbert Turney-High, *The Flathead Indians of Montana*, 41–42; Robert Ignatius Burns, S.J., *The Jesuits and the Indian Wars of the Northwest*, 16; Leslie Spier, *The Prophet Dance of the Northwest and Its Derivatives: The Source of the Ghost Dance*, 30.

12. *Notices & Voyages of the Famed Quebec Mission to the Pacific Northwest*, 36–37.

13. Ibid., 40.

14. Ibid., 40, 47.

15. Charles Wilkes, *Narrative of the United States Exploring Expedition during the Years 1838, 1839, 1840, 1841, 1842*, vol. 4, 307, 354.

16. Dorothy O. Johansen and Charles M. Gates, *Empire of the Columbia*, 2d ed., 164.

17. *Notices & Voyages*, 59, 60, 64, 99. For a general discussion of important communication problems between missionaries and Indians, see Michael C. Coleman, "Not Race, but Grace: Presbyterian Missionaries and American Indians, 1837–1893," 48.

18. *Notices & Voyages*, 59.

19. Ibid., 60, 65, 70.

20. Wilkes, *Narrative*, 480.

21. *Notices & Voyages*, 99, 190, 194.

22. Ibid., 196.

23. Schoenberg, *History of the Catholic Church*, 129, 153.

24. E. A. Starling to Isaac I. Stevens, December 4, 1853, Letters from Agents, WSIA, No. 5, Roll 9. Other diseases also struck the tribes. In his annual report of August 31, 1879, the physician for the Puyallup Reservation, on which some Squaxins lived, reported the most prevalent diseases as syphilis, rheumatism, diarrhea, and those cutaneous in nature. Also prevalent and deadly were venereal, ocular, and scrofulous diseases, the latter being the most fatal. (Franklin C. Purdy to Calvin H. Hale, Washington Superintendent of Indian Affairs, November 25, 1862, Letters from Employees Assigned to the Skallam Agency [Skokomish Reservation] Serving Tribes Parties to the Treaty of Point No Point, April 30, 1861–June 1, 1874, WSIA, No. 5, Roll 13; Byron Barlow to R. W. Milroy, October 1, 1873, in Barlow, Annual Report, 1873, Letters from Employees Assigned to the Puyallup Agency [Puyallup, Nisqually, and Squaxin Reservations] Serving Indian Parties to the Treaty of Medicine Creek, December 31, 1856–August 31, 1874, WSIA, No. 5, Roll 11)

25. Wesley B. Gosnell to Isaac Stevens, March 31, 1857, WSIA, No. 5, Roll 13; Gosnell to Col. J. W. Nesmith, June 30, 1857, in *Annual Report of the Commissioner of Indian Affairs*, 1857, 626–27. John Slocum may have been at Medicine Creek when the treaty was signed, along with

his brothers, Tom and Jack, and Old Slocum. Other important figures in Shakerism were also there, including Chief Old Bob, Mud Bay Louis, Mud Bay Sam, and Dick Johnson. See *Mason County Journal*, May 31, 1901.

26. For information on the Peace Policy, see Robert H. Ruby and John A. Brown, *Indians of the Pacific Northwest*, 175n., 229 ff.

Chapter Three The World of John Slocum

1. For the whereabouts of Squaxins during the war, see Robert H. Ruby and John A. Brown, *A Guide to the Indian Tribes of the Pacific Northwest*, 221–22. By Resolution T-053-94, enacted on January 14, 1994, the Yakama people changed the official spelling of their name. Where it appears in quoted material the authors have retained the use of "Yakima"; in all other instances, the term "Yakama" is used in referring to the tribe.

2. Johansen and Gates, *Empire of the Columbia*, 607; George Ficken and Charles LeWarne, *Washington: A Centennial History*, 25.

3. See Robert H. Ruby and John A. Brown, *Indian Slavery in the Pacific Northwest*; Quincy A. Brooks to Wesley B. Gosnell, September 30, 1857; Gosnell to Nesmith, September 30, 1857, WSIA, No. 5, Roll 1. Later, Squaxin children were sent to the Skokomish Indian Reservation for schooling. Reverend Eells discussed the population makeup of the Skokomish Indian Reservation in his "Indians of Puget Sound," 3.

4. Chouse reportedly died about 1877 (*Mason County Journal*, March 11, 1887). Because many Indians bore the title "chief" and early records sometimes did not give both native and English names, it is difficult to learn more about Chouse's identity. It is possible that Chouse was Old Kettle, a prominent Squaxin chief of the 1850s. (See *Mason County Journal*, June 22, 1900.) Chouse's name may have been taken from Father Chirouse, who by the 1860s was well known among Puget Sound Indians. Origins of the name "Slocum" are equally uncertain. Fort Nisqually records of the 1840s list a Mr. Slocum, probably Polly Slocum, an Indian chief who supervised a work gang for the Hudson's Bay Company's Puget Sound Agricultural Company, which headquartered at Fort Nisqually only a few miles from John Slocum's homeland. In the spring of 1847, Mr. Slocum and his six-man crew took the Dolphes Brice Hannah party in a large canoe through Puget Sound and out to present-day Port Townsend, Washington, on the Strait of Juan de Fuca. See Victor J. Farrar, ed., "The Nisqually Journal," 206–207; Elwood Evans, *History of the Pacific Northwest: Oregon and Washington*, vol. 2, 363.

5. There were also two girls in the family (Gunther, "Shaker Religion," 38n; *Mason County Journal*, March 11, 1887; Jean Todd Fredson, "Auntie Slocum," ISCR).

6. Fredson, "Auntie Slocum," ISCR.

7. Mooney, "Shakers of Puget Sound," 751; Edwin Eells, Autobiography Supplement. Head flattening continued among some Puget Sound Indians into the 1870s. See D. N. Egbert, Annual Report, 1869, WSIA, No. 5, Roll 13.

8. *Council Fire* (Washington, D.C.) 1 (December 1878): 184. A group of thirty Indians from British Columbia canoed down to work in the large Port Blakely mill on the southern end of Bainbridge Island. They held religious services every Sunday and weekday evenings (*Council Fire* 1 (March 1878): 47).

9. For a listing of wages paid in logging camps in 1887, see *Mason County Journal*, March 11 and October 7, 1887. See also *Annual Report*, U.S. Commissioner of Indian Affairs, 1882, 226; Edwin Eells, Autobiography Supplement, 7–9, 33. It is likely that few Squaxins worked in the mills because there were few such operations in the area, and most of the logs cut were sent to mills elsewhere.

10. *Annual Report*, U.S. Commissioner of Indian Affairs, 1864, 205.

11. John T. Knox to Wm. W. Waterman, Washington Superintendent of Indian Affairs, November 6, November 7, 1865, WSIA, No. 5, Roll 13. In the latter half of 1856 and first half of 1857, eighteen to twenty Squaxins died from consuming whiskey (Gosnell to Nesmith, September 30, 1857, WSIA, No. 5, Roll 11). A decade later, whiskey peddlers remained in the area. Indians at Port Townsend on the Strait of Juan de Fuca were described as being in a "deplorable condition" and "drunk all the time," "cutting and killing one another almost every day," (Knox to Calvin H. Hale, May 24, 1864, WSIA, No. 5, Roll 13).

12. Edwin Eells, Autobiography, Box 1, Book 3, Folder 5, 177.

13. Myron Eells, Journal 6, August 1, 1873; Journal 7, February 18, 1878.

14. Ibid.

15. Edwin Eells, Autobiography, Box 1, Book 4, Folder 7, 200.

16. Eells, Notebook 6, 63. For an explanation of the Peace Policy in the Pacific Northwest, see Ruby and Brown, *Indians of the Pacific Northwest*, 228 ff.

17. Myron Eells, Journal 6, August 22, 1875.

18. Myron Eells, *Ten Years of Missionary Work among the Indians at Skokomish, Washington Territory*, 158. Pascal Ricard, O.M.I., chose Priests Point on Budd Inlet, near Mud Bay, for the new mission. The Diocese of Nisqually was created in Rome on May 31, 1850, to which Reverend Eugene Chirouse, O.M.I., was sent in 1857. Schoenberg, *History of the Catholic Church*, 121, 129, 152.

19. Historian Harry W. Deegan wrote that Chirouse came to Hood

Canal as early as 1850, establishing missions among Twana and Skokomish Indians, baptizing a number of natives, and consecrating several
to the priesthood (Harry W. Deegan, *History of Mason County, Washington*, 46).

20. Myron Eells, Journal 6, December 9, 1874, January 18, 1876.

21. Records of the Memorial Meeting, August 21, 1913, Folder 27, Skokomish Indian Reservation, ISCA.

22. Myron Eells, Journal 7, August 15, 1881.

23. Ibid., "Indians of Puget Sound," Notebook 6, 66; Spier, *Prophet
Dance* 49; Myron Eells, Journal 7, May 10, 1880, June 21, 1881.

24. According to Eells, who called the experience "perhaps a night-
mare," Big Bill's vision occurred about fourteen weeks before his natural
death in mid-June 1881. See Myron Eells, Journal 7, June 21, 1881. Big
Bill's prophecies were made in 1880 after he had been ill from tuberculosis for a long time. (Yvonne Klan, "The Shakers," 20)

25. Myron Eells, Journal 7, June 21, 1881; idem., "Indians of Puget
Sound," Notebook 6, 68–75.

26. Myron Eells, "Indians of Puget Sound" Notebook 6, 71–80.

27. Ibid., 75.

28. Ibid., 79, 80.

29. Ibid., 71–80, 85–89. Though one account says that Sandyalla wrote
Big Bill's name in a book, another says that he placed the name in "something egg-shaped" and "sent" it to heaven. In files of the Indian Shaker
Church archives is a short account of Big Bill's death as given by Tenas
Pete, titled "The Sermon of Big Bill," which was related on October 7,
1913, almost two months after the August 1913 Memorial Meeting. The
account was rewritten in a somewhat refined form and retitled "The
Prophecy of Big Bill." According to this account, the prophecy was given
when Big Bill tried to commit suicide, supposedly in August 1879, although other accounts date it to March 1881.

30. Myron Eells, "Indians of Puget Sound," Notebook 6, 75. Paraphras-
ing Eells, Spier wrote that Big Bill repudiated shamanism (Spier, *Prophet
Dance*, 49).

31. Myron Eells, "Indians of Puget Sound," Notebook 6, 49–52.

32. Ibid., Eells, Journal 7, August 15, 1881.

33. Edwin Eells to Gen. O. O. Howard, September 21, 1876, 159; Edwin
Eells to Edward P. Smith, Commissioner of Indian Affairs, February 14,
1877, 182; Edwin Eells to Howard, March 9, 1877, 184–85; all in Edwin
Eells, Record Book of Skokomish Indian Affairs, 1869–1878, 159, Edwin
Eells Papers.

34. George A. Pettitt, "The Quileute of La Push, 1775–1945," 97.

35. "Shaker Faith Nearing Its End, " *Seattle Post-Intelligencer*, Decem-

ber 24, 1907, 15.

36. Myron Eells, Journal 8, December 7, 1882.; Gunther, "The Shaker Religion," 40; Rakestraw, "Shaker Indians," 704; *Mason County Journal*, December 10, 1897.

37. Edmond S. Meany, "Twana and Clallam Indians, Aborigines of Hoods Canal," pamphlet file, Northwest Collections, University of Washington Libraries, Seattle.

38. Rakestraw, "Shaker Indians," 704.

Chapter Four Reviving a Struggling Church

1. Annie James, "Beginning of Shaker Faith," ISCR. On April 9, 1944, at Taholah, Annie James, sister-in-law of John Slocum and an eyewitness to the events, gave her story to Bishop Frank F. Bennett who recorded it. The same story appeared in the *Seattle Times*, May 2, 1971.

2. Gunther, "Shaker Religion," 40. Of the many explanations for the cause of Slocum's illness, only one specifically mentions trauma. Another suggests trauma in a report of a possible head injury. At the Memorial Meeting, August 21, 1913, an unidentified Shaker said that "blood was coming from [Slocum's] mouth and his nose and ear." (Records of the Memorial Meeting, Folder 27, ISCA) There are several mentions of Slocum succumbing to a broken neck, and one specifically mentions a fall from a horse. See Olive Branson, "True Shakers Faith Has Not Been Shaken," *Oregon Journal* (Portland), December 23, 1945. Joe Simons cited a broken neck caused by a shaman with whom Slocum had argued. See Minutes of the Annual Convention, Taholah, October 20–22, 1950, 8, Folder 50, ISCA. Although the details of Slocum's two crises may never be clarified, it is fairly well established that Mary Thompson played a role in his survival of these critical illnesses. Dick Lewis corroborated her words in Records of the Memorial Meeting, ISCA, Folder 27.

3. Harris Teo, interview with authors, Moses Lake, Washington, April 24, 1991; James, "Beginning of Shaker Faith," ISCR.

4. Myron Eells, Journal 8, December 7, 1882; Barnett, *Indian Shakers*, 32–33.

5. Barnett, *Indian Shakers*, 33; *Seattle Times*, May 2, 1971; James, "Beginning of Shaker Faith," ISCR. The beach at Church Point (now called Lighthouse) where the shake came to Mary Thompson was dedicated by church officials on June 30, 1995.

6. Barnett, *Indian Shakers*, 33; James, "Beginning of Shaker Faith," ISCR.

7. Barnett, *Indian Shakers*, 33; James, "Beginning of Shaker Faith,"

ISCR, Pettitt, "Quileute of La Push," 97; Fredson, "Religion of the Shakers," ISCR, Folder 1.

8. Annie James said that on becoming a prophet Slocum foretold several events. See Bennett, "Beginning of Shaker Faith," ISCR. If he did make prophecies, he did not do so for long. He may have had some vision of future conditions and happenings, since visions were more personal expressions of divine guidance than they were predictions and a pattern for all Shakers. (Spier, *Prophet Dance* 50)

9. Statement of Joe Young, August 23, 1913, Records of the Memorial Meeting, Folder 27, ISCA.

10. Statements of Dick Lewis, August 23, 1913, and Billy Adams, August 25, 1913, ISCA, Folder 27.

11. June McCormick Collins, "The Indian Shaker Church: A Study of Continuity and Change in Religion," 410. The belief in Thompson's power so weakened shamanism in the area that some of its practitioners became Shaker healers. Perhaps it was symbolic of the change that Shakers replaced the sounds of shaking rattles and rhythmic beating of sticks that accompanied shamans' incantations with the tintinnabulation of bells.

12. Darleen Fitzpatrick, "Indian Shakerism: God, the Spirit and Other Sacred Symbols," 12.

13. T. T. Waterman, "The Shake Religion of Puget Sound," 505.

14. Waterman, "Paraphernalia of the Duwamish," 553–54. Waterman discussed the arrangement of shamans and their trappings, explaining the sequence of the three-phase journey: (1) journey to the Land of the Dead, singing patients' supernatural songs as their souls or minds sank down through the earth to reach the trail of the dead; (2) confrontations with ghosts, and (3) their return journeys. Waterman reported that shaking occurred with soul recovery in ceremonies in which shamans sought certain spirit power "helps" for their clients.

15. Waterman, "Shake Religion," 506.

16. Jay Miller, *Shamanic Odyssey: The Lushootseed Salish Journey to the Land of the Dead*, 17.

17. Smith, "Shamanism in the Shaker Religion," 121.

18. William C. Miller, Agency Farmer, Skokomish Reservation, to William B. Freer, Superintendent, Klamath Agency, March 4, 1917; Klamath Indian Agency (hereafter cited as KIA); Pamela Amoss, *Coast Salish Spirit Dancing: The Survival of an Ancestral Religion*, 44–45; Dale Valory, *The Focus of Indian Shaker Healing*, 89.

19. Collins, "Indian Shaker Church," 403.

20. "Chaddon" is the spelling Shakers first used in 1892 (Finley, "As My Sun Now Sets," 225). Non-Shaker Indians called Shakerism the "shake" (or the "shakes"). See *Mason County Journal*, October 27, 1893. Fred-

son provided information on "Slocum Tum-Tum" in her "Religion of the Shakers" (ISCR, Folder 1). Mooney used the spelling "Tschaddam" in his "Shakers of Puget Sound," 751. See also Chalcraft, "Memory's Storehouse," 27–28; Myron Eells, "Indians of Puget Sound," Notebook 6, 63. Helen Clark, a missionary among the Makahs, wrote, in a manuscript in possession of the authors, "When the Tamahnous performances were forbidden by the government the Indians started a new religion called the 'Shake'" (Clark, "Chips from an Old Block," 6).

21. Klan, "The Shakers," 21; Myron Eells, Journal 8, September 8, 1883.

22. Myron Eells, Journal 8, September 8, 1883; Mooney, "The Shakers," 748; Myron Eells, "Indians of Puget Sound," Notebook 6, 94.

23. Myron Eells, Journal 8, September 8, 1883; idem., "Indians of Puget Sound," Notebook 6, 104–105.

24. Mooney, "The Shakers," 748.

25. Myron Eells, Journal 8, September 8, 1883.

26. Ibid., October 25, 1883.

27. Ibid., September 8, 1883; February 27, 1884. After the Big Meeting, Billy Clams began having visions of angels. Because Agent Eells was said to have dealt "squarely" with him, Clams reportedly gave up shaking and Catholic practices as the reverend had directed.

28. Ibid., April 13, November 27, 1884; idem., "Indians of Puget Sound," Notebook 6, 63, 96.

29. George Pierre Castile, *The Indians of Puget Sound*, 436; Myron Eells, "Indians of Puget Sound," Notebook 6, 99. Mowitch Man walked out on his young wife when she refused to clean fish and cook for him. See *Mason County Journal*, June 1, 1888, 2. He filed for divorce in Olympia.

30. Myron Eells, Journal 8, September 8, 1883.

31. Ibid., February 27, 1884; Spier, *Prophet Dance*, 50; Barnett, *Indian Shakers*, 56.

32. Edwin Eells, Autobiography Supplement, 22.

33. Ibid., Autobiography, 202.

34. Meany, "Twana and Clallam Indians."

35. Castile, *Indians of Puget Sound*, 436.

Chapter Five The Formative Years of the Church

1. Lida W. Quimby, "Puget Sound Indian Shakers," 189.

2. Myron Eells, "Indians of Puget Sound," Notebook 6, 106; Mooney, "Shakers of Puget Sound," 759; Dawley, "Some Ante-Mortem Good Indians," 22; Alex Teio to William B. Freer, December 6, 1915, KIA; Julius Hanke to S. A. Young, March 21, 1911, Yakama Indian Agency, (hereafter

cited as YIA).

3. Richen, "Legitimacy and Resolution," 45; Myron Eells, "Indians of Puget Sound," Notebook 6, 106–107.

4. Ober, "A New Religion," 584.

5. "Klamath Reservation Oregon, December 3, '17," Folder 43, ISCA; Otto Strom, "Memoirs," vol. 2, 27–29. Strom's descendants are prominent in the Shaker Church. Perhaps the most prominent white figure in Shaker history is Wade Le Roy, who joined the church in the early 1930s and later became the Shakers' secretary-organizer and aide to bishops Horton Capoeman and Bill Martin.

6. Smith, "Shamanism in Shaker Religion," 119; Spier, *Prophet Dance*, 14.

7. Edwin L. Chalcraft, "The 'Shaker' Religion of the Indians of the Northwest," 75.

8. Chalcraft, Diary, June 21, 1891.

9. Ruth Kirk and Carmela Alexander, *Exploring Washington's Past: A Road Guide to History* (Seattle: University of Washington Press, 1990), 263; Charles M. Buchanan, "Some Phases of Religious Beliefs among Puget Sound Indians; Buchanan to Commissioner of Indian Affairs, May 9, 1914, Tulalip Indian Agency (hereafter cited as TIA).

10. William Whitfield, *History of Snohomish County, Washington*, 1: 821.

11. Albert B. Reagan, "The Shake Dance of the Quilente Indians," 73.

12. Pettitt, "Quileute of La Push," 96, 98.

13. U.S. Commissioner of Indian Affairs, *Annual Report*, 1896, 398.

14. DeKoven Brown, "Indian Workers for Temperance," 23–24.

15. Dawley, "Some Ante-Mortem Good Indians," 22.

16. Ibid.

17. Gunther, "Shaker Religion," 75. By 1892, when the Shaker Church was organized, the word "priest" had given way to the word "preacher," a term borrowed from Protestants, especially Presbyterians, who sought to make preachers of Indian converts in much the same way that Catholics made priests of some of theirs.

18. Ibid.

19. Mooney, "Shakers of Puget Sound," 751, 754, 760; Paul Lehnhoff, "Indian Shaker Religion," 284. Mooney reported that Mud Bay Louis Yowaluch (Aiyal) was a member of the Squaxin tribe (Mooney, "Shakers of Puget Sound," 746). Anthropologist Darleen Fitzpatrick, however, claimed that both Mud Bay Louis and his younger brother, Sam, were Cowlitz Indians (Fitzpatrick, interview with authors, Seattle, April 14, 1992).

20. Barnett, *Indian Shakers*, 23; Mooney, "Shakers of Puget Sound,"

754.

21. Myron Eells, "Indians of Puget Sound," Notebook 6, 105; Mooney, "Shakers of Puget Sound," 754.

22. Mooney, "Shakers of Puget Sound," 754–55.

23. Chalcraft, "Memory's Storehouse," 26; Barnett, *Indian Shakers*, 23; Mooney, "The Shakers of Puget Sound," 748.

24. Chalcraft, Diary, February 19, 1888. On July 26, 1901, the *Mason County Journal* reported that John Smith had "by far the best farm on the Chehalis reservation, with a large amount of bottom land cleared, in wheat and oats, with a self-binder." Prophecies of such a flood were common among native prophets. For example, the Sanpoil Skolaskin prophesied that God would rescue his followers on an ark, and Skolaskin had his people whipsaw lumber for the craft (Robert H. Ruby and John A. Brown, *Dreamer-Prophets of the Columbia Plateau*, 138 ff). Gunther wrote that Heck was converted a year following his wife's conversion (Gunther, "Shaker Religion," 43).

25. Chalcraft, "Memory's Storehouse," 32–33.

26. Chalcraft, Diary, February 19, 1888. Marvin Davis attempted to test the zeal of Skookum Bay Shakers by putting a plug of tobacco in his mouth. When the Shakers did not detect it, he questioned their powers of discernment (ibid.) Peter Stanup, an opponent of Agent Eells, was involved in a conflict over a railroad line on the Puyallup Reservation and was murdered, reportedly by drowning, in May 1893 (unlabeled news clipping, Oct. 31, 1893, in Myron Eells scrapbook; Robert H. Ruby and John A Brown, *Myron Eells and the Puget Sound Indians*, 108).

27. Chalcraft, "Memory's Storehouse," 27.

28. Ibid., 28–29.

29. Chalcraft, "Memory's Storehouse," 29–30. Pike Ben was an avid Shaker and was one of three associate judges who had not revealed their Shaker affiliation to Chalcraft.

30. Ibid., 32; idem., Diary, March 16, 1884.

31. Chalcraft, "Memory's Storehouse," 35; idem., Diary, April 12, 1884.

32. Chalcraft, "Memory's Storehouse," 36.

33. Ibid., 37.

34. Ibid., 39.

35. Ibid., 41.

36. Chalcraft, Diary, August 8, 1884.

37. Chalcraft "Memory's Storehouse," 42.

38. Chalcraft, Diary, February 28, March 1, 1887; idem., "Memory's Storehouse," 42–43. They explained Puyallup Bill's failure to receive the gift of healing as due to stiffness in one of his sides.

39. Chalcraft, Diary, March 6, 1887.

40. Chalcraft, Diary, March 6, 1887, March 2, 1889; idem., "Memory's Storehouse," 45.

Chapter Six Healing the Sick

1. The Shaker creed appearing in the *Quilente Independent* was borrowed by Albert B. Reagan for his article "The Shake Dance of the Quilente Indians," 71–73. The creed reproduced here is taken from Reagan's, "The Shaker Church of the Indians," 448. Reagan omitted the phrase "Get 'even' with those who mistreat you" and added "all of us pledging ourselves to abstain from using intoxicating liquor in any form." See also Reagan's "Notes on the Shaker Church," 115–16.

2. Fitzpatrick, "Indian Shakerism," 4, 8.

3. Myron Eells, *Ten Years of Missionary Work*, 170.

4. Amoss, "Resurrection, Healing, and 'the Shake,'" 99.

5. Gunther, "Shaker Religion," 58–59.

6. Waterman, "Paraphernalia of the Duwamish," 548, 551, 553.

7. Gunther, "Shaker Religion," 59; Fitzpatrick, "Indian Shakerism," 5–6. It is difficult to trace handkerchief use in Shaker worship, but it is similar to the use of Catholic vestments. Shakers would probably not have acquired the use of cloth pieces from Presbyterians or Methodists, though later the use of the handkerchiefs may have come from Pentecostal influences.

8. William J. Garfield to Bishop Heck, March 25, 1916, Folder 8, ISCA; Valory, *Focus of Indian Shaker Healing*, 95; Amoss, *Coast Salish Spirit Dancing*, 82; Harris Teo, interview with authors, White Swan, Washington, September 22, 1990.

9. Helen Clark, "The Shaker Religion and Its Influence among the Makah Indians," 92.

10. Richard A. Gould and Theodore Paul Furukawa, *Aspects of Ceremonial Life among the Indian Shakers of Smith River, California*, 62–63.

11. Chalcraft, "Memory's Storehouse," 25.

12. Gunther, "Shaker Religion," 59; Amoss, "Resurrection, Healing, and 'the Shake,'" 92.

13. Smith, "Shamanism in the Shaker Religion," 120.

14. Ibid., 121.

15. Helen Clark, "Shaker Religion," 92; Albert Reagan, "The Secret Dances and Medicine Ceremonies of the Quileute Indians," 10.

16. Harold Patterson, interview with authors, Aberdeen, Washington, June 23, 1993.

17. Ibid.; Reagan, "Secret Dances," 18; Finley, "As My Sun Now Sets," 250. Shamans often produced objects such as quartz crystals as visual

evidence of pantomimed exorcism of illness that they believed were produced by intrusive elements (Waterman, "Shaker Religion," 503). Burning
is one means of disposing of sin, which is thrown, by pantomime into the
flame of a candle on an altar. Brushing is done moving one or both hands
over the contours of a patient's limbs and body, either lightly or in sharp
sweeps. Some healers do not touch the patient; when they make a gesture
of brushing from several inches away, their rapid arm movements are a
series of counterclockwise revolutions. There are other movements used
in conjunction with brushing: scooping, patting, scraping, smoothing, and
fanning a candle flame to splash the light over and along a person's body.

18. Barnett, *Indian Shakers*, 141.

19. Teo interview, April 24, 1991; Myron Eells, Journal 10, October
7, 1903; Myron Stutsman, interview with authors, Malaga, Washington,
March 14, 1992.

20. Waterman, "Shake Religion," 504; Teo interview, April 24, 1991.
Blowers made the sign of the cross and used candles and a variety of
other Catholic accoutrements. Twelve Shakers circled those in need of
helps; they wore crowns of cedar bark on which were fixed lighted candles,
and they carried small cloths in their right hands and lighted candles in
their left. By fastening colored cloth screens over the candles, they could
make the light appear to be yellow, white, or blue. Yellow light symbolized celestial glory; white, terrestrial light; and blue, the sky. The Blower
emphasis on the symbolism of color appears to have been borrowed from
native religions of the lower Columbia River and Columbia River Plateau
in the decades of the 1870s and 1880s when Smohalla was advancing
his Washani religion and Jake Hunt was promoting the Feather Dance.
(Mooney, "Shakers of Puget Sound," 760–71) A similar practice, called
breathing, is practiced by some present-day faith healers.

21. Collins, "Indian Shaker Church," 406.

22. Wade Le Roy, interview with authors, Quincy, Washington, November 30, 1991.

23. Katherine Sheldon Berkeley, interview with Winona Weber, March
7, 1981, Washington Women's Heritage Project; Le Roy interview, November 30, 1991; Gould and Furukawa, *Aspects of Ceremonial Life*, 57;
Oregonian (Portland), July 30, 1987.

24. Le Roy interview, November 30, 1991.

25. William J. Garfield to Bishop Heck, March 25, 1916, Folder 8, ISCA;
Valory, *Focus of Indian Shaker Healing*, 83.

26. For a discussion of Shaker illnesses among the Nooksacks, see
Amoss, *Coast Salish Spirit Dancing*, 82–86.

27. Chalcraft, "Memory's Storehouse," 25; idem., "'Shaker' Religion,"
75.

28. Mooney, "Shakers of Puget Sound," 749.

29. Spier, "Prophet Dance," 49–52.

30. Ibid.

31. Valory, *Focus of Indian Shaker Healing*, 82; Beatrice Black, interview with Winona Weber, January 3, 1981, Washington Women's Heritage Project.

32. Valory, *Focus of Indian Shaker Healing*, 85–86.

33. Ibid., 86–87.

34. Gould and Furukawa, *Aspects of Ceremonial Life*, 63; Valory, *Focus of Indian Shaker Healing*, 80.

35. Gould and Furukawa, *Aspects of Ceremonial Life*, 62–63. In "crisis situations," Richard Kenyon Pope wrote, shamans tell patients what the problems are. Because the shamans' explanations are in large part supernatural, patients undergo a catharsis that enables them to be healed (Pope, "The Indian Shaker Church and Acculturation at Warm Springs Reservation," 24).

36. Phoebe Condon, "Shaker Religion of the Northwest Indians."

37. Within one's central and peripheral nervous system are cells capable of secreting endogenous peptides. These endorphins produce a spontaneous "high" as well as pain relief. This internal analgesia is produced with increasing exercise and may account for the manner in which the elderly, presumably otherwise out of condition, are able to maintain such a vigorous activity as shaking for hours.

38. Helen Clark, "Shaker Religion," 92.

Chapter Seven Worship and Ritual

1. Ober, "A New Religion," 585.

2. Gould and Furukawa, *Aspects of Ceremonial Life,* 61; Helen Clark, "Indian Shakers," 496.

3. Myron Eells, "Indians of Puget Sound," Notebook 6, 83, 99, 100; Mooney, "Shakers of Puget Sound," 749; Spier, *Prophet Dance*, 52.

4. "Indian Shaker Church Rules," Folder 48, ISCA.·

5. The first religious pictures introduced to Indians of the Pacific Northwest by Catholics were printed in France, glued to cloth, and rolled up. They were hung on trees and later in church houses. Protestants used pictures that illustrated printed materials and some that were hand-drawn by the missionaries before such materials were mass-produced in the United States. (Wilfred Schoenberg, S.J., interview with authors, Portland, Oregon, May 17, 1993; Kenneth J. Ross, Department of History, Presbyterian Church U.S.A., to authors, June 2, 1993)

6. E. B. Merritt, Commissioner of Indian Affairs, to Sargent Brown,

October 23, 1915, KIA.

7. Patterned largely after Congregational Church services, Shaker services were held more frequently than those of the Catholic Church (Myron Eells, "Indians of Puget Sound," Notebook 6, 95).

8. Patterson interview, June 23, 1993; Fitzpatrick, "Indian Shakerism," 9; Mooney, "Shakers of Puget Sound," 754–55.

9. The speakers' testimony tends to affirm the nonjudgmental attitudes so common in Shakerism. Sunday services once began at about ten o'clock in the morning, but the time was later moved to eleven o'clock. They can continue until two o'clock in the afternoon, depending on the spontaneity of the members.

10. Harold Patterson, interview with authors, Aberdeen, Washington, April 1, 1994. Prayer meetings were originally held on Thursday and Saturday nights; later, the nights were switched to Fridays and Saturdays.

11. Shakers, exhibiting great enthusiasm in a church house with poor flooring, have been known to stomp through a floor.

12. John Kew, "Coast Salish Ceremonial Life: Status and Identity in a Modern Village," 273.

13. It was the singing along with accompanying ringing of bells that drew the venerable, long-time Shaker leader Charlie Bighead into the Smith River church (Gould and Furukawa, *Aspects of Ceremonial Life*, 56).

14. Mooney, "Shakers of Puget Sound," 755–56.

15. Gunther, "Shaker Religion," 55–56.

16. Pettitt, "Quileute of La Push," 103; Gunther, "Shaker Religion," 55.

17. Gunther, "Shaker Religion," 55; Loran Olsen to authors, October 28, 1991; Willard Rhodes, "The Christian Hymnology of the North American Indians," 327–28.

18. Loran Olsen to authors, October 28, 1991.

19. Prayer offered by John Smith, August 23, 1913, Records of the Memorial Meeting, ISCA, Folder 27.

20. Reagan, "Shaker Church of the Indians," 448.

21. Stutsman interview, March 14, 1992.

22. Gould and Furukawa, *Aspects of Ceremonial Life*, 60–61.

23. Amoss, *Coast Salish Spirit Dancing*, 136; Leotah Bustillo, interview with authors, Tulalip Reservation, May 2, 1991; Wade Le Roy, interview with authors, Quincy, Washington, December 5, 1991.

24. John Johnson, Acting Minister, La Push, to Milton Giles, January 15, 1912; Peter Heck to Giles, March 30, 1912, Folder 78, ISCA; Gunther, "Shaker Religion," 45; Barnett, *Indian Shakers*, 63. Gunther spelled Kallapa's name "Lance"; Barnett spelled it "Lans Kalapa." The spelling here is that found in the church archives.

25. Minutes of the Annual Convention at Taholah, Washington, October 12–13, 1984, Folder 2, ISCA; Teo, interview, April 24, 1991; Alex Teio to Bishop Heck, February 15, 1910, Folder 54, ISCA.

26. Myron Eells, "Shaking Religion," 157. Indians on the Strait of Juan de Fuca and Puget Sound used small brass bells in pre-Shaker days for ornamentation, but apparently not for worship. See Wilkes, *Narrative*, vol. 4, 246–47.

27. Finley, "As My Sun Now Sets," 246–47.

28. Pettitt, "Quileute of La Push," 98.

29. Robert E. Lee and John Johnson to Milton Giles, March 10, 1911, Folder 2, ISCA.

30. Brown, "Indian Workers for Temperance," 24.

31. Reagan, "Secret Dances," 13.

32. Myron Eells, Journal 8, December 7, 1882; Ober, letter to the editor, *Seattle Times*, May 1, 1933.

33. Gunther, "Shaker Religion," 52–53. It appears that dreams may have been at least one influence. Years after Mud Bay Louis dreamed that a robe would keep him from dying and he introduced the practice, a woman claimed that she had dreamed that robes should not be worn and Jamestown Shakers discontinued their use.

34. Francis Starr, assistant minister, interview with authors, Oakville, Washington, May 11, 1990; Gunther, "Shaker Religion," 53; Wade Le Roy, interview with authors, Quincy, Washington, December 5, 1991. Pamela Amoss reported that each joiner received a gown ("Indian Shaker Church," in Wayne Suttles, ed., *Handbook of North American Indians*, 638). Some Shakers still have gowns, but few wear them.

35. "Indian Shaker Rules," Folder 48, ISCA.

36. David Nanamkin, interview with authors, Wapato, Washington, May 1, 1991; Wade Le Roy, interview with authors, Quincy, Washington, December 4, 1991.

37. Myron Eells, "Indians of Puget Sound," Notebook 6, 94–5.

38. Myron Eells, Journal 10, October 7, 1903. Notwithstanding his zeal, Riddle remained in sufficient good grace among the Shaker hierarchy to offer the opening prayer at the annual convention at Mud Bay on October 29, 1926. See Minutes, Annual Convention, Mud Bay, October 29–31, 1926, Folder 25, ISCA.

39. Harris Teo, interview with authors, White Swan, Washington, October 16, 1990.

40. This continuity was perhaps both the cause and the effect of increased attendance at annual conventions and other meetings. The attendance at these meetings was also unquestionably facilitated by improved transportation and communication in the Puget Sound region.

41. Rakestraw, "Shaker Indians of Puget Sound," 706.

42. Ibid., 706–708.

43. Ibid., 707–709.

44. Gunther, "Shaker Religion," 57–58; Myron Eells, "Indians of Puget Sound," Notebook 6, 104; idem., Journal 8, September 8, 1883.

45. Ober, "A New Religion," 586.

46. Joe Connor to Bishop Heck, April 3, 1930, Folder 22, ISCA; Le Roy interview, December 5, 1991; Robert Pope, interview with authors, Aberdeen, Washington, June 23, 1993; Joe Daner to Bishop Heck, March 20, 1935, Folder 52, ISCA. Amoss's contention that Shaker baptism enjoyed only a brief period of popularity can no longer be supported, since it is practiced in the present-day church (Amoss, "Symbolic Substitution," 233). The Indian Shaker Church began recording baptisms in June 1967.

47. Teo interview, April 24, 1991; Bustillo interview, May 2, 1991; Le Roy interview, December 5, 1991.

48. In an article entitled "Marriage among the Northwest Indians," Tommy Bobb, a Skagit Indian, tells of young men at dances placing feathers behind the ears of prospective brides. The women either accepted the proposals or threw the feathers to the ground. It is uncertain whether this ceremony is from an early Shaker period or a time even earlier. There is no evidence that Shakers used either feathers or drums in their ceremonies.

49. Enoch Abraham to Bishop Heck, January 19, 1931, Folder 22, ISCA.

50. Minutes, Annual Convention, White Swan, October 6–7, 1939, Folder 67, ISCA. There are two other drafts of the 1939 convention minutes in the ISCR. They vary slightly from the copy in the ISCA, which favors William Kitsap's followers. This was during a stormy time for the church with the two competing factions.

51. Gunther, "Shaker Religion," 58.

52. R. J. Harvey, Regional Manager, Region 2, Ministry of Health, B.C., to Teo, January 25, February 24, April 9, April 28, 1986, Folder 79, ISCA; Tillie George, Secretary, British Columbia Shakers, to Teo, January 30, 1986, Folder 84, ISCA; Minutes, "Re: Information on the Perf[ormance] of Marriage in B.C.," La Push, Washington, May 3, 1986, Folder 84, ISCA; Registration of Marriage, Joseph Michael Siah and Carol Joan O'Brien, May 25, 1985 (photocopy), "Information for Guidance of Clergymen Registered under the 'Marriage Act' of British Columbia," Form M. 23, "Requirements Respecting Marriage in British Columbia," Form V.S. 76, Division of Vital Statistics, Victoria, B.C., Folder 79, ISCA.

53. The authors attended these ceremonies in March 1992. The three people being ordained were Steven Iukes, Sr., as minister, Fred Manual as assistant minister, and Steven Iukes, Jr., as church secretary.

54. Quimby, "Puget Sound Indian Shakers," 189.

55. Mooney, "Shakers of Puget Sound," 749; Statement of Mary Thompson, August 21, 1913, Records of the Memorial Meeting, Folder 27, ISCA.

56. Spier, *The Prophet Dance*, 50. Amoss implied that Slocum was a prophet when she wrote, "What was it about the Shaker movement which allowed it to grow and flourish when other local prophets had failed?" See Amoss, "Symbolic Substitution," 293; Meany, "Twana and Clallam Indians," 6.

57. Finley, "As My Sun Now Sets," 245; Robert H. Ruby, "A Healing Service in the Shaker Church," 348.

58. Gunther, "Shaker Religion," 58.

59. Patterson interview, April 1, 1994; Teio to Bishop Heck, April 3, 1918, Folder 12, ISCA.

60. Katherine Sheldon Berkeley, tape-recorded interview by Winona Weber, March 7, 1981; Harris Teo, interview with authors, White Swan, WA, May 1, 1991; Dan Hart to Bishop Heck, March 15, 1914, Folder 6, ISCA.

61. *Valley Daily News* (Renton, WA), April 22, 1992.

Chapter Eight A Mantle of Formality

1. Eells had been appointed agent for the Skokomish Agency on March 20, 1871. His jurisdiction included the Skokomish and Squaxin Reservations. (Myron Eells, "Traditions and History," 104) The Reservations removed from Edwin Eells's jurisdiction in July 1883 were those of the Tulalip Agency: the Tulalip, Lummi, Swinomish, Port Madison, and Muckleshoot. George Pierre Castile wrote that the Quinault Agency came within the Puyallup Consolidated Agency in 1888. See Castile, "Edwin Eells, U.S. Indian Agent, 1871–1895," 64. Records of the Pacific Northwest Region of the National Archives in Seattle, however, indicate that the Quinaults came under the Consolidated Agency in 1882 ("Puyallup Indian Agency, 1885–1920, Introduction," 5). See also Edwin Eells, Autobiography, Book 4, Folder 7, 200–217.

2. Both Edwin Eells and his brother, Rev. Myron Eells, had come by their Congregationalism and strong sense of duty naturally. Their father, Rev. Cushing Eells, had labored among the Spokane Indians for a decade (1838–1848) under the Congregationalist wing of the American Board of Commissioners for Foreign Missions. See Clifford M. Drury, *Nine Years with the Spokane Indians*.

3. The Washington state legislature, with congressional approval, could also remove restrictions on sales of these lands. On achieving statehood in 1889, Washington voted to do just that. Congress established commissions in 1890 and 1893 to facilitate the sale of Puyallup lands. Un-

der the Dawes Act, allotted land (usually in 160-acre parcels) was given to each Indian, with surplus land sold to non-Indians. By 1934, approximately 85 million acres of U.S. reservation land had been removed from tribal ownership. See National Lawyers Guild, Law Student Indian Summer Project Report; see also Castile, "Edwin Eells," 62–66.

4. U.S. Commissioner of Indian Affairs, *Annual Report*, 1887, 297; *Daily Tacoma* (Washington) *News*, December 4, 1884.

5. Edward Curtis, *North American Indians*, 9: 116–7.

6. Ober, "A New Religion," 585; Pettitt, "Quileute of La Push," 96; Minutes, Annual Convention, Taholah, Washington, October 20–22, 1950, Folder 50, ISCA; Mooney, "Shakers of Puget Sound," 756.

7. Finley, "As My Sun Now Sets," 237–38. There were several places in the general Puget Sound area where Shakers were incarcerated. In addition to Steilacoom, Shakers were kept at Olympia, the Puyallup Agency near Tacoma, the Tulalip Agency near Marysville, and the town of Chehalis. (Charles M. Gates, *Messages of the Governors of the Territory of Washington to the Legislative Assembly*, 255).

8. See Chalcraft, Diary, June 21, 1891; *Mason County Journal*, May 25, 1888, 3; U.S. Commissioner of Indian Affairs, *Annual Report*, 1887, 297. Reasons for Eells's political survival are delineated in Castile, "Edwin Eells," 179 n. It should be noted in Eells's defense that in incarcerating the Indians he believed he was faithfully following Indian Office guidelines for "civilizing" its "wards."

9. Murray Morgan, *Puget's Sound: A Narrative of Early Tacoma and the Southern Sound*, 318. The liquor problem would also cause friction between the two men. Although it was illegal to sell liquor to Indians, in 1892 Wickersham was able to have charges dropped against a white man accused of that crime. He argued before federal judge Cornelius H. Hanford that although the buyer was an Indian he was also a landowning citizen and therefore had the right to purchase liquor. See Mooney, "Shakers of Puget Sound," 757. The major legislation to prohibit such sales was the Indian Trade and Intercourse Act of 1834, passed the year the Department of Indian Affairs was organized. Over the years, the laws changed, and liquor sales were prohibited in Indian Territory, within buffer lands (or boundaries) outside reservations, and on reservations. On July 23, 1892, Congress prohibited sales or gifts of liquor to allotted Indians, since allotments were restricted or held in trust by the government. Sales were also prohibited to Indians who were "wards" under guardianship of the United States. (Felix S. Cohen, *Handbook of Federal Indian Law*, 352–55)

10. U.S. Commissioner of Indian Affairs, *Annual Report*, 1888, 227.

11. Chalcraft, "Memory's Storehouse," 47.

12. Frank C. Ross to E. E. Ellis, March 11, 1893, Letterpress Book, James Wickersham Papers, Ms. 107, Box 23, Vol. 8, 120–21; Chalcraft, "Memory's Storehouse," 47; *News-Tribune* (Tacoma, WA), January 13, 1980.

13. In his zeal for Eells, Chalcraft interpreted the Indians' response as a celebration against Wickersham (Chalcraft, "Memory's Storehouse," 47). For more on the confrontation between Wickersham and Edwin Eells, see Thompson, "Shakers and Indian Shakers," 5–22.

14. Mooney, "Shakers of Puget Sound," 750. Shakers wanted no association with the Ghost Dance in their effort to legitimize their church. To help put the Ghost Dance in context, see Ruby and Brown, *Dreamer-Prophets,* and Spier, *Prophet Dance,* 50. According to L. L. Langness, Shakerism was a reform movement more than a genuine native movement. "It achieved its success," Langness wrote, "because its moral tenets were compatible with those already held; it united conflicting elements, and offered a means, of curing for which there was a felt need." See Langness, "A Case of Post-Contact Reform," 75–76. The Ghost Dance and the Prophet Dance, both revitalization movements, are no longer an issue for the Shaker Church.

15. Mooney, "Shakers of Puget Sound," 747.

16. Wickersham to John W. Simmons, minister of the Puyallup Reservation, May 9, 1892, 534, Wickersham to D. M. Duckworth, Sheriff, November 25, 1892, 456, Letterpress Book, Wickersham Papers, Box 22, Vol. 7. Wickersham advised Slocum to have money ready to pay taxes on the property, undoubtedly indicating that the decision on the sale would be reversed (Wickersham to John Slocum, December 31, 1892, 11, Letterpress Book, Wickersham Papers, Box 23, Vol. 8).

17. Wickersham to John Hilton, December 5, 1892, 473, Wickersham to Sam Yowaluch, December 8, 1892, 477, Letterpress Book, Wickersham Papers, Box 22, Vol. 7.

18. Wickersham to Charles Francis Adams, March 20, 1890, 268, Letterpress Book, Wickersham Papers, Box 22, Vol. 5.

19. Edwin Eells, Autobiography, 259–62.

20. U.S. Commissioner of Indian Affairs, *Annual Report,* 1893, 333; Myron Eells, Journal 9, July 16, 1888.

21. Gunther, "Shaker Religion," 48.

22. Wickersham appears to have kept a low profile during the proceedings. His name does not appear in any minutes of the meeting. (Finley, "As My Sun Now Sets," 225–26).

23. Ibid.

24. Wickersham to Whom It May Concern, July 20, 1892, 579, Wickersham Papers, Box 22, Vol. 7.

25. Mooney, "Shakers of Puget Sound," 758-59.

26. Ibid. 760; Minutes, Annual Convention, Taholah, Washington, October 20-22, 1950, 10, Folder 50, ISCA.

27. Spier, *The Prophet Dance*, 49; Mooney, "Shakers of Puget Sound," 759.

28. See Coleman, "Not Race, but Grace"; Barnett, *Indian Shakers*, 105; Mooney, "Shakers of Puget Sound," 760. As late as 1912, Milton Giles, Shaker secretary-organizer, informed Bishop Peter Heck and elders that a Presbyterian missionary wanted Chehalis Shakers to donate a stated sum of money to his church. In response, Heck explained that his Shakers were no longer Presbyterians, but had an established church of their own. (Milton Giles to Bishop Heck and Elders, March 13, 1912, Folder 38, ISCA).

29. Mooney, "Shakers of Puget Sound," 750, 759. It was suggested that Shakers affiliate with "some church," and John Slocum, Mud Bay Louis, Iyell We-haw-wa of the Cowlitz, John Simmons, and James Walker visited the Olympia Presbytery with this option in mind. Nothing was resolved at the meeting. See *Mason County Journal*, October 27, 1893.

30. *Mason County Journal*, June 30, 1893.

31. Myron Eells, Journal 9, October 20, 1895; November 28, 1895; October 19, 1898.

32. U.S. Commissioner of Indian Affairs, *Annual Report*, 1896, 398.

33. *Mason County Journal*, February 4, 1897; March 11, 1897; December 10, 1887; May 12, 1893.

34. *Mason County Journal*, October 11, 1901.

35. Myron Eells, Journal 10, January 2, 1905.

36. Edwin Eells, Autobiography Supplement, 26-27.

37. Ibid., 24-25.

38. Smith, "Shamanism in the Shaker Religion," 122.

Chapter Nine A New Era

1. Gunther, "Shaker Religion," 62. Gunther stated that Oregon Shakers incorporated in 1907 when Bishop Heck was forbidden by the Warm Springs Reservation agent to meet there, but Heck did not assume the activities of the bishop's office until 1911. In 1939, during the Bible-use controversy in Washington state, Jerry Bruno, a Warm Springs Shaker, claimed that Oregon Shakers had incorporated on the basis of their belief in the Bible, although the incorporation documents do not specify that. Bruno's statement may have been made to support the Bible-use group, which boldly overstepped the bounds of ISC authority when it amended its constitution. This "Warm Springs Branch of the Indian Church of Oregon"

elected its own bishop. See Minutes, Special Meeting, Concrete, Washington, June 17, 1939, ISCR.

2. *Mason County Journal*, October 18, 1901; Barnett, *Indian Shakers*, 110.

3. Myron Eells, Journal 10, October 7, 1903; Le Roy interview, December 4, December 5, 1991. At this writing there are female assistant ministers at Queets and Chehalis, and there is a woman evangelist on the Tulalip Reservation. Women are ministers in British Columbia and California congregations.

4. *Seattle Post-Intelligencer*, June 22, 1910, section 2, p. 2.

5. Indian Shaker Church, Articles of Incorporation, ISCA.

6. Webster H. Hudson to Bishop Heck, January 27, 1912, Folder 78, ISCA,

7. Thompson had gotten along fairly well with Mud Bay Louis, perhaps because he was a church leader with her husband's blessing, but her relationship with Mud Bay Sam was a different matter. After his brother's death in 1905, Sam directed the church with a functionless staff of elders from the 1892 organization. He was elected bishop and selected Enoch Abraham to serve as his clerk. Sam died in 1911, and Peter Heck replaced him as bishop. (Barnett, *Indian Shakers*, 109–10) Bennett credits Sam for the 1910 organizational meeting where Peter Heck first suggested incorporation.

8. Milton Giles to Bishop Heck, April 26, 1912, Folder 52, ISCA; Le Roy interview, April 23, 1992.

9. Although the term "delegate" is used here to describe persons attending Shaker conventions, Shakers did not use the term. Shaker members who took it upon themselves to attend a meeting acted in the capacity of a delegate with full privileges to take part in discussions and votes. (Minutes of the Annual Convention, White Swan, October 6–7, 1939, ISCR).

10. Peter Joe to Bishop Heck, November 30, 1917, Folder 11, ISCA.

11. R. C. Lowe, Barrister, to Bishop Heck et al., December 1, 1919, Folder 14, ISCA.

12. The official certification number of the subsequent incorporation was 4414.

13. Richen, *Legitimacy and Resolution*, 37. Bible-reading Shakers of the Klamath Reservation refiled for incorporation in 1925, electing their own bishop and other officers (Theodore Stern, *The Klamath Tribe*, 226).

14. Indian Shaker Church of Washington, in California, ISCA; Articles of Incorporation of Indian Shaker Church of the State of California, ISCA.

15. Enoch Abraham to Bishop Heck, May 2, 1911, Folder 2, ISCA.

16. Marilyn Claire Richen, "Authority and Office Leadership in the

Shaker Church," 8, 9.

17. One early bishop suggested that conventions be held in more populous places (Minutes of the Annual Convention, Yakama Reservation [White Swan or Toppenish?], October 18–19, 1912, ISCR).

18. Harris Teo, interview with authors, White Swan, Washington, August 20, 1991. It is uncertain as to how much other Shaker occupations were affected by attendance at conventions. Among these occupations could have been oystering, which was a big industry in the heart of Shaker country, where Mud Bay and Big Skookum Bay workers shipped out as many as ten tons of oysters a week. Traditional domestic chores performed by women, such as gardening, fabricating clothing and baskets, and housekeeping (often for whites), would not have been disrupted as much. Logging was still a major occupation for Shaker men.

19. Gunther, "Shaker Religion," 64; Le Roy interview, November 30, 1991.

20. Minutes of meetings, Musqueam Reserve Shaker Church, December 10, 14, 19, 1963, Harold Stevens, Secretary, Folder 43, ISCA; E. B. Meritt, Assistant Commissioner to William B. Freer, Superintendent, Klamath Agency, October 23, 1915, KIA.

21. William C. Miller, Farmer, Skokomish Agency, to Freer, March 4, 1917, KIA; *Mason County Journal*, October 27, 1916.

22. Gunther, "Shaker Religion," 65.

23. Minutes of the Annual Convention, Yakama Reservation, October 18–19, 1912, ISCR.

24. *Mason County Journal*, March 2, 1917.

25. Minutes of the Annual Convention, Warm Springs, Oregon, November 3, 1913, ISCR.

26. Minutes of meetings, June 20, July 3, 1914, ISCR; Minutes of the Annual Convention, Chehalis Reservation, Oakdale, October 9, 1911, ISCR.

27. Minutes of Annual Convention, n.p., October 16, 1915, ISCR.

28. Ibid.

29. *Mason County Journal*, October 27, 1893.

Chapter Ten Extending the Boundaries

1. Teo interview, September 22, 1990.

2. Gunther, "Shaker Religion," 42–43.

3. Alex Teio to Bishop Heck, March 25, 1912, Folder 78; Teio to Milton Giles, February 27, 1912, Folder 78, ISCA. Teio's father, a Hawaiian, was married to a Wishram woman living near The Dalles.

4. A Quileute tribal judge, Webster H. Hudson, stated that a Landes (Lance) (Kallappa?) from Neah Bay introduced Shakerism to the Quileute, although it appeared among the people at La Push before it did among Makahs of Neah Bay.

5. Pettitt, "Quileute of La Push," 98; Samuel G. Morse, Agent, to A. Wesley Smith, April 28, 1902, Neah Bay Indian Agency Records (hereafter cited as NBIAR), Roll 3. Gunther confirmed that it was David Hudson who introduced Shakerism on the Quileute Reservation in 1901 from the Quinault, where it had begun a decade earlier (Gunther, "Shaker Religion," 45). Initially, the Shakers "shook" for everything they desired–fair weather, favorable winds, and such things as success in hunting and fishing (Ober, "A New Religion," 588). Regarding the means of weather control, Wade Le Roy, supervising minister, secretary-organizer, and counselor in the Shaker Church, told of Rev. William Hall's calming the stormy seas. As Hall told it, when he and his people were in a large boat, with six oarsmen on each side, high waves suddenly splashed into the boat. Hall stood up and raised his hands to calm the storm. When his hands fell from fatigue, others held them up for him, and they all reached shore safely. (Le Roy interview, April 23, 1992).

6. Another such edifice was built piecemeal in the 1920s, after which there was an increase in membership from a little over thirty to eighty-five; membership then began to drop. (Pettitt, "Quileute of La Push," 98; *Seattle Post-Intelligencer*, April 6, 1909)

7. Myron Eells, "Indians of Puget Sound," Notebook 6, 106; Ronald L. Olson, *Quinault Indians and Adz, Canoe, and House Types of the Northwest Coast*, 171, 179.

8. "Record of Church Property," ISCR; Teo interview, April 24, 1991; Gunther, "Shaker Religion," 43; Morse to Smith, April 28, 1902, NBIAR, Roll 3.

9. William Hall, Minister, Jamestown, to Bishop Heck, October 9, 1916, Folder 9, ISCA; Langness, "A Case of Post-Contact Reform," 51.

10. Helen Clark, "The Shaker Religion," 496; idem., "Chips from an Old Block," 6.

11. Lewis St. John, "The Present Status and Probable Future of the Indians of Puget Sound," 19; Joe Sly to Bishop Heck, August 4, 1919, Folder 13, ISCA.

12. Sara Crickenberger, "Shakers," *Seattle Times* and *Post-Intelligencer*, September 17, 1989; Finley, "As My Sun Now Sets," 226.

13. "Ledger of Members, 1911–1923," ISCR; Martin Sampson, *Indians of Skagit County*, 16.

14. O. C. Upchurch, "The Swinomish People and Their State," 294–95; Sampson, *Indians of Skagit County*, 16. Sampson wrote that the Skagit

church was established by Thomas W. McLeod and that the church house was constructed by Gaspar Dan.

15. June Collins reported that when the Smohalla Dreamers danced, the whites looked upon it as a "preparation for war," adding that the "developments [of the dance] contributed to attitudes of suspicion and distrust on the part of Whites in the area toward Indians in general." It stands to reason that Shakers would have been looked upon in the same way. See Collins, "Indian Shaker Church," 400.

16. Gunther, "Shaker Religion," 43; Peter Joe, British Columbia bishop, to Bishop Heck, October 1, 1926, Folder 20, ISCA; Minutes of the Annual Convention, 1915, ISCR; "Roster of Shakers," January 18, 1911, Folder 38, ISCA.

17. Ober, "A New Religion," 588. One anthropologist claimed that the spread of Shakerism to the Vancouver, British Columbia, area came from the south, from across the border, rather than from Vancouver Island. A license hanging on the church wall in Musqueam until the 1970s was issued to Charlie Saleeculton. The Musqueam church was apparently a converted home built on land donated to the church by Alex Peters. After the building was dismantled as a hazard, meetings were again held in homes. An interesting difference between Musqueam ceremonies and those of other Shakers was that as late as 1948 men were positioned on the right in services and women on the left, from which locations they ceremoniously trod in place (Gunther, "Shaker Religion," 47n; Kew, "Coast Salish Ceremonial Life," 240)

18. Mooney, "Shakers of Puget Sound," 761; Gunther, "Shaker Religion," 44. In 1908 almost eighty acres of reservation land were set aside by the federal government for the White Swan church three miles east of White Swan. Another church house on the reservation was built on Lizzie Shuster's allotment on Satus Creek. Enlarged and refurbished in 1971, the Satus church house sits on an acre of land. By 1943, most Shaker churches sat on an acre or less. (*Toppenish Review*, December 1, 1971).

19. Gunther, "Shaker Religion," 44; Cora Du Bois, "The Feather Cult of the Middle Columbia," 22; Ray Harmon, "Indian Shaker Church of The Dalles," 151–52.

20. Spier, *Prophet Dance*, 54; Pope, "Indian Shaker Church," 35, 63, 69.

21. Faye Compo, interview with authors, Lapwai, Idaho, August 31, 1991; John L. Schultz and Deward E. Walker, Jr., "Indian Shakers on the Colville Reservation," 168.

22. Barnett, *Indian Shakers*, 70; Gunther, "The Shaker Religion," 46. Spier reported that Shakers established themselves on the Siletz in 1923. (Spier, *Prophet Dance*, 69)

23. Lee Sackett, "The Siletz Indian Shaker Church," 123; Harris Teo,

interview with authors, White Swan, Washington, October 17, 1990; Minutes of [Weitchpec] business meeting, March 20, 1971, Wade Le Roy Papers.

24. Sackett, "Siletz Indian Shaker Church" 12–3; Gould and Furukawa, *Aspects of Ceremonial Life*, 51; Le Roy interview, April 23, 1992.

25. Edwin Eells, Autobiography, 206.

26. Wilbur Martin to Bishop Heck, November 4, 1933, Folder 56, ISCA. Although this letter was dated November 4, 1933, it mentioned that missionary Joe Conner (*sic*) read a letter from Heck in the Siletz Shaker church on Thanksgiving evening. The envelope cancellation time was 7:00 A.M., December 6, so it would have been sent on December 4. (Sophie Johnson, minister at Siletz, to Bishop Heck, December 4, 1933, Folder 56, ISCA)

27. Joe Connor to Bishop Heck, January 22, January 27, 1934, Folder 57, ISCA; Valory, *Focus of Indian Shaker Healing*, 73; Sackett, "Siletz Indian Shaker Church," 126.

28. Gould and Furukawa, *Aspects of Ceremonial Life*, 59.

29. Pettitt, "Quileute of La Push," 103; "'What Hath God Wrought'" Sarah Endicott Ober to Bishop Heck, May 23, May 5, 1919, Folder 13, ISCA.

30. Amoss, *Coast Salish Spirit Dancing*, 81. Teo drew the line on Pentecostal pressures, speaking bluntly in 1990: "We finally got rid of them" (Teo, interview, October 16, 1990).

31. Ober to Bishop Heck, June 24, 1919, Folder 13, ISCA.

32. Ober to Bishop Heck, August 2, 1919, Folder 13, ISCA.

33. Ibid.

34. U. G. Murphy, Seattle agent, San Francisco–based American Bible Society, to Bishop Heck, August 16, 1933, Folder 56, ISCA.

Chapter Eleven   The Klamath Connection

1. Stern, *Klamath Tribe*, 223–24; Spier, *Prophet Dance*, 68; Hiroto Zakoji, "Klamath Culture Change," 119; A. M. Reynolds, Superintendent, Warm Springs Agency, to Wm. B. Freer, October 14, 1915, KIA. Henry Jackson had also brought the Earth Lodge cult (Warm House Dance) to the Klamath Reservation in 1874. Members of this cult in northern California and southern Oregon abandoned the concept of a world cataclysm, emphasizing instead concepts of an afterlife and a supreme being.

2. Reynolds was also concerned with Jake Hunt's "disgusting" Feather cultists along the lower Columbia River, who had established themselves on the Warm Springs Reservation. Where shaking was the hallmark of Shakerism, for Hunt and his followers feather waving symbolized the

power of cleansing, with the suggestion that feathers were the seat of supernatural powers. Moreover, many Feather cultists, unlike Shakers, continued wearing long hair in the traditional manner, which the government sought to discourage in order to get on with the "civilizing" process. (Reynolds to Freer, October 1915, KIA). For an account of the Feather religion, see Du Bois, "Feather Cult."

3. John W. Lozier, Special Officer, to Freer, October 5, 1915, KIA.

4. Lozier to Freer, October 5, 1915, Freer to G. W. O'Neil, November 8, 1915, E. B. Meritt to Sargent Brown, October 23, 1915, KIA.

5. Meritt to Freer, December 1, 1915, Freer to G. W. O'Neil, December 22, 1915, Reynolds to Freer, February 5, 1916, KIA.

6. Alex Teio to Freer, n.d., Freer to Teio, July 14, 1916, KIA.

7. Statement of Mrs. David Copperfield, July 15, 1916, KIA. During the healing services, Stanley Pedro's wife went around slapping people on the head until they shed their coats, suspenders, and neckties. She also confiscated chewing and smoking tobacco. At the same time, Stanley Pedro slapped women on the head, took their hairpins, and even knocked off their glasses. Taking offense at such treatment, Lessie Lobert reported it to agency authorities, which helped precipitate Freer's investigation of the meeting. (Statement of Hiram Moore, July 16, 1916, KIA)

8. Fred A. Baker, Examiner of Inheritance, to Freer, September 11, 1916, KIA.

9. Teio to Heck, March 12, 1917, Folder 10; Seeley L. Griffen to Thomas H. Lang, December 6, 1927, Folder 21, ISCA.

10. Statement of Mrs. David Copperfield, July 15, 1916, KIA; Zakoji, "Klamath Culture Change," 119, 120.

11. Freer to Commissioner, September 18, 1916, KIA; Helen Clark, "Shaker Religion," 496.

12. E. B. Ashurst to Freer, September 30, 1916, KIA; Statement of Hiram Moore, n.d.; Pettitt, "Quileute of La Push," 100; Mrs. William Jarnaghan, Assistant Minister, Hoopa, California, to Bishop Heck, September 13, 1932, Folder 55, ISCA; Similar complaints came from other quarters in the early 1920s, for example, from the Quileutes far to the north of the Klamaths. Complaints also came from the south in places like the Hoopa Valley in northern California. As late as the 1930s a Hoopa Agency superintendent stated that Indians could be healed by "common sense treatments" and not by ringing bells over the tops of their heads. The superintendent may not have known that in one curing session on the Hoopa Reservation in September 1932 the mouth was used instead of the hand to extract pain from a sick person.

13. Ashurst to Freer, September 30, 1916, KIA.

14. Pettitt, "Quileute of La Push," 100; Freer to Commissioner, October

24, 1916, KIA.

15. Freer to Cookman, Klamath Agency Chief of Police, November 16, 1916, Freer to William Moore, n.d., KIA. The church was unnamed.

16. Freer to Jackson et al., January 2, 1917; Stanley N. Pedro to Commissioner Cato Sells, January 23, 1917; Freer to Sells, February 16, 1917; Pedro to Sells, January 23, 1917, KIA.

17. Freer to Sells, February 16, 1917, KIA; "Remarks of Johnnie Johnson of Yakima Reservation," Klamath Agency, Oregon, January 6, 1917, KIA.

18. Freer to Cookman, January 22, 1917; Statements of Mabel Brown, Charlie Brown, Robert Wilson, Shakespeare Hicks, Edward Cookman, January 24, 1917, KIA.

19. Freer to Commissioner, February 16, 1917, KIA. This group represented about half the Klamath. It should be remembered that when considering numbers in attendance at Shaker services all those participating were not members of the church.

20. Pedro to Commissioner, January 23, 1917, KIA.

21. Meritt to Mrs. Robert Wilson, February 21, 1917; Statement of Mabel Brown, January 24, 1917; George Q. Jacks to Freer, February 2, 1917; Meritt to Jacks, February 26, 1917; Freer to Teio, February 2, 1917, KIA.

22. Waters to Freer, February 21, 1917; Freer to Stwire G. Waters, February 26, 1917, KIA.

23. William G. Miller, Farmer, Skokomish Reservation, to Freer, March 4, 1917, KIA.

24. Freer to Miller, March 11, 1917, KIA.

25. Asbury to Don M. Carr, Superintendent, Yakima Agency, May 15, 1917; Carr to Asbury, May 24, 1917; Asbury to Dan M. Hart, June 8, 1917, KIA.

26. Hart to J. M. Johnson, Superintendent, Klamath Agency, September 17, 1917; Johnson to Hart, September 18, 1917, KIA.

27. Hart to Bishop Heck, December 22, 1917, Folder 11, ISCA; Johnson to Joseph Jackson, May 13, 1918, Meritt to Walter G. West, Supervisor, Klamath Agency School, n.d., KIA.

28. Sargent Brown to Heck, October 17, 1924, Folder 19, ISCA.

29. Richen, *Legitimacy and the Resolution*, x; Joseph Jackson et al. to Johnson, March 12, 1918, KIA.

30. Minutes of the General Assembly in Special Convention, White Swan, Washington, July 5–8, 1918, Folder 27, ISCA.

31. Ibid.

32. Ibid.; Stern, *Klamath Tribe*, 226.

33. Minutes of the General Assembly in Special Convention, White Swan, July 5–8, 1918, Folder 27, ISCA.

34. The Warm Springs group was reinstated on April 5, 1950, and was finally dissolved on March 8, 1960, at the request of the Warm Springs church itself. The church, which had let its corporate charter lapse, had been incorporated on June 7, 1954, as the "Indian Shaker Church of Washington." The Warm Springs corporation continued except for a brief lapse for failing to file papers on time on June 14, 1983, but was quickly reinstated. (Twila Harlan, Office of Oregon Secretary of State, Salem, Oregon, to authors, September 10, 1991, March 4, 1992).

35. Harlan to authors, September 10, 1991.

36. The ISC of Washington on the Klamath Reservation continued to decline and failed to reestablish a viable church in the face of the stronger Chiloquin Bible readers and other healing-oriented Pentecostal groups (Richen, *Legitimacy and Resolution*, 37).

37. Tom Lang to Bishop Heck, January 28, 1924, Folder 74, ISCA; Richen, *Legitimacy and Resolution*, 37. But Richen reported that in 1925 the Bible users incorporated as the ISC of Oregon under Sam Williams's bishopric. At the time of filing, however, on December 18, 1925, Dan Hart was bishop.

38. Authentication of December 19, 1925, Articles of Incorporation of The Indian Shaker Church of Oregon, Maurice Hudson, Corporation Commissioner, State of Oregon, October 8, 1951, Folder 63, ISCA. Ironically, the name Annie Lee Shakers does not appear in their articles of incorporation, although section e of article 2 states that their sect originated in England in 1847 and came to the United States twenty-seven years later under the leadership of Mother Ann Lee. Despite this declaration, the group had no connection with the Shakers of the eastern United States. Few similarities are shared by Indian Shakers in the West with the United Society of Shakers, those followers of Mother Ann in the East. The latter group began in England in 1706 as an offshoot of Quakers. They immigrated to America in 1774. Each group has shaking in their worship, and visions that play a role in their living, as does emphasis on moral behavior. Each group has elders and eldresses who are charged with safeguarding their members' morals. Both have circling in their ceremonials with gender grouping and use of arm gesturing. Both have a strong sense of egalitarianism. Shakers in the West were dubbed as such by whites, as Eastern Shakers were given the epithet Shakers in derision by those outside their group, although it now serves the group well as a name. (Marguerite Fellows Melcher, *The Shaker Adventure*, 117) We still find no connection between the followers of Slocum and Mother Ann. The possibility of a viable connection between the two groups was probed at length by a scholar, Darryl Thompson, who finally gave the search up.

He wrote: "In the end, of course, I had only a theory [presented in his report] that there was a historical link between the Shakers and the Indian Shakers. Unfortunately, I lacked the essential evidence that was necessary to verify any of the various alternative scenarios which I envisioned as possible explanations for the link. After 20 years of research I had to admit that I had still not yet proved that there was a 'lost' historical tie between the Shakers and the Indian Shakers." (Thompson, "Shakers and Indian Shakers," 5–22)

39. Zakoji, "Klamath Culture Change," 123.

40. Ibid., 124–25; Stern, *Klamath Tribe*, 225–26.

41. Le Roy interview, November 30, 1991.

Chapter Twelve Schism within the Indian Shaker Church

1. Chalcraft, "'Shaker' Religion," 75. According to journalist Le Roy Williamson, "Indians could not read the Bible so they rejected its authority." See Williamson, "His Vision of Heaven Started a Church." See also Richen, *Legitimacy and Resolution*.

2. Gunther, "Shaker Religion," 67.

3. William Kitsap to Abe Logan, July 9, 1936, Folder 52, ISCA; Gunther, "Shaker Religion," 67.

4. William Hall to Bishop Heck, April 6, 1910, Folder 54, ISCA.

5. Andrew P. Peterson to Bishop Heck, January 12, 1914, Folder 38, ISCA.

6. Gunther, "Shaker Religion," 66–67.

7. Minutes of the Annual Convention, Skokomish Reservation, October 13, 1927, Folder 25; Deposition of Johnnie James, November 14, 1927, Folder 20, ISCA.

8. Gunther, "Shaker Religion," 66–67.

9. Deposition of Johnnie James, November 14, 1927, Folder 20, ISCA.

10. Jerry Keenum to Bishop Heck, November 14, 1927, Folder 20, ISCA.

11. Carl Jones to Bishop Heck, October 24, 1931; William Guss to Bishop Heck, November 19, 1931; Harry Hobucket to Bishop Heck, November 18, 1931, Folder 23, ISCA.

12. Boome's minutes were transcribed and notarized on December 5, 1932. Before long, Boome would switch his loyalties to the non-Bible users. At the same time, the action of the Bible-use group was sufficiently incendiary to cause the Heck forces to take off their kid gloves and openly argue the Bible-use and bishopric questions. (Deposition of Charley Boome, Folder 75, ISCA)

13. *Peter Heck et al. v. William Kitsap*, Thurston County, Washington, Case Number 14933, April 1933, Memo Opinion filed, September 27,

1933, John M. Wilson, Judge, Folders 72, 56, ISCA. The trial was held on September 21–27, 1933. No one questioned Judge Wilson's possible involvement in a conflict of interest. As an attorney, Wilson had notarized signatures of Mud Bay Sam and Milton Giles when Shaker articles of incorporation were filed with the Washington secretary of state on December 15, 1919.

14. Gunther, "Shaker Religion," 67.

15. Ibid., 68; Minutes of the Annual Convention, Neah Bay, Washington, October 9, 1937, ISCR.

16. Pettitt, "Quileute of La Push," 101.

17. At the 1933 trial, testimony was given that no election had been held for the bishop's office in 1915, but the report of that October annual meeting reflects otherwise.

18. Minutes of a Special Meeting, Concrete Church, June 17, 1939, ISCR.

19. Minutes of the Annual Convention, White Swan, Washington, October 6–7, 1939, ISCR.

20. Minutes of a Special Meeting, Port Gamble, Washington, March 21, 1942, ISCR. During the 1933 case, when Heck brought charges against Kitsap for acting as bishop, Judge Wilson pointed out that Kitsap had taken it upon himself to hold elections of bishops by ballot, thereby violating the articles of incorporation. Kitsap's method of electing bishops, Wilson pointed out, would have required changes in those articles. When Kitsap submitted his constitution and bylaws to Shakers in 1939, he did not include such changes. See Folder 72, ISCA.

21. Minutes of the Annual Convention, Tulalip Reservation, October 26, 1940, ISCR.

22. Bishop Heck received many letters from those who complained about Kitsap as well as promotion of Bible use in services. See, for example, letters to him from John Johnson, January 4, 1933; Edward Hudson, March 31, 1933; Thomas McDonald, November 27, 1933; Folder 56, ISCA.

23. It is possible that Amundson was asked to resign as secretary after Kitsap had seen her notes on the meeting (Minutes of the Annual Convention, White Swan, October 5–8 [sic], 1940, Folder 82, ISCA). Amundson's notes and comments were rewritten and typed from her original longhand and appended to the minutes, Folder 82, ISCA. See also Minutes of the Special Meeting, Tulalip, February 8, 1941, ISCR. Amundson resigned her position as ISC secretary on February 8, 1941.

24. Minutes of the Special Meeting, Neah Bay, Washington, March 16, 1941, ISCR.

25. Teo interview, April 24, 1991; the letter from a group of Heck supporters was signed just "Keep our names from Kitsap," January 1933,

Folder 56, ISCA.

26. The official ISC seal, used to signify authenticity of church documents, is made of iron, with an elongated handle and a circular face. The seal makes an impression on Church documents and other papers with the words "Indian Shaker Church of Washington," with a cross below the word "Incorporated" and above the year, "1910."

27. Minutes of the Special Meeting, Neah Bay, Washington, March 16, 1941; Minutes of the Special Meeting, La Conner, Washington, May 17, 1941, ISCR.

28. Minutes of the Special Meeting, White Swan, October 4–6, 1941, ISCR. This meeting, called mostly by non-Bible users, would substitute for an annual meeting, since neither Heck nor Kitsap had enough clout to call for a meeting of all members.

29. In addition to ministerial duties, Bennett had been a professional ballplayer in Port Angeles. The reasons for his leaving the apostolic faith are discussed in Pettitt, "Quileute of La Push," 103. See also Bennett to Bishop Heck, May 7, 1934, Folder 57, ISCA. Shortly after Christmas 1934, Bennett was embroiled in an argument with Joe Daner over the question of the legitimacy of the two Shaker factions. Bennett believed that the Bible-use question had been settled in convention. Daner denied the validity of the issue based on the 1910 ISC articles of incorporation. (Daner to Heck, March 20, 1935, Folder 52, ISCA.) In 1925, Bennett became affiliated with the fundamentalist ISC and became a licensed minister in the Lower Elwah Reservation church. In 1934, he informed Heck of new officers at Elwah who had led the vote against Heck.

30. Minutes of Special Meeting, White Swan, October 4–6, 1941, ISCR. Although a non-Bible user, Cush had to work with an existing board of elders, most of whom were Bible-reading Kitsap supporters.

31. Minutes of the annual convention, Oakville, Washington, October 16–18, 1942, Folder 71, ISCA.

32. Ibid.

33. Ibid.

34. When Bennett became bishop, he appointed Sam Ulmer (Elmer) to fill the vacancy in the board of elders. He did not list the name of the fifth elder, missionary John Logan, since he was an Oregonian. ("Bishop's Report," Folder 2 of 7, ISCR)

35. Minutes of the meeting, Tulalip, October 8–9, 1943, ISCR.

36. Ibid.

37. Minutes of the meeting, Tulalip, November 6, 1943, ISCR

38. Minutes of the meeting, Tulalip, February 26, 1944, ISCR.

39. Minutes of the meeting, Tulalip, July 3, 1944, ISCR.

40. *Frank F. Bennett v. William Kitsap*, Snohomish County, Wash-

ington, Case No. 41504, Complaint in Quo Warranto, October 4, 1944; Answer, January 20, 1945; Stipulation, March 5, 1945; Answered and Cross-Complaint; Stipulation for Dismissal, November 16, November 26, 1945; Order for Dismissal, November 29, 1945.

41. Copy Deed, Priest Point Park Snohomish County parcel, Tax Acct #5480-000-004-0608, 804360-63, including 804364 and 804365-68, Vol. 362, p. 410.

42. *State of Washington v. William Kitsap, Carl Jones, and Full Gospel Church, Snohomish County, Washington*, Case No. 43799, Complaint, June 20, 1946; Order, July 5, 1946; Summons, December 18, 1946; Notice of Assignment for Trial, December 18, 1946; Stipulation, February 1, 1947; Judgement, February 1, 1947.

43. Richen, *Legitimacy and Resolution*, 55, 86.

Chapter Thirteen Schismatic Fallout

1. Bishop Jasper Andy, interview with authors, White Swan, WA, September 24, 1991.

2. Dorothy Chamblin, interview with authors, Neah Bay, WA, November 28, 1991.

3. Business Meeting, Pendleton Shaker Members, White Swan, Washington, February 23, 1970, Folder 60, ISCA.

4. Teo interview, August 20, 1991.

5. David Nanamkin, interview with authors, Wapato, WA. September 2, 1991.

6. Mattie Charles, Assistant Minister, to Bishop Heck, March 18, 1933, Folder 56, ISCA.

7. Teo interview, August 20, 1991.

8. Minutes of the Annual Convention, Taholah, October 20–22, 1950, Folder 50, ISCA. After Bennett's death Gilbert Sotomish of the Quinault Reservation was appointed to act as temporary bishop until a new bishop was elected at the 1950 annual convention, which was moved from Queets to Taholah to accommodate Horton Capoeman.

9. Interview with Horton Capoeman, August 1980, Marvin N. Fisher Papers.

10. Minutes of Special Meeting, White Swan, November 26, 1950, Folder 84, ISCA.

11. Le Roy interview, April 23, 1992.

12. Le Roy interview, December 4, 1991.

13. Teo interview, April 24, 1991; Clifford Tulee, interview with authors, Moses Lake, Washington, April 24, 1991; Minutes of the Annual Convention, Warm Springs, Oregon, October 15–17, 1965, Folder 70,

ISCA.

14. ISCA, Folder 67, records reveal considerable correspondence from Wade Le Roy to Shaker leaders in November 1965: to Clifford Tulee, November 18; to William Martin, State Elder, November 18; to Florence Strom, November 19; to Theodore Pulsifer, secretary-organizer, November 19; and to Bishop Horton Capoeman, November 18. See also William Martin to Harris Teo, November 15; Minutes of the Special Meeting, Skokomish Reservation, December 4, 1965, Folder 67, ISCA.

15. William Martin et al. to Wade Le Roy, November 25, 1965, Folder 67, ISCA.

16. Minutes of the Annual Convention, Oakville, October 12, 1968, Folder 86, ISCA.

17. An exception to this practice was the appointment of Gilbert Sotomish in 1950 to fill out Frank Bennett's term. Sotomish was so ill that he could not even serve as chairman of the 1950 annual convention. He died on December 19, 1950.

18. Teo's son, who might have carried on the family name in church circles, was not a Shaker.

19. When interviewed July 20, 1992, in Wapato, Washington, Bishop David Nanamkin said that he did not know that the Full Gospel's Washington state corporate status had lapsed on May 24, 1982, for lack of annual reports. The Full Gospel's amended constitution and bylaws had been neither adopted nor discussed in meeting. Interestingly, Nanamkin lived in Wapato, Washington, a scant seven miles from ISC Bishop Clifford Tulee of Toppenish. The Oregon ISC, originally incorporated on December 28, 1925, was administratively dissolved on June 20, 1973. It became the Indian Full Gospel Church, incorporated on June 5, 1979. Effective on May 9, 1983, it had another corporate name change to Klamath Full Gospel Church Inc.

20. Compo interview, August 31, 1991; Bustillo interview, May 2, 1991.

21. John L. Schulze wrote that he was advised by George Nanamkin on July 7, 1966, that the Shaker faith was brought to the Colville Reservation by Ed Walsh in the 1920s (John Schultz, "Shaker Field Notes for Summer 1966"). Schultz and Deward E. Walker, Jr., wrote that Shakerism was introduced on the Colville Reservation in 1914. See Schulze and Walker, "Indian Shakers," 168.

22. Schultz and Walker, "Indian Shakers," 170. Suzie Williams donated two acres from her allotment to the church in 1972. In 1984, she requested a change to accommodate a building project by her children on another part of her land. After her death her children tried to get the land returned since no church house had been built on it. ISC members then acted promptly and vigorously, even obtaining donations from foreign

countries, to build their church house.

23. Bustillo interview, May 2, 1991.

24. Teo interview, April 24, 1991; Leotah Bustillo, interview with authors, Tulalip Reservation, October 15, 1991.

25. Kew, *Coast Salish Ceremonial Life*, 252, 254; Amoss, "Symbolic Substitution," 227; Bustillo interviews, May 2, October 15, 1991.

26. For an explanation of the spiritual relationship between Shakers and Spirit Dancers, see Amoss, "Symbolic Substitution." Other information from Patterson interview, June 23, 1993.

27. This 1913 smokehouse, torn down in the mid-1950s, was rebuilt in 1967 (*Everett* (Washington) *Herald*, March 23, 1991).

28. Joe Sly to Heck, April 20, 1914, Folder 6; Joseph Jefferson to Heck, December 12, 1916, Folder 9; Jefferson to Heck, January 20, 1917, Folder 10, ISCA.

29. Minutes of the Special Meeting, White Swan, October 4–6, 1941, ISCR.

30. *Skagit Valley Herald* (Mt. Vernon, WA), December 14, December 15, 1976.

31. Teo interview, April 24, 1991.

32. *Everett* (Washington) *Herald*, December 29, 1983.

33. *Washington, Geraldine Bill for Isadore Tom, Sr., et al. v. Arthur Humphreys Sr. et al.*, Lummi Tribal Court, Case No. 84-CA-773, Temporary Restraining Order and Order to Show Cause, January 17, 1984; American Indian Religion Freedom, P.L. 95–341, 95th Cong., 92 Stat. 469, Joint Resolution August 11, 1978, Folder 61, ISCA.

34. Minutes of the Annual Convention, White Swan, October 10–11, 1986, p. 7, Folder 69, ISCA.

35. Ibid.

36. Untitled, unsigned statement in longhand, updated; voluntary statement of Joseph L. Washington, January 17, 1984, Folder 61, ISCA. Washington said: "This is a problem that has been brought to the front that stood for 8 months before action was taken about our Lummi Smoke house and now our friend Isadore Tom's house is being attacked by the same man and wife along with Clara's dad, Art Humphreys. I personally would like these people to be barred from the Saoyonin people or even the Lummi Tribe." Smokehouse people have been accused of murdering those whom they believed were interfering with their practices. (Jo Anne Hall to Harris Teo, April 9, 1984, Folder 61, ISCA). One ceremony of the Smokehouse Spirit Dancing was that involving the initiation of young people. This is similar to the ancient Black Tamahnous, the secret society of wealthy clanspeople. Initiates are chosen, and initiation involves physical injury and deprivation. The ceremonies, like others suppressed

by the United States and Canadian governments, went underground for years, surfacing more recently when tolerance toward them increased and legislation allowed for greater expression by all people.

37. *Seattle Post-Intelligencer*, May 12, 1990.

38. Shaker ceremonies and those of Smokehouse Spirit Dancers are complementary among Indians of northwestern Washington and British Columbia. Activity among Shakers, while not limited to any time of the year, has full membership participation during summers and falls. Those Shakers practicing both religions join Spirit Dancers in winter months.

Chapter Fourteen Ashes, Activists, and Attrition

1. *Indian Shaker Church of Washington v. Howonquet Community Association et al., Del Norte County, California*, No. 77-078, Complaint to Quiet Title, March 22, 1977, Folder 46, ISCA.

2. Ibid.; "Resolution 1-16-77" of the Shaker Church, White Swan, Washington, signed by Bishop Harris Teo and Secretary Clifford B. Tulee, Folder 46, ISCA. It is of some interest that the Howonquet Community Association's Smith River Rancheria was restored to trust status in 1983.

3. Nadine Gutierrez et al., Smith River, California, to Harris Teo, June 6, 1978; Minutes of the Smith River August Annual Convention, Smith River, California, August 1983, Folder 82, ISCA. At the Smith River meeting, Bishop Teo looked for someone to be the California secretary-organizer to replace Wade Le Roy. Teo remarked, "Mr. LeRoy is getting old, and needs an Assistance." California held its annual convention in August, Oregon in September, and British Columbia in January. The bishop and state head elders from Washington state attended these meetings when possible. The Washington convention was the official annual meeting for all Shakers, and members attended from other states and British Columbia. California, Oregon, and British Columbia no longer elect their own bishop, but when they did that bishop had authority over certain matters in the state or province in which he resided. The Washington bishop has always been the ultimate authority in the church. The British Columbia church allows more leeway in the election and appointment of church officers and in the disciplining of members and handling of problems. For example, when Theresa Sam did not mail reports to the provincial offices as required by law, members of her Saanich church removed her and appointed another member to her position. (Saanich Meeting, August 26, 1988, Folder 80, ISCA)

4. Teo interview, April 24, 1991.

5. Clifford Tulee, interview with authors, Toppenish, Washington, September 28, 1991; Tillie George, Secretary, British Columbia Shaker

Church, interview with authors, Nespelem, Washington, February 2, 1992.

6. George interview, February 2, 1992. Alex deserted the building before it was demolished. He then met with his congregation in his home until he turned the church over to his daughter, Ann Bob, from Nanose. After Alex left the Chemainus church house, it was used by Catholics and native dancers until it was demolished. According to anthropologist John Kew, the dancers were Vancouver Island Salish speakers who practice the black face *xunxenitl* dance. (Kew to authors, June 22, 1993)

7. Kew, *Coast Salish Ceremonial Life*, 241; George interview, February 2, 1992.

8. *Indian Voice* (Sumner, Washington) 9 (July 1979). Rumor laid the 1979 burning of the church house to a controversy over the Shakers' refusal to grant to a nearby resident a right-of-way across Mud Bay church land. (Marilyn Bode, interview with authors, Seattle, February 17, 1992; *The Globe* (Marysville, WA), October 26, 1972.)

9. Memo, "Indian Shaker Church Smith River California," typescript, n.d., Folder 62, ISCA; Wade Le Roy Papers.

10. Minutes of the Annual Convention, White Swan, October 17, 1964, Folder 83, ISCA; Le Roy Papers; Le Roy interview, April 23, 1992.

11. Memo from Tillie George, Secretary, Duncan, B.C., November 5, 1888, Folder 84, ISCA; Johnnie Bastian, interview with authors, Moclips, Washington, January 19, 1993; Patterson interview, June 23, 1993; Pamela Amoss, telephone interview with authors, Leavenworth, Washington, May 6, 1992.

12. Minutes, Annual 4th of July Camp Meeting, Mud Bay, Washington, June 16, 1971, Le Roy Papers.

13. Patterson interview, June 23, 1993.

14. *Marvin N. Fisher v. Bishop Clarence Solberg et al., King County, Washington*, No. 80-2-01227-4, Notice of Readiness of Deposition for Reading and Signing, 54, 56, Marvin N. Fisher Papers; Marvin N. Fisher, interview with authors, Kirkland, Washington, December 6, 1991.

15. Robert Wallace, "Fuss over Church Proposal."

16. Marvin N. Fisher, interview with authors, Kirkland, Washington, October 14, December 6, 1991, February 10, 1992.

17. Marilyn Bode, *Christians and Native American Concerns in the Late 20th Century: A Study for Congregations.*

18. Fisher interview, December 6, 1991; *Fisher v. Solberg*, Notice of Filing (Deposition of Robert James), April 14, 1980, Marvin N. Fisher Papers; Joe DeLaCruz, interview with authors, Taholah, Washington, October 19, 1991.

19. "Deeds for Church," photocopy statement by Robert James, n.d.,

Marvin N. Fisher Papers; Fisher interview, February 10, 1992. Robert James claimed that after visiting the county courthouse in Montesano, Washington, in April 1979 to secure a copy of the deed to church property, he was advised that two "tribal leaders" had removed the papers concerning the church and destroyed them. They had told county officials that they were having the church property put in trust in order to remove it from tax rolls.

20. Minutes of Special Meeting, Taholah Shaker Church, January 27, 1979, Marvin N. Fisher Papers.

21. Robert James et al. to Marvin Fisher, November 30, 1979, Marvin N. Fisher Papers.

22. *In the Superior Court of the State of Washington, In and for the County of King, Marvin N. Fisher, Plaintiff vs Bishop Clarence Solberg, et al., Defendants*, No. 80-2-01227-4, Notice Filing, April 14, 1980. The February 1980 *Contact*—news notes published by the North Pacific District of the American Lutheran Church—carried the district bishop's acknowledgement that the conflict should receive no publicity in the national American church. Lutheran public relations man Herb David, however, responded that when a bishop of the American Lutheran Church was sued for a million dollars, there was no way of keeping the news out of the paper.

23. *Fisher v. Solberg*, Amended Complaint, September 30, 1980, Fisher Papers; *Aberdeen* (Washington) *World*, October 7, 1980.

24. See *Seattle Times*, May 2, July 11, 1981; Fisher interview, March 10, 1992; Robert Comenout, interview with authors, Tacoma, Washington, March 23, 1992. The Boldt decision in the 1974 judgment of a suit, *United States v. State of Washington* (384 F. Supp. 312), permitted fourteen tribes (subsequent to the decision, three additional tribes were included) to assert their 1954–1955 treaty-granted fishing rights. The decision confirmed the use of off-reservation customary fishing places for treaty Indians, as distinct from others, and reserved their right to 50 percent of the harvestable fish, exclusive of on-reservation harvests or fish taken for subsistence and ceremonial use. It also excluded the classification and treatment of steelhead as a "game fish" for Indians.

25. *Seattle Times*, May 31, 1981, September 27, 1980; *Seattle Post-Intelligencer*, September 27, 1980; Marilyn Bode to Friends, October 20, 1980, photocopy, Marvin N. Fisher Papers.

26. Fisher interviews, March 10, March 21, 1992.

27. Ibid.; Marilyn Bode to Friends, October 20, 1980, Marvin N. Fisher Papers.

28. Joe DeLaCruz, President, Quinault Indian Nation, to Bishop Teo, October 8, 1980, Folder 59, ISCA.

29. DeLaCruz interview, October 19, 1991.

30. Ibid.

31. Andy interview, September 24, 1991.

32. Le Roy interview, December 5, 1991.

Afterword

1. Patterson interview, June 23, 1993.

2. Upchurch, "Swinomish People," 295.

Bibliography

Amoss, Pamela *Coast Salish Spirit Dancing: The Survival of an Ancestral Religion*. Seattle: University of Washington Press, 1978.

———. "Resurrection, Healing, and 'the Shake': The Story of John and Mary Slocum." *JAAR Thematic Studies* 48 (September, December 1980): 87–109

———. "Symbolic Substitution in the Indian Shaker Church." *Ethnohistory* 25 (summer 1978): 225–49.

Bagley, Clarence. Scrapbook 6. Northwest Collections, University of Washington Libraries, Seattle.

———, ed. "Documents-Journal of Occurrences at Nisqually House." *Washington Historical Quarterly* 6 (October 1915): 264–78; 7 (January 1916): 59–75; 7 (April 1916): 144–67.

Barnett, Homer G. *Indian Shakers*. Carbondale, IL: Southern Illinois Press, 1957.

Berkeley, Katherine Sheldon. March 7, 1981, Interview by Winona Weber, for Washington Women's Heritage Project, August, 1982. Tape recording. Suzzalo Library, University of Washington, location T0420d-422a.

Betts, William J. "How the 'Shakers' Found Religion." *The West* 16 (February 1973): 16–45

Bobb, Tommy. "Marriage among the Northwest Indians. A Shaker Ceremony." Pamphlet file, General, "Indians N.A.," Northwest Collections, University of Washington Libraries, Seattle.

Bode, Marilyn. *Christian and Native American Concerns in the Late 20th Century: A Study for Congregations. Leaders Guide and Study Papers*. Seattle: The American Lutheran Church, 1981.

Branson, Olive. "True Shakers Faith Has Not Been Shaken." *Oregon Journal* (Portland), December 23, 1945.

Brown, DeKoven. "Indian Workers for Temperance." *Colliers*, September 3, 1910, 23–24.

Bryant, Hilda. "Indians Add Tribal Customs to Traditional Religious Rites." *Seattle Post-Intelligencer*, December 7, 1969.

Buchanan, Charles M. "Some Phases of Religious Beliefs among Puget Sound Indians." Microcopy. Buchanan Papers, University of Washington Libraries, Seattle.

Buchanan, Iva. "Lumbering and Logging in the Puget Sound Region in Territorial Days." *Pacific Northwest Quarterly* 27 (January 1936): 34–53.

Burns, Robert Ignatius, S.J. *The Jesuits and the Indian Wars of the Northwest*. New Haven, CT.: Yale University Press, 1966.

Castile, George Pierre. "Edwin Eells, U.S. Indian Agent, 1971–1895." *Pacific Northwest Quarterly* 72 (April 1981): 61–68.

———. *The Indians of Puget Sound*. Seattle: University of Washington Press, 1985.

Chalcraft, Edwin L. Diary, 1884, 1887, 1888, 1889, 1891. Chalcraft Papers, Holland Library, Washington State University, Pullman.

———. "Memory's Storehouse." Typescript. Chalcraft Papers. Holland Library, Washington State University, Pullman.

———. "The 'Shaker' Religion of the Indians of the Northwest." *The Assembly Herald* 19 (February 1913): 74–75.

Clark, Ella. *Indian Legends of the Pacific Northwest*. Berkeley: University of California Press, 1969.

Clark, Helen. "Chips from an Old Block." Typescript. In possession of the authors.

———. "The Indian Shakers." *Literary Digest*, 48, no.10, March 7, 1914.

———. "The Shaker Religion and Its Influence among the Makah Indians." *Home Mission Monthly* 28 (February 1914): 92.

Cohen, Felix S. *Handbook of Federal Indian Law*. 1941. Albuquerque: University of New Mexico Press, n.d.

Coleman, Michael C. "Not Race, but Grace: Presbyterian Missionaries and American Indians, 1837–1893." *Journal of American History* 67 (June 1980): 44–60.

Collins, June McCormick. "The Indian Shaker Church: A Study of Continuity and Change in Religion." *Southwestern Journal of*

Anthropology 6 (Winter 1950): 399–411.

Condon, Phoebe. "Shaker Religion of the Northwest Indians." *Tacoma* (Washington) *Sunday Ledger–News Tribune*, April 24, 1960.

Crickenberger, Sara. "Shakers." *Seattle Times* and *Post-Intelligencer*, September 17, 1989.

Curtis, Edward. *The North American Indian*. 22 vols. New York, Johnson Reprint, 1907-1930.

Dawley, Daniel L. "Some Ante-Mortem Good Indians." *The Northwest* 12 (October 1894): 22.

Deegan, Harry W. *History of Mason County, Washington*. Shelton, WA. Self-published, 1971.

Drury, Clifford M., ed. *Nine Years with the Spokane Indians: The Diary, 1838–1848, of Elkanah Walker*. Glendale, CA: Arthur H. Clark, 1976.

Du Bois, Cora. "The Feather Cult of the Middle Columbia." *General Series in Anthropology*. 7. Menasha, WI: George Banta Publishing, 1938.

Eells, Edwin. Autobiography. Typescript. Box 1, Book 3, Folder 5; Book 4, Folder 7; Book 5, Folder 9, Edwin Eells Papers, Washington State Historical Society, Tacoma.

———. Autobiography Supplement. Typescript. Box 1, Folder 19A, Edwin Eells Papers, Washington State Historical Society, Tacoma.

———. Record Book of Skokomish Indian Affairs, 1869–1878. Box 3, Edwin Eells Papers, Washington State Historical Society, Tacoma.

———. "Skokomish and Clallam Tribe Attitudes towards U.S. Government and Religion." With notes by Myron Eells, March 15, 1878. Box 3, Folder 8, Edwin Eells Papers, Washington State Historical Society, Tacoma.

Eells, Myron. "Do-Ki-Batt: Or, The God of the Puget Sound Indians." *American Antiquarian* 6 (November 1884): 389–393.

———. "The Indians of Puget Sound." *American Antiquarian* 9 (January 1887): 1–9.

———. "The Indians of Puget Sound." Handwritten copies. Notebook 6, Box 3, Myron Eells Papers, Penrose Library, Whitman College, Walla Walla, Washington.

———. Journals 6–10. Handwritten copies. Myron Eells Papers, Penrose Library, Whitman College, Walla Walla, Washington.

———. Papers. Penrose Library, Whitman College, Walla Walla, Washington.

———. "The Religion of the Clallam and Twana Indians." *American Antiquarian* 2 (July 1879): 8–14.

———. "The Religion of the Indians of Puget Sound." *American Antiquar-*

ian" 12 (March 1890): 69–84.

———. "Shaking Religion." *American Missionary* 46 (May 1892): 157–58.

———. *Ten Years of Missionary Work Among the Indians at Skokomish, Washington Territory.* Boston: Congregational Sunday-School and Publishing Society, 1886.

Elmendorf, W. W. "The Structure of Twana Culture." *Monographic Supplement 2. Research Studies* (Pullman, Washington) 28 (September 1960): 1–576.

Evans, Elwood. *History of the Pacific Northwest: Oregon and Washington.* 2 vols. Portland, OR.: North Pacific History, 1889.

Farrand, Livingston. *Traditions of the Quinault Indians.* New York; 1902.

Farrar, Victor J., ed. "The Nisqually Journal." *Washington Historical Quarterly* 10 (July 1919): 205–30.

Ficken, George, and Charles LeWarne. *Washington: A Centennial History.* Seattle: University of Washington Press, 1988.

Finley, Werdna. "As My Sun Now Sets." Typescript in possession of the Finley family.

Fisher, Marvin N. Papers. In possession of Marvin Fisher, Kirkland, WA.

Fitzpatrick, Darleen. "Indian Shakerism: God, the Spirit and Other Sacred Symbols." M.A. thesis, University of Washington, Seattle, 1968.

Fredson, Jean Todd. "Auntie Slocum." Indian Shaker Church Records, Folder 1. Washington Room, Washington State Library, Olympia.

———. "The Religion of the Shakers." Indian Shaker Church Records, Folder 1. Washington Room, Washington State Library, Olympia.

Gates, Charles M. *Messages of the Governors of the Territory of Washington to the Legislative Assembly.*

Gould, Richard A., and Theodore Paul Furukawa. *Aspects of Ceremonial Life among the Indian Shakers of Smith River, California. Kroeber Anthropological Society Papers.* Berkeley: University of California Press, 1962.

Gunther, Erna. "The Shaker Religion of the Northwest." In *Indians of the Urban Northwest.* Edited by Marian W. Smith. New York: Columbia University Press, 1949.

Harmon, Ray. "Indian Shaker Church of The Dalles." *Oregon Historical Quarterly* 72 (June 1971): 148–58.

Herrick, Huldah. "Strange Rites and Ceremonies of Redman's New Religion." *Seattle Post-Intelligencer*, Magazine Section, July 19, 1908.

Indian Shaker Church Archives (ISCA). Washington State Historical Society, Tacoma.

Indian Shaker Church Records (ISCR). Mss. 118, Washington Room,

Washington State Library, Olympia.

James, Annie. "Beginning of the Shaker Faith among the American Indians." Indian Shaker Church Records, Washington Room, Washington State Library, Olympia.

Johansen, Dorothy O., and Charles M. Gates. *Empire of the Columbia.* 2d ed. New York: Harper and Row, 1967.

Kew, John Edward Michael. "Coast Salish Ceremonial Life: Status and Identity in a Modern Village." Ph.D. diss., University of Washington, Seattle, 1970.

Klamath Indian Agency (KIA). Numerical Correspondence File 438–447. Box 96, RG 75. Federal Archives and Records Center, Seattle.

Klan, Yvonne. "The Shakers." *Raincoast Chronicles* 7 (1977): 20–24.

Langness, L. L. "A Case of Post-Contact Reform among the Clallam." Ph.D. diss., University of Washington, Seattle, 1959.

Lehnoff, Paul. "Indian Shaker Religion." *American Indian Quarterly* 6 (Fall and Winter 1982): 283–90.

Le Roy, Wade. Papers. In possession of the authors.

Majors, Harry M. *Exploring Washington.* Holland, MI: [publisher], Van Winkle Press, 1975.

McWhorter, Lucullus V. "Petition of Alex Teio, Head Elder of the Yakima Shaker Church, and Its Followers Asking the White Man to Keep His Word." No. 301. McWhorter Papers, Holland Library, Washington State University, Pullman.

Meany, Edmond S. "Twana and Clallam Indians: Aborigines of Hoods Canal." *Seattle Post-Intelligencer,* October 11, 1905.

Melcher, Marguerite Fellows. *The Shaker Adventure.* Princeton, NJ: Princeton University Press, 1951.

Miller, Jay. *Shamanic Odyssey: The Lushootseed Salish Journey to the Land of the Dead.* Menlo Park, CA: Ballena Press, 1988.

Moody, Raymond A., Jr. *Life after Life.* New York: Mockingbird Books, 1975.

———. *The Light Beyond.* New York: Bantam Books, 1975.

———. *Reflections on Life after Life.* New York: Bantam Books, 1977.

Mooney, James. "The Shakers of Puget Sound." *In Fourteenth Annual Report of the Bureau of American Ethnology to the Secretary of the Smithsonian Institution, 1892–1893,* part 2. Washington, D.C., 1896.

Morgan, Murray. *Puget's Sound: A Narrative of Early Tacoma and the Southern Sound.* Seattle: University of Washington Press, 1979.

Morse, Melvin. *Closer to the Light.* New York: Villard Books, 1990.

National Lawyers Guild. "Law Student Summer Project: Project Report" (Seattle, 1973). Pamphlet in possession of the authors.

Notices & Voyages of the Famed Quebec Mission to the Pacific Northwest, Portland, Ore., 1956.

Ober, Sarah Endicott. Letter to the Editor. *Seattle Times*, May 1, 1933.

———. "A New Religion among the West Coast Indians." *Overland Monthly* 56 (July-December 1910): 583–94.

Olson, Ronald L. *Quinault Indians and Adz, Canoe, and House Types of the Northwest*. Seattle: University of Washington Press, 1976.

Pettitt, George A. "The Quileute of La Push, 1775–1945." *Anthropological Records* (University of California, Berkeley), 14 (May 19, 1950): 95–105.

Pope, Richard Kenyon. "The Indian Shaker Church and Acculturation at Warm Springs Reservation." M.A. thesis, Reed College, Portland, Oregon, March 1953.

"Puyallup Indian Agency, 1855–1920, Introduction." *Washington State Centennial Microfilm Resources for Research at the National Archives, Pacific Northwest Region*, February 1989. Federal Archives and Records Center, Seattle.

Quimby, Lida W. "Puget Sound Indian Shakers." *The State* 7, no. 6 (January 1901): 188–89.

Rakestraw, Charles D. "The Shaker Indians of Puget Sound." *Southern Workman* 29 (December 1900): 702–9.

Reagan, Albert B. "Notes on the Shaker Church of the Indians." *Proceedings of the Indiana Academy of Science* (1910): 115–16.

———. "The Secret Dances and Medicine Ceremonies of the Quileute Indians." *Alaska-Yukon Magazine* 5 (March 1908): 10–18.

———. "The Shaker Church of the Indians." *Southern Workman* 56 (1927): 446–48.

———. "The Shake Dance of the Quilente Indians." *Proceedings of the Indiana Academy of Science* (1908): 71–74.

Rhodes, Willard. "The Christian Hymnology of the North American Indians." International Congress of Anthropological and Ethnological Sciences, University of Pennsylvania, Philadelphia, 1960.

Richen, Marilyn Claire. "Authority and Office Leadership in the Shaker Church." In *University of Oregon Anthropological Papers*. vol. 7. Edited by James J. McKenna et al. Eugene: University of Oregon, 1974.

———. "Legitimacy and the Resolution of Conflict in an Indian Church." Ph.D. diss., University of Oregon, Eugene, June 1974.

Ring, Kenneth. *Heading toward Omega*. New York: William Morrow, 1984.

———. *Life at Death*. New York: Coward, McCann and Geoghegan, 1980.

Ruby, Robert H. "A Healing Service in the Shaker Church." *Oregon*

Historical Quarterly 67 (December 1966): 347–55.

Ruby, Robert H., and John A. Brown. *The Chinook Indians: Traders of the Lower Columbia River*. Norman: University of Oklahoma Press, 1976.

——. *Dreamer-Prophets of the Columbia Plateau*. Norman: University of Oklahoma Press, 1989.

——. *A Guide to the Indian Tribes of the Pacific Northwest*. Norman: University of Oklahoma Press, 1986.

——. *Indian Slavery in the Pacific Northwest*. Spokane, WA: Arthur H. Clark 1993.

——. *Indians of the Pacific Northwest*. Norman: University of Oklahoma Press, 1981.

——. *Myron Eells and the Puget Sound Indians*. Seattle: Superior Publishing, 1976.

Sackett, Lee. "The Siletz Indian Shaker Church." *Pacific Northwest Quarterly* 64 (July 1973): 120–26.

Sampson, Martin J. *Indians of Skagit County*. Mt. Vernon, WA: Skagit County Historical Society, 1972.

Schoenberg, Wilfred P., S.J. *A History of the Catholic Church in the Pacific Northwest, 1743–1983*. Washington, DC: Pastoral Press 1987.

Schultz, John L. "Shaker Field Notes for Summer 1966." Photocopy. Yakama Indian Nation Library, Toppenish, Washington.

Schulty, John L. and Deward E. Walker, Jr. "Indian Shakers on the Colville Reservation." *Research Studies, Washington State University* 35 (June 1967): 167–72.

Smith, Marian W. *The Puyallup-Nisqually*. Columbia University Contributions to Anthropology, vol. 43, New York: Columbia University Press, 1940.

——. "Shamanism in the Shaker Religion of Northwest America." *Man: The Journal of the Royal Anthropological Institute* 54 (August 1954): 119–22.

——. "Towards a Classification of Cult Movements." *Man: The Journal of the Royal Anthropological Institute* 59 (January 1959): 8–12.

Spier, Leslie. *The Prophet Dance of the Northwest and Its Derivatives: The Source of the Ghost Dance. General Series in Anthropology*. vol. 1. Menasha, WI: George Banta Publishing, 1935.

Stern, Theodore. *The Klamath Tribe*. Seattle: University of Washington Press, 1966.

St. John, Lewis. "The Present Status and Probable Future of the Indians of Puget Sound." *Washington Historical Quarterly* 5 (January 1914): 12–21.

Strom, Otto. "Memoirs." In *Told by the Pioneers: Reminiscences of Pio-*

neers. 3 vols. Olympia: Washington Pioneer Project, 1936.

Suttles, Wayne, ed. *Handbook of North American Indians*. Vol. 7. Washington, DC: Smithsonian Institution, 1990.

Thompson, Darryl. "The Shakers and the Indian Shakers." *The Shaker Messenger* 17, no. 1 (July 1995): 5–22.

Turney-High, Harry Holbert. *The Flathead Indians of Montana. Memoirs of the American Anthropological Association*. vol. 48 Menasha, WI: George Banta Publishing, 1937.

United States. Bureau of Indian Affairs. Neah Bay Indian Agency Records, (NBIAR), 1876–1907. U.S. Bureau of Indian Affairs. Roll 3. Microcopy in Wesley A. Smith Papers, Washington State Library, Olympia.

———. Secretary of the Interior. *Annual Reports of the Commissioner of Indian Affairs*. 1857, 1864, 1882, 1887, 1888, 1892, 1893, 1896, 1899. Washington, DC: Government Printing Office.

———, Tulalip Indian Agency (TIA). Press Copies of Letters Sent to the Commissioner of Indian Affairs, March 20, 1914, to June 3, 1914. Federal Archives and Records Center, Seattle.

———, Yakama Indian Agency (YIA). Press Copies of Letters Sent to the Commissioner of Indian Affairs, March 3, 1911, to August 31, 1911. Federal Archives and Records Center, Seattle.

Upchurch, O. C. "The Swinomish People and Their State." *Pacific Northwest Quarterly* 27 (October 1936): 283–310.

Valory, Dale. *The Focus of Indian Shaker Healing*. Kroeber Anthropological Society Papers, no. 35. Berkeley: University of California Press, 1966.

Wallace, Robert. "Fuss over Church Proposal Lacked Sense of Proportion." *Journal American* (Bellevue, WA), June 14, 1991.

Washington Superintendency of Indian Affairs (WSIA). Records, 1853–1874. no. 5, Rolls 9, 10, 11, 13. Federal Archives and Records Center, Seattle.

Washington Women's Heritage Project. University of Washington Libraries, Seattle.

Waterman, T. T. "The Paraphernalia of the Duwamish 'Spirit-Canoe' Ceremony." *Indian Notes* 7 (April 1930): 129–48; 7 (July 1930): 295–312; 7 (October 1930): 535–61.

———. "The Shake Religion of Puget Sound." *Smithsonian Institution Annual Report for 1922*, 499–507. Washington, DC: Smithsonian Institution, 1924.

"'What Hath God Wrought': A Message to All Indian People." Pamphlet. Circa 1960.

Whitfield, William. *History of Snohomish County, Washington*. 2 vols.

Chicago: Pioneer Historical Publishing, 1926.

Wickersham, James. Letterpress Book, 1884–1979. James Wickersham Family Papers, Box 22, Vol. 5, April 1889–March 1891; Box 22, Vol. 7, April 1890–December 1892; Box 23, Vol. 8, December 1892–July 1901. Microcopies. Alaska Historical Library, Juneau.

Wilkes, Charles. *Narrative of the United States Exploring Expedition during the Years 1838, 1839, 1840, 1841, 1842.* 5 vols. Philadelphia: Lee & Blanchard, 1845.

Williams, Johnson. "Black Tamanous, The Secret of the Clallam Indians." *Washington Historical Quarterly* 2 (October 1916): 296–300.

Williamson, LeRoy. "His Vision of Heaven Started a Church." *Sunday* (Portland) *Oregonian*, December 20, 1942.

Zakoji, Hiroto. "Klamath Culture Change." Ph.D. diss., University of Oregon, Eugene, June 1953.

Index

www.ingramcontent.com/pod-product-compliance
Lightning Source LLC
Chambersburg PA
CBHW021845270825
31755CB00002B/88